Princess Sultana's Daughters

A Saudi Arabian princess reveals intimate
revelations about sex, love, marriage
—and the fate of her beautiful daughters—
behind the veil

JEAN SASSON

Windsor-Brooke Books

Cover photograph © Mohamad Itani / Trevillion Images

Jacket design by www.HotDamnDesigns.com

Interior book design by Judith Engracia

Windsor-Brooke Books
Tower Place 100, Suite 1775
3340 Peachtree Road NE
Atlanta, GA 30326

This Windsor-Brooke Books edition of *Princess Sultana's* Daughters was previously published by Doubleday in 1994 and by Dell in 1995.

The Doubleday hardcover edition contains the following Library of Congress Cataloging-in-Publication Data:

Sasson, Jean P.
Princess Sultana's daughters / Jean Sasson — 1st edition
p. cm.
Sequel to: Princess
1. Women—Saudi Arabia—Social conditions. 2. Princesses—Saudi Arabia—Biography I. Title.

Printed in the United States of America

To Mom and Dad, I miss you.

Your baby girl, Jean

For additional information about Jean Sasson and her books,
or for updates on Princess Sultana, women's issues, and
Saudi Arabia, please visit www.JeanSasson.com
and www.PrincessSultanasCircle.com

Princess Sultana's Daughters is available for purchase in bookstores
and online retailers.
It is also available as an e-book at all e-bookstores.

Other Works
by Jean Sasson

Non-Fiction:
The Rape of Kuwait
*Princess: A True Story of Life Behind the Veil in Saudi
   Arabia*
Princess Sultana's Daughters
Princess Sultana's Circle
Mayada, Daughter of Iraq
Love in a Torn Land: A Kurdish Woman's Story
*Growing up Bin Laden: Osama's Wife and Son Reveal their
   Secret World*
*For the Love of a Son: One Afghan Woman's Quest for her
   Stolen Child*
American Chick in Saudi Arabia (first in a series of five)

Historical Fiction:
Ester's Child

To learn more about author Jean Sasson and the subjects
of her books, log on to: www.JeanSasson.com

Readers can follow Jean Sasson on Facebook, Twitter, and
her blog.

AUTHOR'S NOTE:

Princess Sultana's Daughters is a true story. Names have been changed and various events slightly altered to protect the safety of recognizable individuals. In telling this true story it is not the intention of the author nor of the princess to demean the rich and meaningful Islamic faith. Princess Sultana and the author believe that it is the male-dominated culture of the region, as well as the habit of some men to misinterpret the words of Prophet Mohammed are the main problems when it comes to women's lives.

An earlier book, *Princess: A True Story of Life Behind the Veil in Saudi Arabia* set the stage for this work by depicting the life of Princess Sultana from early childhood to the Gulf War of 1991. This book is the continuing story of Princess Sultana, her daughters, and other Saudi Arabian women they personally know. While readers are encouraged to read the first book about Sultana, Princess Sultana's Daughters is a story in itself and can be read on its own.

Additionally, the third and last book in the trilogy is titled *Princess Sultana's Circle.* Although many facts are revealed about a land that is little understood by the Western world, none of these three books propose to be a history of Saudi Arabia, or to reflect the lives of all women who live there.

Know that these three books, linked by one woman, come to one conclusion: that the degradation of women is a worn-out habit. Though the double standard is still alive and well in most countries, it is time for male dominance over women to end.

Table of Contents

Appendices

The Monarchs of Saudi Arabia

King Abdulaziz
(also known as Ibn Saud)
Born: 1876 - Reigned 1932-1953

King Saud
(son of King Abdul Aziz)
Born: 1902 - Reigned 1953-1964; deposed

King Faisal
(son of King Abdul Aziz)
Born 1904: Reigned 1964-1975; assassinated

King Khalid
(son of King Abdul Aziz)
Born: 1912 - Reigned 1975-1982

King Fahd
(son of King Abdul Aziz)
Born 1922 - Reigned 1982-2005

King Abdullah
(son of King Abdul Aziz)
Reigned 2005-Present

Map of Saudi Arabia

Key People

ABDUL: Egyptian employee of Princess Sultana (married to Fatma).

King ABDUL AZIZ AL SA'UD: Grandfather of Princess Sultana. Was the first king and founder of Saudi Arabia. Died in 1953.

ABDULLAH AL SA'UD: Son of Princess Sultana.

AISHA: Girlfriend of Princess Maha.

ALHAAN: Egyptian girl who is sexually mutilated against the wishes of her grandmother, Fatma.

ALI AL SA'UD: Brother of Princess Sultana.

AMANI AL SA'UD: Youngest child and daughter of Princess Sultana.

ARAFAT, YASSIR: Chairman of the PLO.

ASAD AL SA'UD: Brother-in-law of Princess Sultana (husband of Sara).

CONNIE: Filipino maid who was employed to work in the home of Saudi friends of Princess Sultana's.

CORA: Filipino maid of Princess Sultana.

ELHAM: Egyptian woman who is daughter of Abdul and Fatma (employees of Princess Sultana).

King FAHD: Current ruler of Saudi Arabia who is highly regarded by Princess Sultana, his niece.

FATMA: Egyptian housekeeper of Princess Sultana (married to Abdul).

FAYZA: Daughter of Saudi friends of Princess Sultana's. She elopes with Jafer, a Palestinian.

FOUAD: Father of Fayza.

HANAN: Younger sister of Prince Kareem (sister-in-law of Princess Sultana).

HUDA: African slave who worked in the childhood home of Princess Sultana. Huda is now deceased.

JAFER: Palestinian employee of Prince Kareem and close friend to his son, Abdullah. Jafer elopes with Fayza.

KAREEM AL SA'UD: A prince in the ruling family who is Sultana's husband.

King KHALID: Fourth king of Saudi Arabia who was greatly loved by his people. Died in 1982.

KHOMEINI: Iranian religious leader who led the revolution against the shah of Iran and succeeded in establishing an Islamic Republic.

LAWAND AL SA'UD: First cousin of Kareem who was confined to the woman's room.

MAHA AL SA'UD: Oldest daughter of Princess Sultana.

MAJED AL SA'UD: Son of Ali (nephew of Princess Sultana).

MISHA'IL: Royal cousin of Princess Sultana who was put to death for the moral crime of adultery.

MOHAMMED: Brother-in-Law of Princess Sultana. Mohammed is married to Kareem's sister, Hanan.

MOUSA: Egyptian driver for Princess Sultana's family.

NADA: Childhood friend of Princess Sultana who was killed by her father for a crime against "honor."

NASHWA: Niece of Princess Sultana. Nashwa is the teenage daughter of Princess Sara.

NASSER: Son-in-law of Fatma.

NOORAH: Mother-in-law of Princess Sultana.

NURA AL SA'UD: Oldest sister of Princess Sultana.

REEMA: Child bride from Yemen.

REEMA AL SA'UD: Sister of Princess Sultana.

SALEEM: Brother-in-Law of Princess Sultana. Saleem is married to Reema.

SAMEERA: Childhood friend of Tahani, who is sister of Princess Sultana. Sameera was confined to the woman's room until her death.

SAMIA: Member of the royal family who married Fouad and is the mother of Fayza.

SARA AL SA'UD: Sister of Princess Sultana. Sara is married to Asad, brother of Kareem.

TAHANI AL SA'UD: Sister of Princess Sultana.

WAFA: Childhood friend of Princess Sultana who was married at a young age to an old man.

YOUSIF: Egyptian man who was college friend of Prince Kareem and who later joined radical Islamic group in Egypt.

Foreword from the Author

I lived in Saudi Arabia from 1978 until 1990, and visited there regularly until 1992, a country well known for its segregation of the sexes. I quickly came to see that forced gender segregation created a close bonding between women.

During that time I met and befriended a number of Saudi Arabian women. After living in the country for five years, I came to know an extraordinary woman the world now knows as Princess Sultana in *Princess: A True Story of Life Behind the Veil in Saudi Arabia*. What a brave woman! I admire Sultana's strength and courage more than I can say for she literally risked her life for her story to be told.

After the amazing success of *Princess*, Princess Sultana requested that I continue to write the stories of abuse that continue to occur in her homeland, Saudi Arabia. And so I have. Like most women who are mothers, Sultana's deepest concerns are for her own daughters, yet I believe that Sultana's determination to "right wrongs" also stems from a basic goodness and desire to help mankind.

Although my small town American life has been nothing like the royal life of Princess Sultana, we do share several common bonds: both of us want to help all women who are unable to help themselves; both of us are relentlessly determined to continue fighting the men and women who have made numerous efforts to stop us from revealing these truths; and, both of us are optimistic in character. Princess Sultana and I both truly believe that by the telling of these true stories that we can make a difference in women's lives.

When I was young, my optimism in all things knew no bounds. I truly believed that I could solve every problem and right every wrong. In part I believe this optimism stemmed from the fact that I grew up in America's deep south in a tiny town of only 800 people. Small town life carries a happy innocence that clings to its inhabitants forever. And, the people in my little community were for the most part, decent and kind. Due to this inherent "goodness", I can't recall a single incident in my youth where I felt females were less valued than males, although when I was a child, most women I knew remained home to raise their children.

Although Sultana grew up in a wealthy environment that I could not have begun to imagine in my poverty-stricken youth, I now know that I was more fortunate than a royal princess, for I never felt I was second-class in any way, to anyone. This wonderful confidence instilled a great sense of optimism in my every emotion and action.

After years of living an adventurous life that, thus far, has taken me to 68 countries, my optimism has survived, although it has been battered by the reality of life for so many women of the world. I have found that the oppression of women and the social pressures to which they are exposed, are a worldwide problem and is not limited to the Islamic world. Sadly, some governments and social systems are downright hostile to their female population. Too many women of the world are condemned to a life of heart-breaking and even cruel discrimination. Too many men, who are the world's social or political leaders, turn a blind eye to this "war" against women.

How *anyone* with an ounce of feeling can turn a

blind eye to the horrors inflicted on women is beyond my comprehension. I know that I am haunted by many incidents of abuse against women. I am sad to report that I have personally seen the following:

- While working at a hospital in Saudi Arabia, I personally knew of young girls admitted to the hospital to give birth. "Babies having babies," as we often sadly observed. For the most part, those young girls were the third or fourth wife of an aging man.
- I have seen young Asian women auctioned off to the highest bidder for the purposes of unlimited sex. I witnessed young girls, some that looked no older than eight-years-old, stand weeping as heartless men inspected their bodies. I was shocked to see that most of the men buying the young girls were citizens from Western countries.
- I visited a brothel in Asia where beautiful young women had been bought to serve men as sex slaves. During the day the "owners" of these young girls forced them to work in a clothing factory located on the premises. At night they were compelled to return to the brothel on the ground floor to allow strangers to take possession of their bodies.
- I once saved a young woman from a slave-like existence an supported her for years. This same woman later gave her own three-year-old daughter away to a group of men so that she could devote herself solely to supporting her treasured son.
- I interviewed women of several nationalities who had been kidnapped and held as sex slaves by Iraqi soldiers during their occupation of Kuwait. Their agony haunts me to this day.

Many well-meaning people have often advised me to temper my reactions to such abuses, that social change comes slowly, and that I must be patient. Although history tells me this is true, as far as I am concerned, change cannot come quickly enough for young females who are so brutally mistreated.

And so a princess from Saudi Arabia and an American woman from small town America continue to tell the stories that we hope will provide knowledge to readers, and that this knowledge will compel people to gather their courage and take action to bring change to our planet.

At this moment, the princess and I are making plans to write a fourth book about her life. We are also outlining a book that is to be an adventure story about her only granddaughter.

So long as there are readers who want to know about Princess Sultana and her family, and so long as the world ignores the plight of women, we will never stop. Princess Sultana al-Sa'ud is the most determined woman I have ever known, and I am proud to be her voice. And, I am proud to present the second book in the Princess Trilogy: *Princess Sultana's Daughters.*

Jean Sasson

May 2013

Prologue

*A great rock is not disturbed by the wind; the mind of a wise
man is not disturbed by either honor or abuse.*
—BUDDHA

Once, I read that any good pen can stab any king.
As I study the photograph of my uncle, Fahd ibn Abdul
Aziz, the king of Saudi Arabia, I contemplate the fact that I
harbor no desire to stab our king, or even to spark the
wrath of a man I know to be kindly.

I trace my fingers across his face, calling to mind
the man, Fahd, from the days of my childhood. The photograph portrays the king in maturity and reveals not a
spark of the youthful figure I remember. The king's stern
brow and strong jaw belie the charming man I wistfully
summon into my mind. My thoughts wander back in time,
remembering the king before he was crowned. Standing
tall and broad-shouldered, with his large hand outstretched, he had offered a sweet date to a child in awe.
That child had been me. Fahd, like his father before him,
was a robust man, and, to my young eyes, had looked
more like the son of a bedouin warrior he was than like
the statesman he would become. Contrary to my bold
character, I had reacted in a timid manner, reluctantly accepting the desert fruit from his fingers, then running

away to the arms of my mother. I overheard Fahd's fond laughter as I tasted the sweetness of the date.

As is our Saudi custom, I have not been unveiled in the presence of the king since the age of puberty. Since that time he has grown into a man of age. Acknowledging that the king now appears somber, I decide that while the years of statesmanship have strengthened him, the responsibilities of leadership have chastened him. And, though massive and regal, our king cannot be judged handsome. His eyelids droop too heavily over his bulging eyes; his nose overshadows his upper lip, which tightly frames a delicate mouth. In the picture so familiar to all Saudis and visitors to the kingdom, the official photograph that hangs conspicuously in every business and institution in my country, I think the king appears to be what I know he is not: forbidding, insensitive.

In spite of his unquestioned power and vast wealth, his position is not to be envied. As absolute sovereign of one of the wealthiest nations on earth, King Fahd's rule over the hot, dreary land of Saudi Arabia is a perpetual struggle between old and new.

While most nations maintain themselves by abandoning or recasting the old ways, growing slowly into newer and better systems that advance civilization, our king has no such options. He, a mere mortal, must force into unity and peace four divided and completely distinct groups of citizens: the religious fundamentalists, stern, unyielding men of power who demand a return to the past; the prominent, well-educated middle class who cry out for release from the old traditions that stifle their lives; the Bedouin tribes who struggle against enticements to abandon their roving ways and yield to the lure of the cities; and, finally, members of the vast royal family who desire nothing more than wealth, wealth, and more wealth.

Bridging these four factions is the one group of natives who have been forgotten, the women of Saudi Arabia, as diverse in our desires and demands as the individual men who rule our daily lives.

Yet, strangely, I, a woman of great frustrations, have little anger with the king over our plight, for I know that he must have the loyal backing of ordinary husbands, fathers, and brothers before moving against the disciplined men of religion. These clerics claim that they correctly interpret the historic code of laws to allow men to rule harshly over their women. Too many ordinary men of Saudi Arabia are content with the status quo, discovering that it is easier to ignore the complaints of their women than to follow their king in negotiating change.

In spite of the difficulties, the bulk of Saudi citizens support King Fahd. It is only the religious fundamentalists who call for his downfall. To the remainder of Saudi citizens, he is known as a man of generosity and good cheer.

And, I remind myself, the women of our family know the king is well loved by his wives, and who knows a man better than his wives?

While King Fahd rules with a milder hand than did his father and his three brothers, it does not require the wisdom of a sage to know that Princess, the book that tells the story of my life, will be viewed as a slap in the face to the man who rules my country.

That, alone, I regret. I bluntly admonish myself that I, under no duress, made the decision to break the precedent of generations by flinging family secrets to the wind. Now, for the first time, I wonder if I acted with passion rather than wisdom; perhaps my earnestness and enthusiasm led me to overestimate my capacity for intrigue.

In an attempt to soothe my conscience and calm my fears, I vividly recall the intensity of my anger with the men of my family, the rulers of Saudi Arabia, who appeared so oblivious to the suffering of the women in the land they ruled.

Chapter One:
Unveiled

Despair weakens our sight and closes our ears. We can see nothing but specters of doom, and can hear only the beating of our agitated hearts.
—KAHIL GIBRAN

It is October of 1992, and I, Sultana al Sa'ud, the princess featured in a tell-all book, follow the days of the calendar with a mixture of feverish excitement and morose depression. The book that exposed the life of women behind the veil was released in the United States in September. Since its publication, I carry with me a somber presentiment of my doom, feeling as though I were precariously suspended in space, for I am aware that no deed great or small, bad or good, can be without effect.

While taking a deep breath, I hopefully remind myself that I am likely to be safe in the anonymity of the extended al Sa'ud family. Still, my trusty instincts warn me that I have been discovered.

Just as I conquer my conflicting guilt and fear, my husband, Kareem, enters our home in a rush, shouting out that my brother, Ali, has returned early from his trip to

Europe and that my father has called an urgent family meeting at his palace. With black eyes glaring in a pale face marked with blotches of fiery red, my husband looks madder than a mad dog.

I am struck with a horrifying thought. Kareem has been told of the book!

Imagining suffocating confinement in a subterranean dungeon, deprived of my beloved children, I surrender to my agitation for a moment, and in a thin, high voice that bears no similarity to my own, I implore, "What has happened?"

Kareem shrugs his shoulders, answering, "Who can know?" His nostrils flare with irritation when he remembers, "I informed your father that I have an important appointment in Zurich tomorrow, that you and I could see him when I return, but he was adamant that I cancel my plans and escort you to his home this evening."

Like a windswept figure, Kareem charges into his office, exclaiming, "Three meetings have to be canceled!"

Weak-kneed, I collapse on the sofa with relief, thinking that all conclusions are premature. Kareem's anger has nothing to do with me! My courage flickers hopefully.

Still, the threat of discovery persists, and I have many long hours before the unexpected family meeting.

Feigning a gaiety I do not feel, I smile and chat as Kareem and I walk through the wide entrance hall, over the thick Persian carpets, into an enormous and grand sitting room in my father's newly constructed palace. Father has not yet arrived, but I see that Kareem and I are the last of the family to make an appearance. The other ten living children of my mother, without their spouses, have also been summoned to my father's home. I know that three of my sisters had to fly into Riyadh from Jeddah, while another two sisters flew in from Taif. Looking around the room, I verify that Kareem is the only outside member of the family present. Even Father's head wife and her children are nowhere to be seen. I surmise that they have been dismissed from the premises.

The urgency of the meeting leads me back to the book, and my chest tightens from fear. My sister Sara and I exchange worried glances. As the only member of my family aware of the book's publication, her thoughts seem the same as mine. Each of my siblings greets me warmly except my only brother, Ali, and I catch a glimpse of his sly eyes following me.

Within moments of our arrival, Father enters the room. His ten daughters rise respectfully to their feet, and each of us expresses her greetings to the man who has given her life without love.

I have not seen my father in some months, and I think to myself that he looks exhausted and prematurely old. When I lean to kiss his cheek, he impatiently turns away, failing to return my greeting. Giving my fears full range, I know at that moment that I have been naïve, thinking that the al Sa'uds are too busy accumulating wealth to care much for books. My trepidation mounts.

In a stern voice Father asks us to sit, saying that he has some disturbing news to relay.

Lured by a stare, I see that Ali, with his morbid interest in the suffering of others, is gloating, regarding me with a pitiless stare. There is little doubt in my mind that Ali is privy to the evening's business.

Father reaches into his large, black briefcase and retrieves a book none of us can read. It is written in a foreign language. My mind in conflict, I think that I have made a mistake with my earlier fears, wondering what this particular book has to do with our family.

In a voice filled with undisguised rage, Father says that Ali recently purchased the book from Germany, and that the book tells about the life of a princess, a stupid and foolish woman who is not aware of the royal obligations that accompany the privileges of royalty. Circling the room, he holds the book in his hands. The picture on the cover is plainly that of a Muslim woman, for she is veiled and is standing against a backdrop of Turkish minarets. I have a wild thought that an aging, exiled princess from Egypt or Turkey has written a revealing book, but quickly realize that such a tale would hold no interest in our land.

When Father steps closer, I read the title: *Ich, Prinzessin aus dem Hause Al Saud.*

It is my story!

As I had not been in touch with the book's author since learning of its sale to William Morrow, a large and respected American publishing house, I was unaware that the book, *Princess*, was a huge success and had sold to numerous countries. The one before me is quite obviously the German edition.

I have a short moment of elation followed by sheer terror. I feel the blood rush to my face. I am numb and can barely hear my father's voice. He explains that Ali had been curious when he saw the book in the Frankfurt airport and had gone to a great deal of trouble and expense to have the book translated because he saw that our family name was written on the cover.

At the time, Ali had an irritating thought that some obscure, disgruntled princess within the al Sa'ud family had divulged the gossipy secrets of her life. Once Ali had read the book and clearly recognized himself from our childhood dramas, the truth was revealed. He canceled the remainder of his holiday and hastily returned to Riyadh in a fury.

Father has had copies of the translated version made for the meeting.

He nods at Ali, giving a small signal with his hand.

My brother grapples with a bulky pile of paper at his side and proceeds to hand each person a bundle secured with a large rubber band.

Confused, Kareem nudges me, raising his eyebrows and rolling his eyes.

Until the last possible second, I express my denial, returning an expression of bewilderment. Shrugging my shoulders, I stare, unblinking and unseeing, at the papers in my hand.

In a soaring voice Father shouts out my name, "Sultana!"

I feel my body jump into the air.

Father begins to speak rapidly, spitting out words as I imagine a machine gun expels bullets. "Sultana, do you recall the marriage and divorce of your sister Sara? The wickedness of your childhood friends? The death of your mother? Your trip to Egypt? Your marriage to Kareem? The birth of your son? Sultana?"

I have stopped breathing.

Relentless, my father continues to accuse. "Sultana, if you have difficulty in recalling these momentous events, then I suggest that you read this book!"

Father throws the book at my feet.

Unable to move, I stare, mute, at the book on the floor.

My father orders, "Sultana, pick it up!" Kareem grabs the book and stares at the cover. He gasps—a deep, ragged breath—and then turns to me. "What is this, Sultana?"

I am paralyzed with fear. My heart stops beating. I sit and listen, longing for the life-giving thump.

Quite out of control, Kareem drops the book to the floor, grabs my shoulders, and shakes me like a rag.

I again feel the familiar heartbeat, though I have a childlike thought—a moment of sorrow that I did not die on the spot and so burden my husband's conscience with lifelong guilt. I hear the muscles of my neck snapping from the force of Kareem's strength.

My father yells, "Sultana! Answer your husband!"

Suddenly the years evaporate. I am a child again, at my father's mercy. How I long for my mother to be alive, for nothing less than maternal fervor can save me from this vicious encounter!

I feel a whimper forming in my throat.

I have told myself many times in the past that there can be no freedom without courage, yet my courage fails me when I need it the most. I had known that if members of my immediate family read the book, my secret would be discovered. Foolishly, I had felt protected by the fact that in my family, only Sara reads books. Even if gossip of the book had spread throughout the city, I assumed that my family would take little note of it, unless mention was made of a particular incident they would recall from our youth.

Now, ironically, my brother, a man who scorns the mention of women's rights, had read the book that focused attention on the abuse of women in my land. My demon of a brother, Ali, had foiled my precious anonymity.

Timidly, I look around the room at my father, my sisters and brother. Together, as if they had practiced, their looks of surprise and anger slowly forge into a united hard stare.

After only one short month, I am discovered!

Finding my voice, I protest weakly, blaming my deed on the highest authority, saying what all good Muslims say when caught in an act that will bring punishment on their heads. I thump the papers with my hand. "God willed it. He willed this book!"

Ali is quick to retort, scoffing, "God? Not so! The

devil willed it! He willed it! Not God!" Ali turns to my father and says with perfect seriousness, "Since the day of her birth, Sultana has had a little devil living inside her. This devil willed the book!"

Quite rapidly, my sisters begin to flip through the pages in their hands, to see for themselves if our family's secrets have been made public.

Only Sara gives me her support. She quietly gets to her feet and slips behind my back, resting her hands on my shoulders, reassuring me with her soft touch.

After his initial outburst, Kareem is quiet. I see that he is reading the translated copy of the book. I lean sideways and see that he has discovered the chapter that tells of our first meeting and consequent marriage. Sitting perfectly still, my husband reads aloud the words that he is seeing for the first time.

Father's angry shouting arouses the enthusiastic hatred of Ali, and my father and brother quite outdo each other in their verbal assaults on my stupidity. Amid the passionate disorder, I hear Ali shout out the accusation that I have committed treason.

Treason? I love my God, country, and king, in that order; and I shout back that "No! I am not a traitor! Only a mediocre mind such as yours, my brother, can reach a conclusion of treason!"

As my anger builds, my fear is receding.

I think to myself that the men in my family are proof that men and women can remain at peace only when one sex is strong enough to completely dominate the other. Now that we women in Saudi Arabia are becoming educated, and are beginning to think for ourselves, our lives will be filled with additional discord and mayhem. Still, I welcome the battle if it means more rights for women, for a false peace does nothing more than further women's subjugation.

Yet, I know that this is not the most opportune moment for argument.

The hot controversy continues to rage, and I become lost in the details. My initial fright had dimmed my memory of why I had requested Jean Sasson to write my story in the first place. Now, I stop listening to the accusations and force myself to remember the drowning death of my friend Nada. I was a teenager at the time, and religious authorities had discovered my good friends Nada and Wafa in the company of men to whom they were not wed nor related. Because both girls were still virgins, they were not punished by the State for their crime against morality; instead they were released to their fathers for punishment. Wafa was wed to a man many years her senior. Nada was drowned. Nada's own father called for the cruel punishment, saying that the honor of his family name had been ruined by the sexual misconduct of his youngest daughter. With Nada's execution, he dubiously reclaimed the honor he had lost.

My thoughts then drifted to the crushing imprisonment of Sameera, the best friend of my sister Tahani. Sameera was a young woman whose parents had died in an automobile accident. She fled to the United States with her lover when she felt threatened by her uncle, who had become her legal guardian at the death of her parents. A great tragedy occurred when Sameera's uncle tricked her into returning to Saudi Arabia. In a rage over her love affair, he married his niece to a man not of her choice. When it was discovered Sameera was no longer a virgin, she was confined to the "woman's room," where she was still locked away even as my own crisis unfolded.

Even before the book was published, I had realized that neither tale seemed credible, unless the book's readers would consider the barbarities that men inflict upon women. Yet, something was telling me that those with genuine knowledge of my land—its customs and traditions—would recognize the truth of my words. Now, I wonder if Nada's and Sameera's tragic lives have yet touched readers' hearts.

The memory of my unfortunate friends and their sad fate renews my strength.

With mounting exasperation I think that those who desire freedom must be willing to pay for it with their lives. The worst has happened. I have been discovered. Now what?

It was a pivotal moment. Feeling my strength return, I stand up and face my foes. I feel the warrior's blood of my grandfather, Abdul Aziz, surge through my body. From the time I was a child, I have been most to be feared when I stand in real danger.

My courage gives me a hardened resolve. Thinking back, I remember the face of a kind man who offered a little girl succulent dates. I have a wild idea. Without hesitating, I shout brave words over the din, "Take me to the king!"

The shouting stops. Incredulous, my father repeats my words, "The king?"

Ali makes an impatient tsking sound with his tongue. "The king will not meet with you!"

"Yes. He will! Take me to him. I wish to tell the king the reasons why the book came to be. To tell him of the tragic lives of the women he rules. I will confess, but only to the king."

My father looks askance at his son, Ali. Their eyes lock. It is as if I could read their minds. "One must be honorable, but not too much!"

"I insist upon confessing. To the king." I know this king well. He hates confrontation. Even so, he will punish me for what I have done. I think to myself that I will need someone from outside Saudi Arabia to keep my memory alive. I say, "But before I go to the king, I must speak with someone at a foreign newspaper to make my identity known. If I am to be punished, I refuse to be forgotten. Let the world know how our country deals with those who unveil the truth."

I walk toward the telephone that sits on a small table next to the hallway door, thinking that I must notify someone of my plight. I am desperate, trying to recall the telephone number of an international newspaper that I had memorized for just such an occasion.

My sisters begin to wail, crying out to our father that he must stop me.

Kareem jumps to his feet, rushing to beat me to the phone. My husband stands tall over me, blocking my path. With a stern face, he holds out his arm and points to my chair as if it were the executioner's block.

Despite the seriousness of the moment, something about Kareem's expression amuses me. I laugh aloud. My husband can be a foolish man and still has not learned that to silence me, he must bury me. That, I know, he can never do. My knowledge of Kareem's inability to commit violence has always given me strength.

Neither Kareem nor I move. Keenly feeling the drama of the moment, I shout out, "When the beast is cornered, the hunter is in danger." The thought enters my mind to ram into his stomach with my head, and I am considering this option just as my oldest sister, Nura, takes center stage and quiets us all with her calm voice.

"Enough! This is not the manner to solve a problem." She pauses, glancing at Father and Ali. "All this shouting! The servants will hear every word. Then we are in a true dilemma."

Nura is the only female child of my father who has gained his love. Father motions for everyone to be quiet.

Kareem leads me by the arm and we return to our

chairs. Father and Ali continue to stand, both quite speechless.

Since the book's publication, I have been weakened by my fear. Now, for the first time in weeks, I feel absolutely fierce, recognizing that the last thing the men want is to turn me over to the authorities.

The meeting continues much more calmly, with serious talk of how to keep my identity a secret. We understand that there will be much talk and speculation within the kingdom as to the identity of the princess in the book. My family decides that it will be impossible for the common men of Saudi to uncover the truth, for they are outside our family circles. And there is no real danger from male relatives within the extended al Sa'ud family, for females and their activities are carefully guarded from male view. In Father's mind, there is genuine concern regarding close female relatives, since they sometimes participate in our intimate gatherings.

There is a moment of panic as Tahani remembers that one old auntie who was closely involved in Sara's calamitous marriage and divorce is still living. Nura calms their fears by revealing that our auntie, just a few days before, had been diagnosed with a disabling brain disorder that affects the elderly. Nura says that our auntie is rarely, if ever, coherent. If by some remote chance she hears of the book, nothing she says or does would be taken seriously by her family.

Everyone breathes easier.

I, myself, have no fear of the old woman. She was an anomaly in her time. I understand her frisky character better than the others. My intimate knowledge has come from past conversations when she whispered in my ear that she supported me in my quest for small female freedoms. This auntie had bragged to me that she was the world's first feminist, long before the European women thought of such matters. She said that on the night of her marriage, she had insisted to her startled husband that she handle the money from the sale of the sheep, since she could figure numbers in her head and he had to use a stick in the sand. Not only that, her husband had never even thought of taking another wife, saying often that my auntie was too much woman for him.

With a toothless laugh, my auntie had confided in me that the secret to controlling a man was in a woman's ability to keep her husband's "leather stick" rigid and ready. I was a young girl at that time and had no idea what a "leather stick" might be. Later, in my adult years, I often smiled, thinking of the lusty activities that must have shaken their tent.

After her husband's early death, my auntie confessed that she missed his tender caresses and that it was his memory that kept her from accepting another mate.

Over the years I have jealously guarded her happy secret, fearing that such a confession would nibble at my auntie's soul.

For several hours my family pore over the translated pages and satisfy themselves that no one else alive, or traceable outside of our immediate family, is aware of the family dramas and squabbles divulged in the book.

I can see that my family feels a keen sense of relief. In addition, I catch a trace of mild admiration that I had so cleverly altered the pertinent information that would have led the authorities directly to my door.

The evening closes with Father and Ali warning my sisters not to tell their husbands of the night's business. Who knows which husband might feel compelled to confide in a sister or mother? My sisters are instructed to say that the meeting involved nothing more than personal female matters not worthy of their husbands' attention.

Father sternly ordered me not to "come out" in

public and announce my "crime." The fact that the book is the story of my life must remain a well-kept secret within our family. My father reminds me that not only would I suffer dire consequences, house arrest, or possibly imprisonment, but that the men of the family, including my own son, Abdullah, would be scorned and shut out by Saudi Arabia's patriarchal society, which values nothing more highly than a man's ability to control his women.

As a token of submission, I lower my eyes and promise compliance. My heart is smiling, for on this night I have made a brilliant discovery that the men of my family are locked to me as if by a chain, that their dominance jails them as surely as it imprisons me.

As I say good night to my father and brother, I think to myself: complete power poisons the hand of the person that holds it.

Cheated of my blood, Ali is displeased and gruff in our parting. He would like nothing better than to see me placed under house arrest, but he cannot risk the wound to his male pride that would come from being associated by blood with such a one as I.

I give him an especially warm farewell, whispering in his ear: "Ali, you must remember that not everyone in chains can be subdued."

It is a great triumph!

Kareem is sullen and stubborn as we make our way home. He smokes one cigarette after another, soundly cursing the Filipino driver on three occasions for not driving to suit his master.

I lean my face against the car window, seeing nothing of what we pass on the Riyadh streets. I brace myself for a second battle, for I understand that I cannot escape Kareem's great anger.

Once locked in our bedroom, Kareem grabs the pages of the book. He begins to read aloud the passages that most insult him: "His facade was wisdom and kindness; his very bowels were cunning and selfish. I was disgusted to discover that he was merely a shell of a man with little to commend him, after all!"

There is a strain of sympathy in my thoughts, for what human would not feel pain and fury at public notification of their weakest traits. I fight the emotion, forcing myself to recall the activities of my husband that led to my own pain and grief so vividly portrayed in the book.

I am in a dilemma, knowing not whether to laugh or to cry.

Kareem solves the problem for me with his exaggerated behavior. My husband waves his arms and stomps his feet. I'm reminded of the Egyptian puppet show I had attended the previous week at my sister Sara's palace, a hilarious event featuring puppets in full Saudi dress. The closer I look, the more Kareem resembles Goha, a lovable but eccentric imaginary figure in the Arab world. Goha the puppet had been his usual foolish self in the play, prancing across the stage, disentangling himself from complex situations.

My lips quiver with the urge to laugh. At any moment now, I expect my husband to fall to the floor and throw a childish temper tantrum.

"He swore, he blushed with shame; I thought perhaps he was angered by his inability to control his wife."

Kareem glares hatefully at me. "Sultana! Do not dare smile! I am truly angry."

Still battling conflicting emotions, I shrug. "Do you deny that what you are reading is the truth?"

Ignoring my words, Kareem foolishly continues to seek out the most damning passages concerning his character, reminding his wife of the particular traits of her husband's temperament that had led her to leave him years ago.

Actually shrieking, he reads aloud, "How I yearned to be wed to a warrior, a man with the hot flame of righteousness to guide his life."

His rage growing with every word, Kareem holds the book under my nose and points with a finger to the words that he deems most insulting, "Six years ago, Sultana was stricken with a venereal disease; after much distress, Kareem admitted that he participated in a weekly adventure of sex with strangers... After the scare of the disease, Kareem promised he would avoid the weekly tryst, but Sultana says she knows that he is weak in the face of such a feast, and that he continues to indulge himself without shame. Their wonderful love has vanished except in memory; Sultana says she will stand with her husband and continue her struggle for the sake of her daughters."

Kareem is so angry at that particular revelation that I fear he will start weeping. My husband accuses me of "poisoning paradise," claiming that, "our lives are perfect."

Admittedly, over the past year I have regained some of my earlier love and trust of Kareem, but it is at moments such as this that my dismay grows over the cowardice of the men of our family. I realize from his behavior that Kareem gives not a thought to the reasons I risked my safety and our happiness to make known the events of my life, or to the very real and tragic events ending the lives of young and innocent women in his own land. Kareem's only concern is for how he is portrayed in the book, and for the fact that he has fared poorly in many passages.

I tell my husband that he and other men of the al Sa'ud family alone hold the power to make change in our country. Slowly, quietly, in their subtle manner, they can pursue and encourage change. When he makes no response to my plea, I understand that the men of the al Sa'ud family cannot risk their power for the sake of their women. They are passionately in love with the crown.

Kareem regains his composure after I remind him that no one outside our family, other than the author, knows who he is! And those persons know him well and are aware of his good and bad traits, even without the publication.

Kareem sits beside me and lifts my chin with his finger. He looks almost appealing as he ponders, "You told Jean Sasson about the disease I caught?"

I wiggle in shame as Kareem slowly shakes his head from side to side, visibly disappointed in his wife. "Is nothing sacred to you, Sultana?"

Many battles end in an outpouring of goodwill. This evening ends with unexpected displays of affection. Strangely, Kareem says he has never loved me more.

I find myself being courted by my husband, and the intensity of my feelings increases. My husband reawakens the desire I had once deemed forever lost. I wonder at my own ability to both love and hate the same man.

Later, as Kareem sleeps, I lie awake by his side and replay in my mind, moment by moment, the events of the day. I realize that despite the evening's end—the guarantee of protection promised by my family (due solely to their own fears of royal banishment and/or punishment) and the renewal of my marriage—I cannot rest peacefully until genuine social adjustment comes to the land I love for the women whose burden I share. The hard necessities of female life are pushing me to continue my efforts to gain personal freedom for the women of Arabia.

I question myself: Am I not the mother of two

daughters? Do I not owe my daughters and their daughters after them every effort to bring transformation?

I smile, once again thinking back on the puppet skit I had watched with Sara's youngest children, and I recall the words of the funny but wise puppet Goha. *"Does a faithful saluki [desert dog] stop barking in his master's defense when a single bone is thrown his way?"*

I shout, "No!" Kareem stirs and I rub the back of his head, whispering sweet words, lulling my husband back to sleep.

I know at that moment that I will not keep the pledge I made under coercion. I will let the world community decide when I should return to silence. Until people choose to close their ears to the plight of women in despair, I will continue to reveal the true happenings behind the secrecy of the black veil. This is to be my destiny.

I make a decision. In spite of the promises I made under threat of detention, when I next travel out of the kingdom I will contact my friend Jean Sasson. There is more to be accomplished.

When I close my eyes to sleep, I am a more focused but much sadder woman than the Sultana who had awakened the previous morning, for I know that I am once again entering a risky arena, and even though my punishment— and possibly even my death— will be cruel, failure will be more bitter, for failure is everlasting.

Chapter Two:
Maha

The more prohibitions you have, the less virtuous people will be.
—TAO TE CHING

Those whom Kareem and I love best have proved the worst. Abdullah, our son and firstborn, troubles us; Maha, our eldest daughter, frightens us; while Amani, our youngest daughter, puzzles us.

I felt no prophecies of doom as our only son, Abdullah, smiled with boyish happiness when he recounted with relish his wonderful success on the soccer field. Kareem and I were entranced, as most parents would be, upon hearing the successful exploits of a well-loved child. From a young age, Abdullah was seldom surpassed in physical games, and this fact was a particular source of glee for his athletic father. While listening with pride, we took no note of his younger sisters, Maha and Amani, who were amusing themselves with a video game.

When Amani, our youngest child, began to scream in alarm, it was with a terrible shock that Kareem and I saw flames licking at Abdullah's clothing.

Our son was on fire!

Acting on instinct, Kareem quickly threw our son to the floor and extinguished the flames by rolling Abdullah in a Persian carpet. After we assured ourselves that our son was unharmed, Kareem tried to find the source of the unexplainable fire.

I cried out that the fire was caused by an evil eye, that we were too boastful of our beautiful son!

Fighting back tears, I turned to comfort my daughters. Poor Amani! Her small frame was wracked with sobs. While I held my baby, I motioned with my free arm to her older sister, Maha, to come to me. Suddenly, I drew back in horror, for Maha's face was a frightful mask of anger and hate.

Investigating the confusing incident, we learned a terrible truth: Maha had set her brother's *thobe* on fire.

Maha, meaning "She Gazelle," has not fulfilled the promise of her gentle name. From the time she was ten, it has been apparent that our eldest daughter is possessed by the demonic energy of her mother. Often I have thought that there must be a battleground of good and evil spirits hovering over Maha, with evil spirits usually overpowering the good. Neither her life amid imperial splendor nor the unconditional love of a devoted family has tempered Maha's spirit.

Without justification, she has tormented her brother, Abdullah, and her younger sister, Amani, for as long as they both can remember. Few children have brought so many crises to one family as Maha.

In appearance, Maha is a stunningly attractive girl, with a frighteningly seductive personality. She has the look of a Spanish dancer, all eyes and hair. Combined with this great beauty is a gifted mind. Ever since her birth, it seemed to me that too many blessings had been bestowed upon my eldest daughter. With so many abilities, Maha is unable to focus on one goal, and lacking a unifying purpose, she has failed to harness her talents in any one direction. Over the years, I have watched as a hundred promising projects have been started and then abandoned.

Kareem once said he feared that our daughter was nothing more than a girl of brilliant fragments, and would fail to accomplish one single goal in her lifetime. My greatest concern is that Maha is revolutionary seeking a cause.

As I too am such a person, I am aware of the turmoil raised by a mutinous character.

In her earlier years, the problem seemed simple. Maha loved her father to distraction. The intensity of her feelings increased with her years.

Whereas Kareem adored his two daughters as he did his one son, and strove to avoid the resentments I endured as a child, the makeup of our society drew Abdullah more closely into Kareem's life outside of our home. This basic fact of our Muslim heritage was the first shock of Maha's young life.

Maha's intense jealousy of her father's affections brought to mind my own unhappy childhood—a young girl who had chaffed under the harsh social system into which she was born. For that reason, I failed to comprehend the seriousness of my child's discontent.

After Maha set fire to Abdullah's thobe, we knew that her possessiveness of Kareem went far beyond normal daughterly affection. Maha was ten years old and Abdullah was twelve. Amani was only seven, but she had watched her sister slip away from their game, fetch her father's gold lighter, and set fire to the edge of Abdullah's thobe. Had Amani not cried out a warning, Abdullah could have been seriously burned.

The second shocking incident occurred when Maha was only eleven. It was the hot month of August.

Our family had left the sweltering desert city of Riyadh and gathered at my sister Nura's summer palace in the cool mountain city of Taif. It was the first time in years that Father had attended a gathering of his first wife's children, and his attentions were devoted to his grandsons. While admiring Abdullah's height and figure, my father ignored Maha, who was tugging on his sleeve to show him an ant farm the children had built and proudly displayed. I saw Father as he brushed her aside and proceeded to squeeze Abdullah's biceps.

Maha was stung by her grandfather's preference for her brother and his indifference to her. My heart plunged for the pain I knew was in her heart.

Knowing Maha's capability for creating a scene, I walked over to comfort my daughter just as she assumed a masculine stance and began to curse my father with fiery invectives of the coarsest indecency, peppered with vile accusations.

From that moment, the family gathering rapidly declined. Though humiliated, I had the quick thought that Maha had expressed to my father his manifest due.

Father, who had never held a high opinion of the female sex, made no pretense of his feelings now. Scornfully, he ordered, "Remove this horrible creature from my sight!"

I saw plainly that my daughter had awakened Father's contempt for me. His eyes were penetrating, and his lips were curled in scorn as he looked from his daughter to his granddaughter. I overheard him mutter to no one in particular, "A mouse can only give birth to a mouse."

In the blink of an eye, Kareem snatched Maha from Father's sight and took her squirming and cursing into the villa to wash out her mouth with soap. Her muffled cries could be heard in the garden.

Father left soon after, but not before announcing to

the entire family that my daughters were doomed by my blood.

Little Amani, who is too sensitive for such accusations, collapsed into hysterics.

My father has not acknowledged the existence of either daughter since that day.

Maha's belligerence and hostility did not prevent her from occasional bouts of kindness and sensitivity, and her temperament cooled somewhat after the incident in Taif. My daughter's angers ebbed and flowed. In addition, Kareem and I doubled our efforts to assure both our daughters that they were as loved and esteemed as our son. While this proved fruitful in our home, Maha could not ignore the fact that she was considered less worthy than her brother in the world outside our walls. It is a distressing habit of all Saudi Arabians, including my own family and Kareem's, to pour attention and affection on the heads of male children, while ignoring female children.

Maha was a bright girl who was hard to deceive, and the uncompromising facts of Arab life burned into her consciousness. I had strong premonitions that Maha was a volcano that would one day erupt.

Like many a modern parent, I had no clear notion of how to help my most troubled child.

Maha was only fifteen during the Gulf War, a time that no Saudi Arabian is likely to forget. Change was in the air, and no one was more tempted by the promise of female liberation than my eldest daughter. When our veiled plight peaked the curiosity of numerous foreign journalists, many educated women of my land began to plan for the day when they could burn their veils, discard their heavy black abaayas, and steer the wheels of their own automobiles.

I, myself, was so caught up in the excitement that I

failed to notice that my oldest daughter had become involved with a teenage girl who took her idea of liberation to the extreme.

The first time I met Aisha I was uncomfortable—and not because she was unrelated to the royal family, for I, myself, had cherished friends outside the circle of royalty. Aisha was from a well-known Saudi Arabian family that had made its fortune importing furniture into the kingdom to sell to the numerous foreign companies that had to stock large numbers of villas for the swarm of expatriate workers invading Saudi Arabia.

I thought the girl was too old for her years. Only seventeen, she looked much more mature, and acted in a tough manner that suggested trouble.

Aisha and Maha were inseparable, with Aisha spending many hours at our home. Aisha had an unusual amount of freedom for a Saudi girl. Later, I discovered that she was virtually ignored by her parents, who seemed not to care about their daughter's whereabouts.

Aisha was the oldest of eleven children, and her mother, the only legal wife of her father, was embroiled in a never-ending domestic dispute with her husband over the fact that he took advantage of a little-used Arab custom called mut'a, which is a "marriage of pleasure," or a "temporary marriage." Such a marriage can last from one hour to ninety-nine years. When the man indicates to the woman that the temporary arrangement is over, the two part company without a divorce ceremony. The Sunni sect of Islam, which dominates Saudi Arabia, considers such a practice immoral, condemning the arrangement as nothing more than legalized prostitution. Still, no legal authority would deny a man the right to such an arrangement.

As an Arab woman belonging to the Sunni Muslim sect, Aisha's mother protested the intrusion of the temporary, one-night or one-week brides her depraved husband brought into their lives. The husband, disregarding the challenge of his wife, claimed validation through a verse in the Koran that says, "You are permitted to seek out wives with your wealth, indecorous conduct, but not in fornication, but give them a reward for what you have enjoyed of them in keeping with your promise." While this verse is interpreted by the Shiite sect of the Muslim faith as endorsement of the practice, these temporary unions are not common with Sunni Muslims. Aisha's father was the exception in our land, rather than the rule, in embracing the freedom to wed young women for the sole pleasure of sex.

Occupied by the plight of helpless girls and women in my land, I questioned Aisha closely about the indecent practice I had heard discussed by a Shiite woman from Bahrain whom Sara had met and befriended in London some years before.

It seemed that Aisha's father did not desire the responsibility of supporting four wives and their children on a permanent basis, so he sent his trusted assistant on monthly trips into Shiite regions in and out of Saudi Arabia to negotiate with various impoverished families for the right of temporary marriages with their virginal daughters. Such a deal could easily be struck with a man who had four wives, many daughters, and little money.

Aisha sometimes befriended these young girls, who were transported into Riyadh for a few nights of horror. After Aisha's father's passion waned, the young brides were sent away, returned to their families wearing gifts of gold and carrying small bags filled with cash. Aisha said that most of the youthful brides were no more than eleven or twelve years old. They were from poor families and were uneducated. She said they seemed not to know what exactly was happening to them. All the girls understood was that they were very frightened, and that the man Aisha called Father did very painful things to them. Aisha said all of the girls pleaded to be returned to their mothers.

The hard-eyed Aisha wept as she related the story of Reema, a young girl of thirteen who had been brought to Saudi Arabia from Yemen, a poverty-stricken country that is home to a large number of Shiite Muslim families. Aisha said Reema was as beautiful as the deer for which she was named, and as sweet as any girl she had ever known.

Reema was from a nomadic tribe that roamed the harsh land of Yemen. Her father had only one wife, but twenty-three children, of whom seventeen were girls. Even though Reema's mother was now shriveled and bent from childbearing and hard work, she had once been a lovely girl and had given birth to seventeen beautiful daughters. Reema proudly said that her family was known as far away as San'a, the capital of Yemen, for the beauty of their women.

The family was very poor, with only three camels and twenty- two sheep. In addition, two of the six sons were handicapped from difficult births. One son's legs were twisted and he could not walk; the other jerked in a strange motion and could do no work. For these reasons, Reema's father strove to sell his sought-after daughters to the highest bidder. During the summer months, the family would travel through high mountain passes, along narrow, tortuous roads into the city, and a deal would be struck for the daughter who had reached marriageable age according to Islam.

The year before, at age twelve, Reema had reached puberty. She was her mother's favorite child, and the girl attended to her handicapped brothers. The family had pleaded with her father to let her remain with them a few more years, but he sadly confessed that he could not. There were two sons after Reema, and the sister closest in age was only nine years old. Reema's younger sister was small and undernourished, and her father feared the girl might not reach puberty for another three or four years. Reema's family could not exist without the marriage money.

Reema was taken to San'a to be wed. While her father scouted the city for a suitable bridegroom, Reema remained in a small mud house with her sisters and brothers. On the third day, her father returned to the hut with the agent of a rich man from Saudi Arabia. Reema said her father had been very excited, for the man represented a wealthy Saudi Arabian who would pay much gold for a beautiful girl.

The Saudi agent insisted upon seeing Reema before he paid the money, a request generally met with the blade of a Yemeni sword rather than humble compliance from a Muslim father. The gold in the agent's hands overcame the religious convictions of the family. Reema said she was inspected in the same way her father inspected the camels and sheep at market. Reema confessed she did not protest the shame, for she had always known she would go to another family, as the purchased property of another man. But she squirmed and pushed when the man insisted upon viewing her teeth.

The agent pronounced Reema satisfactory and paid a portion of the agreed sum. The family celebrated by killing a fat sheep, while the agent had Reema's documents prepared to fly to Saudi Arabia. Reema's father happily announced that the family could now wait out the four years until Reema's younger sister reached the proper age, for the man from Saudi Arabia had paid a large sum for Reema.

Reema herself forgot her anxieties, even becoming

excited, after her father told her that she was the most fortunate of girls. Reema was going to a life of leisure, she would eat meat every day, have servants at her beck and call, and her children would be educated and well fed. Reema asked her father if the man might purchase her a doll, one like she had seen in a discarded European magazine the children had discovered in the trash bins of San'a.

Her father promised that he would make Reema's request a high priority.

When the man returned a week later, Reema first learned the terrible truth, that the marriage would not be honorable, that it was a marriage of mut'a, a temporary union. Her father became angry, for his honor was at stake, his daughter should not be treated in such a lowly manner. He pleaded with the man from Arabia, saying that it would be difficult to find another husband for his daughter, who would no longer be considered fresh and clean. He might be forced to provide for Reema for many years while seeking a man who would accept her as a second, less honored wife.

The man sweetened the deal with a bundle of bills. He said that if Reema's father refused, he would be forced to insist upon the return of the money already paid.

Reluctantly, Reema's father relented, admitting that he had already spent a portion of that sum. Ashamed, he turned his face to the ground and told Reema that she must go with the man, that it was God's will. Reema's father asked the Saudi man to find Reema a permanent husband in Saudi Arabia, since there were many Yemeni laborers working in that rich country.

The agent agreed that he would make an effort. Otherwise, he said, Reema could become a servant in his home.

Reema said good-bye to her family and left the land of her birth, haunted by the pitiful weeping of her two handicapped brothers.

During the trip, the man promised a homesick Reema that he would purchase her a doll, even though such an item was expressly forbidden by the men of religion.

Like most Arab girls, Reema had full knowledge of a wife's responsibilities. She had slept in the same room with her parents since the day of her birth. She understood that a woman must submit to her husband's every wish.

Aisha said it was the girl's calm acceptance of her life of slavery that she found so distressing, recalling that the girl's tears belied her declaration that she was not displeased with her lot. Reema wept for the six days she was in Aisha's home, all the while defending the right of Aisha's father to do with her as he pleased.

Aisha revealed that her father's employee easily located a Yemeni man who was employed as a tea boy in one of their offices, a man who was willing to accept Reema as his second wife. The man's first wife was in Yemen, and he admitted that he needed a woman to cook his meals and serve him.

The last day Aisha saw Reema, the young girl was clutching a small doll, obediently following one man out of their home to go and wed another man she did not know.

Aisha's mother, a pious Sunni Muslim, became so distraught over Reema's situation that she went to her husband's family to complain. This desperate deed created quite a furor in the family, but nothing the man's parents could say or do convinced their son to cease the godless act. Their advice was for Aisha's mother to be patient and to make her husband happy. She should also pray to God for her husband's soul.

I often wondered what became of those children,

the mut'a brides, for it is quite difficult in the Muslim world to arrange a good marriage for a girl who is no longer a virgin. As dispensable girls in fortuneless families, they were, I suppose, eventually married off as the third or fourth wife to a man without wealth or influence, much in the same manner as Reema, or of my childhood friend Wafa, who had been wed to such a one against her will by her own father as punishment for socializing with men not of her family.

Aisha's home life was agony for a thinking girl, and the stress and strain of her father's debauchery pushed her into inevitable teenage decline.

My daughter, Maha, naturally imprudent, was captivated by Aisha's antics. Recalling my own rebellious youth, I knew the futility of forbidding Maha to meet with Aisha.

Forbidden fruit is too tempting for all children, regardless of their nationality or sex.

During the height of the Gulf War, our king harnessed the most aggressive of the roving bands of morals police, forbidding them to harass Western visitors to our land. Quite sensibly, the men of our family knew it would not do for journalists from the West to view life as it really is in our country. Happily, the women of Saudi Arabia benefited from this royal order. The absence of sharp-eyed religious police patrolling the cities of Saudi Arabia, searching for uncovered women to strike with their sticks, or spray with red paint, was too good to be true. This policy endured no longer than the war itself, but for a few months we Saudi women enjoyed a welcome respite from probing eyes. During this heady period, here was a universal call for the women of Saudi Arabia to take their proper place in society, and we foolishly thought that the favorable situation would continue forever.

For some of our women, too much freedom given too quickly proved disastrous. Our men were disappointed that all women did not behave as saints, without understanding the confusion caused by the contradictions in our lives.

Now I know that Aisha and Maha were two Saudi girls not yet psychologically prepared for unfamiliar and complete freedom.

Because of the unusual times brought about by war, Aisha managed to have herself appointed a volunteer at one of the local hospitals, and nothing would do but for my daughter to seek the same appointment at that institution. This she did two days a week after her school day ended. It was a marvelous experience for Maha, for although she was forced to wear her abaaya and head scarf, she was not required to wear the hated veil once she was inside the hospital doors.

When the war ended, Maha refused to go back to the old ways. She held tight to her newfound freedom and begged her father and me to allow her to continue her work at the hospital.

Our approval was reluctantly given. One afternoon when Maha was expected at the hospital, our driver was waiting in the front drive. I decided to go and hurry her along. By some whim of circumstance, I happened to enter Maha's room just as my daughter was putting a small caliber pistol into a brown leather holster strapped to her upper leg.

I was struck dumb! A weapon! Kareem happened to be home for the afternoon siesta, and upon hearing our raised voices, he came to investigate. After an emotional scene, Maha confessed that during the war, she and Aisha had begun to arm themselves, in the event that the Iraqi army broke through to Riyadh! Now that the war was over, she thought she might need protection from the morals police, who had begun to threaten women in the street.

The "morals" or "religious police," sometimes called the mutawwa, are members of the "Committee for Enforcing the Right and Forbidding the Wrong." Now that the foreign journalists had departed the kingdom at the end of the Gulf War, these zealots were more active than we could ever recall, initiating arrests and prosecutions against women in my country.

Maha and Aisha had decided they would not endure the attentions of these zealots let loose upon innocent women.

I looked at my daughter in alarm and disbelief! Was she planning to fire upon a man of religion?

Kareem learned that the weapon belonged to Aisha's father. He, like many Arab men, had quite a collection of firearms and had not missed the two pistols his daughter and Maha had stolen.

Imagine our horror when we learned that the pistol was loaded and that it had no safety feature. Maha tearfully confessed that she and Aisha had practiced firing the pistols in a vacant lot at the back of Aisha's home!

To Maha's dismay, her enraged father confiscated the illegal weapon and bundled her into his Mercedes. Dismissing his driver, Kareem drove like a madman across the city of Riyadh to the home of Aisha in order to return the gun and warn Aisha's parents of our children's dangerous activities.

The result of our bizarre discovery was a hasty conference called between ourselves and Aisha's parents. Both our daughters were sent to Aisha's room.

Aisha's mother and I, covered still by our black veils, sat in our world of separations and discussed the children we had brought into the world. Oddly enough, for once in my life I was pleased to be veiled, for I could stare in undisguised contempt at Aisha's father, a man I knew to be a molester of young girls. Surprisingly, he was a youthful and attractive man of dignified appearance.

I thought to myself, beware of those who look like a rose, for even roses have spikes. With our daughters the main topic of the evening, I had little time to dwell upon the dark secrets of the home we were visiting.

What Kareem and I uncovered that evening about our eldest daughter's shocking convictions will haunt our memories until we cease to walk the earth.

While I question the unjust practices and cruel customs inflicted upon the female population of Saudi Arabia by those who so rigidly interpret—and thus often misinterpret—the laws laid down by the Prophet, there is no doubt in my mind of the existence of one God as preached by his messenger, Mohammed. Our three children have been raised to revere the teachings of the Prophet and the Koran, which was passed down from God. That a child of mine would curse God and denounce his word brought a chill to my heart and numbed me.

When it was announced to Aisha and Maha that their parents had reasonably concluded that the two girls should henceforth avoid each other's company and seek out other friends and new interests, my daughter yanked the veil from her face, raised her head in fury, and displayed such a look of evil that terrorized her own mother, who had carried her in her womb and suckled her at her breast. If I had not heard Maha's words with my own ears, no person could convince me of their validity.

Her full lips tight with determination, our daughter yelled, "I will not do as you say! Aisha and I will leave this land we hate and make our home in another place. We hate it here! We hate it! To be a woman in this awful country you must defile your life with the most tremendous injustices."

Spittle dripped from Maha's lips. Her body shook with uncontrolled rage. Her eyes sought mine. "If a girl lives modestly, she is a fool. If she lives normally, she is a hypocrite. If she believes there is a God, she is an imbecile!"

Unable to move, Kareem did manage to find his voice. "Maha! You blaspheme!"

"Blaspheme? What is there to blasphemy? There is no God!" Kareem jumped to his feet and squeezed Maha's lips together with his fingers. Aisha's mother screamed and fainted, for such a statement can cost a life in the land of my birth.

Aisha's father shouted out for us to remove our unbelieving daughter from his home.

Kareem and I struggled with Maha, who suddenly had the strength of a giant. My daughter had lost her mind! Only the insane have such unnatural power! After much pulling and pushing, Kareem and I managed to shove our child into the back seat of the automobile and we raced back to our home. Kareem drove while I tried to quiet my child, who no longer knew her mother. Finally, she lay still, as someone in a swoon.

We summoned an Egyptian physician, who was trusted by our family physician. In a vain attempt to calm us, he said there were many such disorders in teenage girls the world over, and proceeded to cite statistics on the strange malady that seems to affect females only.

The physician had his own theory. He claimed that at puberty, a girl often receives large spurts of hormones, and such an event drives her crazy for short periods of time. He said that he had treated many such psychological cases within the royal family, without any complications or permanent effects. He grinned and stated that he had not lost a patient yet.

In the doctor's opinion, Maha should be kept sedated for a few days; she would recover from the case of hysterics on her own.

Leaving us with an ample supply of tranquilizers, he said that he would return in the morning to check on his patient.

Kareem thanked the doctor and walked him to the door. When he returned, we exchanged a long and thoughtful look. There were no words necessary between us.

While Kareem arranged for our private plane to be readied, I telephoned my sister Sara and arranged for Abdullah and Amani to stay with her until our return. Kareem and I were taking Maha to London. She was in desperate need of the best psychiatric care available. Sara was asked to keep Maha's condition a secret. If inquiries were made, our families were to be told that Maha was in need of dental care that required a number of visits to London.

Many members of the Saudi royal family routinely travel abroad for medical and dental treatment. Such a trip would arouse little curiosity.

While packing Maha's clothing, I came across disturbing books and documents hidden among her underwear. There were numerous writings on astrology, black magic, and witchcraft. Maha had underlined many passages detailing revelations and prophecies. Most alarming to my mind were malevolent items that were supposed to wreak dire evils upon people who had offended her, or induce love at a glance, or cause death by a spell.

My breath caught in my throat when I saw an item of Abdullah's clothing wrapped around a black stone with some bits of loose, gray-colored substance I could not identify. I stood, hand to forehead, thinking. Could it be true? Had Maha plotted to harm her only brother? If this was the case, I was a failure as a mother.

I moved about in turmoil, collecting damning evidence of my child's barbaric interests. Confused, I traced in my mind Maha's activities from the days of her childhood. From what source had my daughter learned of such matters, accumulating a treasure house of dark paraphernalia?

I remembered Huda, my father's long-deceased slave, and her obvious abilities at predicting the future. But Huda had died before my daughter's birth. As far as I knew, there were no other freed slaves or servants from Africa in our homes who possessed Huda's power of sorcery.

I recoiled, as if hit by a blow, as I thought of my mother-in- law, Noorah. It had to be Noorah! Noorah had disliked me from the first moment we met. When I wed her son, I was a young and foolish girl, whose bold, rebellious character made a bad first impression on my mother-in-law. Disappointed that her son had neither divorced me nor taken a second wife, Noorah had never ceased to hate me, although she was careful to hide her dislike under a thin veneer of false affections.

From Kareem's revelations to his mother, Noorah had detected with her eagle eyes that Maha was my weakest point. From a young age, Maha's mental life had been one of conflict and pain, and Noorah had seized on that pain and in it found a vulnerability.

It was plain to see that Noorah had always favored Maha over her other granddaughters, and her attention had been gratefully received by the confused child. Maha had spent long hours alone with her grandmother. Noorah, an avid believer in the occult, had clearly lost no time in teaching my daughter her own ominous beliefs. How could I be so stupid as to believe that Noorah had my best interests in mind?

I had been a fool, for my heart had been softened by Noorah's obvious delight in Maha, and I had often expressed my profound appreciation for her generous attentions toward my most troubled child. Noorah, because of her dislike for me, had chosen to lead my emotionally fragile daughter deeper into the abyss.

I knew that I must confide my findings to Kareem. My words would have to be delicate, for Kareem would have great difficulty in believing that his mother was capable of such a shameful deed. The truth could become twisted, and I, Sultana, might bear the brunt of his anger, while Noorah would sit contentedly in her palace gloating at her most hated daughter-in-law's failure as a mother and wife.

Chapter Three:
London

Not forever can one enjoy stillness and peace. But misfortune and obstruction are not final. When the grass has been burnt by the fire of the steppe, it will grow anew in summer.
—WISDOM FROM THE MONGOLIAN STEPPE

Under the influence of strong medication, Maha lay as one dead while her father and I attempted to make some sense of the precarious situation in which we found ourselves. During the airplane trip to London, Kareem sat like a stone, pale-faced as he handled the distasteful objects I had brought in a small bag from Maha's room. He was as appalled as I at our daughter's fascination with the supernatural.

After a few silent moments, Kareem posed the question I had been dreading. "Sultana, where did Maha come across such madness?" His brow furrowed, and he wondered aloud, "Do you believe it was that foolish girl Aisha?"

I squirmed in my seat, not knowing how to answer my husband. Recalling a wise Arab proverb spoken often by my gentle mother, *"A fly will never be able to enter a*

mouth which knows when to stay shut," I felt that this was
not the time to implicate Noorah, my husband's mother.
Kareem had already endured too many shocks for one
day.

Biting my lip and shaking my head, I answered
him, "I do not know. We will tell the doctor what we
found. Perhaps Maha will confide in him, then we will
know who or what is behind her knowledge of such matters."

Kareem nodded his head in agreement. For the remainder of the flight, we took turns sleeping and
watching our child, who appeared in her drug-induced
sleep as sweet as an angel. For some unexplained reason, I
was reminded of another al Sa'ud royal, Princess Misha'il,
a young woman who hid her illicit love. When her secret
was discovered, my royal cousin's life ended in front of a
firing squad.

While Kareem slept, I watched Maha, and remembered Princess Misha'il.

Misha'il was the granddaughter of Prince Mohammed ibn Abdul Aziz, the same Prince Mohammed who
had been passed over for the crown because of his father's
ruling that the ferocious behavior of a warrior had no
place on a throne.

While I did not have a close friendship with
Misha'il, I had met her at various royal functions. She was
known in the family as a rather wild girl. I thought perhaps her unhappy temperament was related to her
marriage to an old man who failed to satisfy her. Whatever it was, she was miserable and became romantically
involved with Khalid Muhalhal, who happened to be the
nephew of the special Saudi Arabian envoy to Lebanon.

Their love affair was hot and filled with the tension caused by the impossible social climate of Saudi
Arabia. Many members of the royal family had heard of

their illicit relationship, and when the young couple were on the brink of discovery, they made a fatal decision to run off together.

My oldest sister, Nura, was in Jeddah at the time and heard the story firsthand from a member of Misha'il's immediate family. Misha'il, fearing the wrath of her family, attempted to stage her own death. She told her family that she was going for a swim at their private beach on the Red Sea. Misha'il piled her clothes on the shore, then dressed herself as a Saudi man and tried to flee the country.

Unfortunately for Misha'il, her grandfather, Prince Mohammed, was one of the shrewdest and most powerful men in the country. He did not believe she had drowned. Officials manning all exits from the country were alerted to search for the granddaughter of Prince Mohammed. Misha'il was caught—intercepted trying to catch a flight from the airport in Jeddah.

Telephones were ringing all over the kingdom, with each royal professing to know more than the next. There was a rumor a minute. I heard that Misha'il had been set free and allowed to leave the kingdom with her lover. Then I was told a divorce would be granted. Later, a hysterical cousin called and claimed that Misha'il had been beheaded, and that it had taken three blows to separate her head from her body. Not only that, Misha'il's lips had moved and had called out her lover's name, causing the executioner to run from the scene! Can you imagine, my excited cousin asked, words from a bodiless head!

Finally, the very real and ugly truth was made known. Prince Mohammed, in a fit of anger, said that his granddaughter was an adulterer and that an adulterer should submit to Islamic law. Misha'il and her lover were going to be executed.

King Khalid, who was our ruler during this time of

tragedy, was known for his indulgent nature. He recommended that Prince Mohammed show mercy, but mercy was not an agreeable emotion for that fierce bedouin.

On the day of the execution, I waited with my siblings for news. My sisters and I hoped for a last-minute reprieve. Ali, not surprisingly, expressed the opinion that adulterous women should submit to the laws of Islam and prepare themselves for death.

On that hot day in July of 1977, my cousin Misha'il was blindfolded and forced to kneel before a pile of dirt. She was shot by a firing squad. Her lover was forced to watch her die. He was then beheaded with a sword.

Once again, unsanctioned love had cost two young people their lives.

The affair was hushed up, and the al Sa'ud clan hoped that talk of a young woman murdered for the simple act of love would soon disappear. It was not to be. Though buried in the sands of the desert, Misha'il was not forgotten.

Many Westerners will recall the documentary about her death, called, appropriately, *Death of a Princess*. As divided as our family was over her punishment, nothing compared with the arguments and hostility generated by the film.

Having comfortably mastered the role of dictators, the men in our family grew furious over their inability to control the news releases and films shown in the West. Offended to the edge of madness, King Khalid ordered the ambassador from Great Britain to leave our country.

I heard later from Kareem and Asad, Sara's husband, that our rulers had seriously considered forcing all British citizens out of our country!

International tensions ran high over the sexual misconduct and execution of one Saudi Arabian princess.

I despaired of the memory. I held my head in my

hands. Now, I was the mother of a child who had gone mad. In her madness, what act might Maha commit that would disrupt our family and introduce the pain of young death into our home? My uncharitable father would surely insist upon the harshest of punishments for the child of my womb who had so spitefully and vigorously pointed out his shortcomings as a grandfather.

Maha stirred.

Kareem awakened, and once again we shared our tortured fears for our daughter.

While we were en route to London, as agreed, Sara had made the necessary medical arrangements via telephone. When we called from Gatwick Airport, Sara reported that Maha was expected at a leading mental institute in London and that her bed was waiting. Sara had thoughtfully arranged for a special medical vehicle to transport us to the institute.

Once we had fulfilled the tiresome admitting procedures, Kareem and I were informed by the hospital staff that Maha's physician would meet with us the following morning, after his initial consultation and his examination of our child. One of the younger nurses was especially kind. She held my hand and whispered that my sister had found one of the most respected physicians in the city, and that he had years of experience with Arab women and their unique social and mental problems.

At that moment I envied the British. In my land shame over a child's madness would close the minds and mouths of my countrymen, and sympathy would never be shown.

Anguished at leaving our precious child in the hands of strangers, albeit capable strangers, Kareem and I walked listlessly to the waiting car that would take us to our apartment in the city.

Aroused from sleep, the permanent staff at our

London home was clearly not expecting us. Kareem was irritated, but I calmed him with the thought that our personal comfort was the last thing on Sara's mind. We could not fault her for not telephoning our servants prior to our arrival.

Because of the Iraqi invasion of Kuwait, and the recent Gulf War, it had been almost a year since we visited London, one of our favorite spots in the Western world. In our absence, our three servants had grown slovenly and careless. Whether we were in London or Riyadh, they had strict instructions to maintain the apartment as if we were in the city.

We were too depressed over Maha's condition to complain. Kareem and I sat on sheet-covered furniture in the sitting room and ordered strong coffee. Servants scurried about the place as best they could, considering they had been awakened at three o'clock in the morning.

I found myself apologizing for intruding on their sleep, and Kareem snapped at me, ordering, "Sultana! Never apologize to those who are paid by us. You will ruin their work habits!"

I felt peevish and wanted to retort that we Saudis could benefit from a little humility. Instead, I changed the subject and began to talk once again about our daughter.

I thought to myself that I too must be coming down with some form of insanity. Twice in one day I had chosen to avoid an argument with my husband.

After our bed was prepared, Kareem and I rested without sleeping.

Never had a night seemed so long.

The British psychiatrist was an odd-looking little man whose head sat large on his small body. His brow was vast, and his nose turned slightly to one side. I could only stare in surprise at the tufts of white hair that strangely sprouted from his ears and nose. While his appearance was disconcerting, his manner was encouraging. With his small, blue, penetrating eyes, I could tell he was a man who took the problems of his patients very seriously. My daughter was in good hands.

Kareem and I quickly discovered that he was a man who spoke what was on his mind. Without caring about our wealth, or the fact that my husband is a high-ranking prince in the royal family of Saudi Arabia, he spoke with fearless honesty about the system in our land that so hobbled the will of women.

Well informed of the traditions and customs of Arab lands, he told us, "As a child I was fascinated by the Arabian explorers: Philby, Thesiger, Burton, Doughty, Thomas, and of course Lawrence. I devoured their adventures. And, quite determined to view what I had read about, I convinced my parents to send me to Egypt. It wasn't Arabia, but it was a start, anyway. To my misfortune, I arrived just as the Suez Crisis occurred. But I was hooked."

His eyes took on a faraway look. "I went back years later...set up a small practice in Cairo...learned a bit of Arabic"—he paused, looking at Kareem—"and found out more than I wanted to know about the way you fellows treat your women."

Kareem's love of his daughter proved stronger than his love of honor. To my relief, he remained quiet, his face free of all expression.

The doctor looked pleased. He seemed to be thinking, here is an Arab who would not spout nonsense about the need to lock females in purdah.

"Will our daughter recover? Fully recover?" Kareem asked.

The worry in his voice told the doctor of his love

for Maha. I moved to the edge of my seat. I could hear my heart pounding in my ears.

The doctor clasped his hands together, rubbing them as if he were lubricating his palms. Looking from Kareem to me, he heaped drama upon an already dramatic situation. His face remained blank as he answered, "Will your daughter recover? Fully recover? I have spoken with her for one hour only. Therefore, it is difficult to summarize her case completely." Looking upon my stricken face, he added, "But, her case seems quite typical. I have treated a good number of Arab ladies who suffered from hysterics, women who were visiting our city. Generally speaking, given time and proper care, I would say that your daughter's prognosis is favorable."

I wept in my husband's arms.

Maha's physician left us alone in his office.

For three months I remained in London while Maha underwent psychiatric evaluation and treatment. Once we understood that our daughter would require lengthy care, that a cure could not be achieved in a matter of days, Kareem traveled back and forth to Riyadh, making a point to be in London on Tuesdays and Thursdays, the two days of the week when we were allowed to visit with our child.

During our visits we offered Maha peace, but she preferred to fight. It was as if a thousand terrors denied her ability to speak calmly and reasonably. Nothing we could say or do pleased her. Following the physician's instructions, Kareem and I refused to argue with our child. At those moments Maha argued with herself, even going so far as to speak in two voices! Maha's doctor assured us that eventually Maha's mental state would improve beyond our expectations.

How we prayed for that moment to arrive!

The intense visits wore poorly on Kareem. I saw my husband age before my eyes. I said to him one evening, "If nothing else, I have learned that aging has nothing to do with the accumulation of years. Aging is the inevitable defeat of parents by their young."

A small twinkle came into Kareem's eyes, the first sign of joy I had seen in many days. He claimed, in all seriousness, that it could not be so. "If that were the case, Sultana, your long-suffering father would appear the oldest living man on the planet."

Pleased that my husband had showed a glimmer of life, I let the reference pass and leaned fondly on his shoulder, relieved that our family tragedy had brought us closer together rather than pushing us further apart. At that moment I reminded myself that no person leads an irreproachable life, and I forgave my husband for the trauma I had endured in his futile quest for a second wife. The event had taken place years before, and we had repaired our damaged relationship, but until now, I had not forgiven my husband for his desire to take another woman into our home. Full of emotions I had assumed I'd lost forever, I congratulated myself on the worth of the man I had wed.

In time, Kareem and I witnessed a miracle. Maha's doctor was, as I had expected, a man of genius and perseverance, a devoted physician whose natural abilities soothed my daughter's frightful demons. In happy obscurity, while locked in the drabbest of offices in the dreariest of hospital wards, he combined his medical knowledge with his experience in the world of Arab women and gained my daughter's trust. With this trust, the physician opened her wounds, and torrents of jealousy, hate, and anger spilled from Maha's trembling hands onto the pages of an ordinary notepad, producing an extraordinary journal.

Weeks later, while reading one of these short but disturbing stories from her notes, given freely from Maha's hands to her parents, Kareem and I discovered the depths of our child's plunge into a world more sinister than either of us could ever have imagined.

Living in the Mirage of Saudi Arabia
or
The Harem of Dreams
by
Princess Maha al Sa'ud

During the dark period of Saudi Arabian history, ambitious desert women could only dream of harems stocked with hard-muscled men, well endowed with instruments of pleasure. In the enlightened year of 2010, when the matriarchal family ascended into power, with the most intelligent woman crowned queen, women became the political, economic, and legal authority of society.

The great wealth accumulated during the oil boom of the year 2000, the boom that had crippled the powers of the United States, Europe, and Japan to that of third world powers, assured the land of Arabia plenty for generations to come. With little but time on their hands, women addressed social issues that had plagued the land for more years than they could remember.

A small minority of women voted to abolish polygamy, the practice of taking four husbands, while the majority, remembering the evils the practice had spawned when the kingdom was a patriarchal society, recognized that while the system was not the best that they could devise, it was the only social system that embittered women would receive. *The pleasures of love that had been forbidden now wormed their way into the mind of every woman, even that of the waiflike Malaak, the daughter of the queen of Saudi Arabia.*

Malaak danced a hot dance of love, challenging her favorite lover, Shadi, with a gold sovereign between her lips, motioning with her head for the man to pull it out with his teeth.

Malaak was small and brown-skinned with delicate features. Her lover was large and heavy with muscles of steel. Wanting desperately to achieve his goal of being appointed the most influential man in the harem, Shadi moved his tongue over every part of Malaak's body, enticing her senses in an agony of passion.

In a frenzy of movement, Shadi removed the coin with his teeth, and lifted Malaak into his arms, taking her behind the flimsy curtains of his assigned section of the harem. There, the lovers pressed against each other, the warmth of their breath spreading over their faces, and down their necks, to their chests. Shutting out the world, they began to kiss.

Malaak opened her eyes to watch her lover perform his rhythmic movements. Her muscles tensed when she saw that the man Shadi had softened into a woman!

Life having produced a cynical soul, Malaak adjusted herself to the power at hand, and she became enamored of the loveliness of the woman who shared her bed. Choosing between being feared without love and being loved without fear, Malaak could not sacrifice the love.

With Machiavellian subtlety, Malaak became what she had to be in the circumstances and atmosphere of her time.

With a pale, sickly look, Kareem laid the pages of Maha's journal on the doctor's desk. Bewildered, he asked, "What does this mean?" He gestured toward the notepad, his tone accusatory. "You said that Maha was much improved. This writing is nothing more than the ramblings of a lunatic."

I know not the source of my instinct, but I knew what the doctor was going to say before he said it. I could not breathe, I could not speak, I saw the room through a haze of blue. The doctor's voice came to me as from a distance.

The doctor was gentle with Kareem. "It's quite simple, really. Your daughter is telling you that she has made the discovery that men are her enemies, and that women are her friends."

Kareem still did not comprehend what the doctor was saying. He was impatient in his ignorance. "Yes? So?"

There was nothing else but to speak bluntly. The doctor verbalized what I already knew. "Prince Kareem. Your daughter and her friend Aisha are lovers."

Kareem was quiet for many minutes. When Kareem regained his senses, he had to be restrained and kept from Maha's side for three days.

Muslims are taught that love and sex between two of the same is wrong, and the Koran forbids experimenting: "*Do not follow what you do not know.*" In Saudi Arabia, love and sex are considered distasteful, even between those of *opposite* sexes, and our society pretends that relationships based on sexual love do not exist. In this atmosphere of shame, Saudi citizens respond to social and religious expectations by *saying* exactly what is expected.

What we *do* is another matter altogether.

Arabs are by nature sensuous, yet we live in a puritanical society. The topic of sex is of interest to everyone, including our Saudi government, which spends enormous amounts of money employing countless censors. These men sit in government offices, searching out what they deem to be odious references to women and sex in every publication allowed into the kingdom. Rarely does a magazine or newspaper make it past the censors without losing a number of pages, or having sentences or paragraphs blacked out by the censor's ever-ready pen.

This form of extreme censorship against all conventional social behavior affects every aspect of our lives, and the lives of those who compete to claim our business.

Asad, who is the younger brother of my husband and the husband of my sister Sara, once contracted with a foreign film company to make a simple food commercial for Saudi Arabian television. The manager of that foreign company was forced to adhere to a list of restrictions that would have been amusing had it not been authentic. The list of restrictions read:

1. There can be no attractive females in the commercial.

2. If a female is included, she cannot wear revealing clothing such as short skirts, pants, or swimming suits. No flesh can be exposed other than the face and hands.

3. No two people can eat from the same dish, or drink from the same cup.

4. There can be no fast body movement. (It is suggested in the contract that if a female is used, she has to sit or stand without moving at all.)

5. There can be no winking.

6. Kissing is taboo.

7. There can be no burping.

8. Unless it is absolutely necessary to sell the prod-

uct (it is suggested) there should be no laughter.

When the normal is forbidden, people fall into the abnormal. That, I believe, is what happened to my daughter.

In my country it is prohibited by religious law for single men and women to see each other. While inside the country, men socialize with men, and women with women. Since we are prevented from engaging in traditional behavior, the sexual tension between those of the same sex is palpable. Any foreigner who has lived in Saudi Arabia for any length of time becomes aware that homosexual relations are rampant within the kingdom.

I have attended many all-female concerts and functions where quivering beauties and suggestive behavior triumph over heavy veils and black abaayas. An orderly gathering of heavily perfumed and love-starved Saudi women festers into spontaneous exuberance, bursting forth in the form of a wild party with singing of forbidden love accompanied by lusty dancing. I have watched as shy-faced women danced lewdly with other women, flesh-to-flesh, face-to-face. I have heard women whisper of love and plan clandestine meetings while their drivers wait patiently in the parking lots. They will later deliver these women to their husbands who are that same evening being captivated by other men.

While the conduct of men is overlooked, the behavior of women, even with other women, is often carefully guarded. This is made apparent by the various rules and regulations governing females. Some years ago I clipped a small item from one of our Saudi Arabian newspapers to show to my sisters. I was particularly irritated by yet another foolish restriction placed upon women. A ban on cosmetics had been announced in a girls' school. Recently I ran across this clipping while throwing out some old papers. This article reads:

> ### Cosmetics Ban in School
>
> The director of Girls' Education at Al Ras, Abdullah Muhammad Al Rashid, urged all students and staff of the school under the directorate to refrain from using cosmetics, dyestuffs, ornaments, and other makeup inside the school compounds.
>
> The director added that some staff and students were noticed of late to have been using transparent garments and cosmetics as well as high-heeled shoes; hence, such adornments are prohibited. While the students must keep uniformity in dress, the teachers should set good examples to the students. The authorities would not hesitate to take punitive measures against violators of school regulations, Al Rashid added.

I remember well what I said to my sisters at the time. I waved the clipping angrily under their noses, raging, "See! See for yourself! The men of this country want to regulate the wearing of our shoes, the ribbons in our hair, the color of our lips!"

My sisters, while their anger did not equal mine, sullenly complained that our men were obsessed with controlling every aspect of our lives, even that part of our daily living that was supposedly private.

In my opinion, the control fanatics who govern our traditional lives had driven my daughter into the arms of a woman! While I was greatly distressed and did not condone my daughter's relationship with another woman, I understood, in view of the harsh restrictions she had inherited by the mere fact of being born female, how she had come to seek solace with one of her own kind.

Knowing the problem, I now felt more capable of

seeking solutions.

Kareem feared that Maha's character was now marred by her experiences. As a mother, I could not agree. I told Kareem that Maha's wanting to share her darkest secret with those who love her best pointed to her recovery.

I was right in my assessment of the situation. After months of professional treatment, Maha was ready for maternal guidance. For the first time in her young life, she drew close to her mother, wanting to communicate, tearfully acknowledging that from her earliest memory she had hated all men but her father. She had no ready explanation for it.

I felt a twinge of guilt, wondering if my own prejudices against the male sex had seeped into the embryo I had given life. It was as if my daughter had been forewarned of the wicked nature of men while lying cradled in my womb.

Maha confessed that the early trauma she had endured on the occasion of her parents' long separation had further eroded her trust in men. "What was so wrong with Father that we had to flee from his presence?" she asked.

I knew that Maha was speaking of the time Kareem had tried to take a second wife. Not wishing to share my wifely status with another woman, I had fled the kingdom, fetching my children from summer camp in the Emirates and taking them with me to the French countryside. France, with its humane people who shelter those in distress, had seemed the perfect spot to protect my young while I negotiated for those long months with my husband over his scheme to wed another woman. How I had tried to shield my children from the trauma of my own failing marriage and our separation from Kareem!

What folly! As a parent, I know now that it is preposterous to believe that even minor parental conflict does not interfere with the emotional well being of a child. Hearing Maha say that my actions had increased her mental pain, allowing abnormal thoughts to creep into her consciousness, caused me more anguish than any previous agony I have known. I had a moment of renewed anger at my husband, remembering the distress he had brought upon our three children.

Maha confessed that even after Kareem and I had patched over our differences and brought our family together again, our continuing strife had pierced the safety of the cocoon in which my children dwelled.

When I prodded my daughter about her relationship with Aisha, Maha confided that she had not known women could love women and men could love men. Such a possibility had never entered her mind, until the day Aisha showed her some magazines she had taken from her father's study. The magazines had displayed photograph after photograph of beautiful women in acts of female love. At first the photographs were a novelty, but later Maha came to see them as beautiful, sensing that the love between women was more tender and caring than the aggressive, possessive love of man for woman.

There were other disturbing revelations.

Aisha, a girl who had experimented with many social taboos before knowing my daughter, thought nothing of spying on her father's sexual misdeeds. The girl had made a small peephole in the study adjoining her father's bedroom. There, she and my daughter had watched as Aisha's father deflowered one young virgin after another. Maha claimed that the cries of those young girls had closed her mind to wanting a relationship with a man.

She told me an unbelievable tale that I would brush aside as fabrication had my own daughter not witnessed the event.

Maha said that on one particular Thursday evening

Aisha had telephoned her, urging her to come over quickly. Maha said that Kareem and I were out, so she'd had one of our drivers deliver her to Aisha's home.

Aisha's father had gathered together seven young girls. Maha did not know if he had wed the girls or if they were concubines.

My daughter watched as those young girls were made to prance naked around the room, each with a large peacock feather stuck up her backside. With these feathers, the girls were forced to fan and tickle the face of Aisha's father. Over the course of a long night, the father had performed sex with five of the seven girls.

Afterward, Maha and Aisha had stolen a feather and played together on Aisha's bed, giggling and tickling each other's bodies. It was then that Aisha showed Maha the pleasure women could have with one another.

Ashamed of her love for Aisha, Maha cried in my arms, sobbing that she wanted to be a happy, well-adjusted girl with a productive life. She cried out, "Why am I different from Amani? We came from the same seed, but we have blossomed into different plants!" She screamed, "Amani is a beautiful rose! I am a prickly cactus."

Ignorant of the ways of God, I could not answer my child. I held her in my arms and comforted her with the thought that the remainder of her life would be that of a beautiful flower.

Then my troubled daughter asked me the most difficult question of my life. "Mother, how can I ever love a man, knowing all that I know of their nature?"

I had no ready answer, yet it was with profound happiness that I understood that Kareem and I had another chance with our daughter. It was time to go home to Riyadh. We did not leave before Kareem offered Maha's British physician a position in Riyadh as our family's personal doctor.

Much to our amazement, the physician refused. "Thank you," he said. "I am honored. Fortunately, or unfortunately, whichever is the case, my aesthetic sensibilities are too keen for Saudi Arabia."

Undaunted, Kareem insisted upon rewarding the doctor with a large sum of cash. He even went so far as to try to put the money into the man's hand.

Maha's physician firmly waved aside the offer, uttering words that would have been a keen insult had they not been spoken softly. "My dear man, please, do not. The shallowness of wealth and power holds no appeal for me."

While staring in awe at one of the least prepossessing figures I have ever beheld, I suddenly had the answer to Maha's earlier, unanswerable question! Later, I told Maha that she would one day meet a man deserving of her faithful love, for such men existed. She and I had met one in London.

Once we were back in Riyadh, the source of Maha's knowledge of black magic was revealed. It was as I had thought. Noorah was the culprit.

Maha told her father, in my presence, that it was her grandmother who had introduced her to the dark world of the occult. Confronted with Abdullah's clothing wrapped around a charm, Maha denied wanting to cast a spell on her brother. Hoping that she had learned a great lesson, we did not press the issue.

I desired nothing more than to confront my mother-in-law, spit in her face, and yank out her hair. Kareem, wisely recognizing the dangers of pent-up anger, refused to let me accompany him when he went to confront her about her misdeeds. Nevertheless, I did coax my unenthusiastic sister Sara into paying a visit to our mutual mother-in-law's palace at the time of Kareem's visit.

Sara arrived at Noorah's villa shortly after my husband. She waited in the garden for Kareem to leave. Sara said that she overheard Kareem's shouts and Noorah's pleas for mercy. Kareem forbade his mother to visit his children without supervision.

Long after my husband had left, Sara said, Noorah's moans of despair could be heard in the garden. "Kareem, most beloved, you came from my womb! Come back to your mother, who cannot live without your precious love."

Sara accused me of being as wicked as Noorah, for I radiated much happiness when she told me of my treacherous mother-in-law's well-deserved wretchedness.

Chapter Four:
Makkah

"God, Great and Glorious is He, said: "And proclaim among men the pilgrimage, they will come to you on foot and on every lean camel, coming from every deep ravine."
—AL HAJ, 22:27

There is no method to calculate the number of pious Muslims who have perished while making the grueling journey across the deserts of Saudi Arabia since the time of the Prophet Mohammed and the first pilgrimage, but the total is estimated to be in the thousands. While I am pleased to report that it is no longer necessary for devout Muslims to do battle with Bedouin raiding parties or even to travel through Saudi Arabia on foot or riding lean camels in order to fulfill their fervent desire to perform one of the basic tenants of Islam, the annual pilgrimage to the holy city of Makkah, known as Mecca to Westerners, still remains a chaotic affair. Each year, hundreds of thousands of pilgrims converge on the cities, airports, and highways of Saudi Arabia for the rite of pilgrimage during the time of Haj. (Haj begins in Dhu Al Qida, the eleventh month of the hejira calendar, and ends during Dhu Al Hijah, the twelfth month of the hejira calendar.)

I performed the traditional pilgrimage many times in my youth, as a laughing child in my mother's arms, and later as a rebellious girl seeking communication with my God, whom I prayed would bestow peace of mind on an unhappy child.

To my great dismay, since Kareem and I wed, I had not worshiped in Makkah during the official time of Haj.

While Kareem and I, along with our children, have made the Umrah, or the lesser pilgrimage, which can be made at any time of year, never had we joined the multitudes in the massive annual celebration of Haj, a time when Muslims remind themselves of the lessons of sacrifice, obedience, mercy, and faith, models of conduct that are required in the Islamic faith.

Many times over the years, I emphasized to my husband that our children should experience the moving occasion of the pilgrimage during the designated time of Haj. Much to my chagrin, Kareem was forever adamant that our family flee the pandemonium of Saudi Arabia during the annual pilgrimage, which brings the largest and most concentrated gathering of human beings on earth into our country.

Each time I requested of Kareem the justification for his non-performance of Haj, my husband would provide me with a multitude of lame explanations that were heavy with contradiction.

Bewildered at his attitude and determined to get to the heart of the matter, I once purposely entangled Kareem in the discrepancy of his excuses, trapping him on the issue. Kareem was groping for a path out of his dilemma when I plainly told my husband, a man who believes in the God of Mohammed, that it seemed to me he abhorred the ritual that brings such joy to all Muslims. There was no other explanation for his bizarre behavior.

I crossed my arms across my chest and waited for his response to this insulting charge, which demanded refutation.

Kareem's face swelled with revulsion at the accusation so vile to a Muslim. Shocked at such a scandalous idea, he swore to me that he did not abhor the pilgrimage.

In the manner all men respond when they are in the wrong, Kareem then yelled out, "Sultana, you are ugly to my eyes," and turned his back on me as if to leave the room, but I ran around his side and with outstretched arms blocked the door with my body, demanding more specifics.

I screamed out that I was displeased with what I had heard, and that I would wait forever for a compelling explanation of his annual flight from the Haj. Sensing that Kareem was in a position of weakness, I became reckless and added a small lie, saying, "Others have noticed your strange distaste for Haj, and people are beginning to talk."

When Kareem saw that I would not let him pass without using physical force, he stared down at me and hesitated for a long moment. I could see that he was examining and weighing the wisdom of his reply. Making a decision, he pulled me by the arm and forced me down on the side of the bed by pushing my shoulders with his hands. He paced for a short time to the balcony doors and back, and then his defenses fell.

Kareem confessed in a rush that as a young man he had once suffered a realistic and terrifying nightmare that he was crushed to death in a crowd of Hajjis (people of the Muslim faith who attend Haj).

I made a sound in my throat. Many baffling aspects of my husband's behavior were now clear in my mind. Since the time I first met him, Kareem had seen crowds where there were none, interpreting the smallest groups of people as a mass of humanity. I shook my head at the perplexing intimacies of my husband's inner life, which I had never known. So! Kareem was frightened of the masses of pilgrims.

Being a strong believer in the powerful message of dreams, I turned my attention to Kareem's words; my mood was grim as I listened to his vivid description of the imaginary yet frightening experience he had endured while sleeping.

My husband's face became pale as he graphically described the feeling of being asphyxiated under the trampling feet of frenzied worshipers. He told me that since the time of his dream, at age twenty-three, he had purposely avoided the congested conditions endured by the faithful in making the annual pilgrimage to Makkah.

Kareem felt so intensely that his nightmare would be fulfilled if he attended Haj, that I had little heart to argue with his visionary forebodings.

Once again, everything was as before, and our family continued to depart the kingdom during the time of Haj.

When the very real and ghastly tragedy of the 1990 Haj occurred, as over fifteen hundred pilgrims were crushed to death in a mountain tunnel in Makkah, Kareem took to his bed in Paris and trembled for an entire day, declaring that the cataclysmic disaster was yet another extraordinary omen from God that he should never again worship at the Holy Mosque.

After the fateful accident of 1990, when hundreds of worshipers died, Kareem's extreme reaction to his dream began to annoy me, and I told him that his fears were inherently unsound. Nothing I could say or do at the time comforted my husband, even when I pointed out the obvious, that his dream had been realized in the death of others. In my opinion, the exact catastrophe was unlikely to occur again.

I saw that my observation failed to quiet Kareem's fierce apprehension when he replied that, evidently, he would be crushed as a singular tragedy if he failed to heed his dream or the recent mishap, which to his mind was nothing less than a direct warning from God.

Since it is true that a number of Hajjis are trampled or crushed to death during each Haj season, I could not reason further with Kareem. I wanted to dismiss his obsession, to ignore his terrors, but I could not.

Sadly, I pushed the possibility of ever again making the happy journey of Haj far into the back of my mind, but not from my heart.

After our triumphant return from London with a loving Maha in our arms, I felt an irresistible desire to embrace the ritual of glorifying God in unison with other Muslims. The time of Haj was upon us, and I gently approached the topic with my husband once again, suggesting that I take our children to Makkah. Since women in our country rarely travel without the protection of a male escort, I wondered aloud about the possibility of accompanying my sister Sara and her family to Makkah.

Much to my surprise, Kareem responded favorably to my ardent wish to undertake a journey to the city of Mohammed. My mouth fell open when he said he would consider taking the journey himself. Kareem acknowledged that he continued to fear personal harm, but that he too shared my need to give special thanks to God for the return of our precious daughter.

We were discussing the upcoming trip with members of Kareem's family when we received a warning from his brother-in-law Mohammed, who was married to Kareem's youngest sister, Hanan. Mohammed said that over two million pilgrims were expected to unite in our holiest city of Makkah, and of that total, a hundred fifty thousand worrisome worshipers were expected from Iran, the Shiite country that makes an annual call to revoke King Fahd's exclusive custodianship over Islam's holiest places.

In 1987 the inflamed Shiites had gone so far as to lead a violent protest during the traditional holy event, and in the process of breaching Saudi laws, they had desecrated the Holy Mosque, causing the deaths of 402 pilgrims. Two years later, in 1989, Tehran had instigated two deadly bombings, killing one person and wounding sixteen others.

In Mohammed's view, Haj was becoming a dangerous religious ceremony for peaceful Muslims. Radical Muslims were on the move the world over, and they favored the holiest of Islamic sanctuaries to make known their political grievances.

Mohammed, a prince of high authority in Public Security, a Saudi public service organization that strives to ensure the security of Saudis and Muslims visiting our country, was privy to knowledge that most Saudis do not have. Blind to my emotion, and absorbed only in our personal safety, Mohammed suggested that Kareem and I wait until the masses of pilgrims left the kingdom. Then, we could take our children and perform the sacred rites.

Kareem sat pale-faced and said little, and I knew that my husband was not in the slightest concerned over Iranian danger but was considering the dreaded effects of four million tramping feet.

Stubborn, and determined to fulfill my personal desires, as is my way, I challenged Mohammed's warning, saying that in my opinion, as a result of the Iranians' past violence, those pilgrims traveling from Iran would be so carefully screened and observed by Saudi Security that they would be of little danger to Haj worshipers.

Mohammed, with a stern and uneasy look on his face, said, "No. The Iranians can never be trusted. Do not let yourself forget, Sultana, that we are dealing with Shiite fanatics who dream of overthrowing our al Sa'ud-led Sunni government!"

Seeing that my reasoning was not going to achieve the reassuring response I was seeking, I used a female tactic, mischievously asking Mohammed and my husband if they failed to remember that according to Islamic teachings, to die while in Makkah ensures immediate ascension to heaven.

My husband and brother-in-law failed to see any humor in the situation, and my religious argument made little impact with Kareem, but obviously he too felt the wonderful release of anxiety that came with Maha's miraculous recovery even more than I had imagined.

Kareem took a deep breath, gave a weak smile, and said, "Sultana, I will face a thousand dangers if it will give you peace of mind. Together, we will take our children and go on the pilgrimage."

Mohammed hid a disappointed face with a smile, and I gave my husband an unexpected kiss on the cheek and began to pull on his earlobes, promising him that he would never regret his decision.

Mohammed looked scandalized at my affectionate display and made some small excuse to leave the room. Kareem's younger sister Hanan, who had been married for some years to Mohammed, gave us a knowing smile and said that we should ignore her husband's prudish facade, that Mohammed was the most loving, affectionate, and attentive of men behind closed doors.

I laughed aloud, wondering about their secret life of sweet sex, for Mohammed had always seemed strict and standoffish, and in the past I had pitied my sister-in-law.

I looked at my husband and saw that his face had reddened at the idea of his sister's marriage bed. I thought to myself that our Saudi men are too uptight and unbearably puritanical when it comes to married passion, even their own.

Remembering that we were soon going to Makkah, I kissed my husband again. I was elated!

Kareem and I invited Sara, Asad, and their growing brood to accompany our family on our long-awaited religious odyssey. Sara never failed to do Haj and was immensely pleased that this year our family would not be traveling abroad during the religious occasion.

We made excited plans to depart Riyadh for Makkah in two days' time.

Finally, it was the day of our trip to Makkah. There was much to be accomplished. Our plan was to meet Sara and her family at the airport in Riyadh at seven o'clock in the evening. Prior to that time, each member of the family had to enter Ihram, which is marked by an all-consuming intention of the heart to fulfill all the rites of pilgrimage.

During the time of Ihram, nothing involving normal life is acceptable. Hair cannot be cut, nails cannot be trimmed, beards cannot be shaved, perfumes cannot be worn, garments with seams cannot be worn, animals cannot be killed, sexual relations must be postponed, and direct contact between men and women avoided, until the sacred time of Ihram has ended.

All the members of our family started their rituals for the pilgrimage before leaving Riyadh. It was important for each person to enter a state of purity even before the long-awaited journey began.

Startling my Filipina maid, Cora, who was dusting in my bedroom, I entered my private quarters chanting the famous cry uttered by all pilgrims as they perform the rites while in the holy city of Makkah, "Here I am, God! Here I am! Here I am to do your bidding."

After Cora recovered herself, I, in a happy frame of

mind, explained the significance of our upcoming religious journey.

Cora, a dedicated Catholic, had little understanding of Muslim traditions, but as a girl of deep religious convictions, she did appreciate my delight at going on a pilgrimage.

I continued to chant my cry to God as a smiling Cora filled my bath. I counted off on my fingers all the tasks I had to accomplish. My face had to be cleansed of all makeup, and I had to take off my jewelry, even the ten-carat flawless diamond earrings given to me by my husband the year before, which I rarely removed from my pierced ears.

After removing my earrings and placing them in the large bedroom safe that holds my collection of precious jewels, I submerged myself for hours in a hot tub, to symbolically cleanse myself of any impurities. While soaking, I prepared myself for the journey by repeating aloud God's command to Muslims to visit Makkah, "And proclaim among men the pilgrimage, they will come to you on foot and on every lean camel, coming from every deep ravine." I put aside any and every thought of my family and myself, concentrating instead on things of peace and feelings of love for my fellow man.

After my long bath, I wrapped myself in a seamless black garment and covered my hair with a lightweight black scarf. Facing the holy city of Makkah, I prostrated myself on the bedroom floor and performed my prayers, appealing to God to accept the rites of Haj from me.

Finally, I was prepared for my journey.

I met my husband and children in the sitting room downstairs. Kareem and Abdullah were immaculate in white seamless robes and plain sandals. Maha and Amani were dressed in modest, dark-colored garments that covered all flesh except their faces, feet, and hands. They, as I, were unveiled. "The true veil is in the eyes of men," runs a saying of the Prophet. Thus, women on pilgrimage are forbidden to cover their faces while on Haj.

As a child, I often asked my mother about the strange necessity of covering her face before man but not before God. My mother, reared never to question the authority of men, appeared baffled and confused at the sane logic put forth by her inquiring daughter, but having spent a lifetime under the rigid jurisdiction of men, she hushed me and made no answer to what I believe is still a justifiable question.

Now, looking at my daughters' faces in all their innocence, the memory came flowing into my mind.

I hugged each of my daughters and said in an irritated tone, "When man comes to share God's wisdom, you can discard the veils you so hate!" I could not help tossing a glance of contempt at my husband and son.

Kareem moaned, "Sultana," admonishing me for what I had done!

I was struck with the horrible thought that I had broken my Haj vow. I had lapsed into a moment of discord, thinking of worldly concerns, when I must rejoice in topics of peace and love.

Embarrassed at my indiscretion, I left the room in a rush, explaining that I must perform my rituals once again.

Kareem was smiling, and my children began to laugh, as they seated themselves on chairs and sofas, patiently awaiting my return.

I prostrated myself on the bedroom floor, asking God to quiet my tongue and assist me in entering Ihram once again.

While I was praying, sad thoughts of my mother once again crept into my mind, and angry images of my father played across my eyes, ending the tranquility so necessary for entering Ihram. With a frown, I began my prayers again, from the very beginning.

I was on the verge of tears when I rejoined my family, and my husband gave me a tender look of love, which I mistook for a sexual thought. I shouted at Kareem, and then burst into tears, declaring that I could not go to Haj, that my family would have to leave without me, for I could not quiet my active and spiteful mind in order to enter the state of Ihram.

Kareem gave a nod to my daughters, for our flesh was forbidden contact, and Maha and Amani laughingly pushed me from the room into the waiting car. We were going to the airport.

Kareem quieted my protests by saying that I could go through my rituals once again on the airplane, or at our home in Jeddah before we made the short drive the following morning to Makkah.

Asad, Sara, and their children were waiting for us at the royal waiting lounge at the King Khalid International Airport, which is a forty-five-minute drive out of the city of Riyadh.

I greeted my sister and her family with strained silence, and after Maha whispered in my sister's ear, Sara gave a knowing smile that told me she understood our delay.

Our family traveled in one of Kareem's private Lear jets to Jeddah. It was a quiet journey, the adults thinking of God and their planned communication with him. The older children played quiet games, while the younger ones slept or looked through books.

Respectful of my inability to control my tongue, I spoke not a word until moments before we landed, and then I spoke too much.

It was night when we arrived at the King Abdul Aziz International Airport at Jeddah, and I was pleased when Kareem instructed the American pilot to take us through the Haj, or Pilgrim's Terminal, which is a surrealistic tent city that covers 370 acres of land. The Pilgrim's Terminal is for incoming pilgrims from other lands, but our royal status made it possible for us to land wherever we might wish.

A few years before Kareem had taken Abdullah to the grand opening of the terminal, but neither of my daughters had yet been inside the spectacular building.

Forgetting my earlier vow to remain silent until my feet touched the streets of Makkah, I felt an unexplained need for my daughters to discover a source of pride in their heritage, even if that pride was linked implicitly with economic wealth.

Initially, I spoke in a quiet voice, which I knew would not be offensive to God. I explained to my daughters that the terminal had won an international award for its unique design and advanced engineering innovation. I felt a surge of pride in the infrastructure that Saudi Arabians had created in one short generation. No longer feeling the shame of my ancestors' wrenching poverty, which had haunted me in my younger days, the old passions left me and my sense of the past was sharpened. What had once seemed bleak and shameful was now lovely and of great value. I thought to myself: from a forbidding land where scarcely fifty years ago warring tribes had fought over camels and goats, we Saudis have arrived as an economic force. My own family had led lawless tribesmen from a stark desert land to become one of the wealthiest peoples and nations on earth.

While Western minds have always claimed that only the oil paved our way to prosperity, I paid that analysis little heed, for oil had been discovered in other lands, and the ordinary citizens of those countries had never enjoyed the abundant life-style experienced by all Saudis. The secret lay in the wisdom of the men who controlled the proceeds from our resources. While I have always found much fault with the men of my family, particularly regarding their stance on women's issues, on this one subject I recognized and commended their clever and insightful leadership.

Thinking the opportunity was ripe to instill ancestral pride into those I had given life, I became enthusiastic and began to speak in a loud voice, reminding the children of past events and the virtues of the ones who came before us: the courage, endurance, self-reliance, and intelligence of our bedouin ancestors. Recalling the impoverished life lived by my parents, and then the extravagant life enjoyed by their children and grandchildren, a reversal that was nothing short of miraculous, I became animated, telling family tales with dramatic intensity and convincing realism.

Thinking myself quite the storyteller, remembering happy moments spent at the feet of my own mother and older aunties, I was immersed in the drama of the founding of our country when, suddenly, I realized that I had no audience.

Sara, Asad, and Kareem shared pained looks, but as I had quite forgotten the purpose of our journey, their expressions of disbelief at my conduct made no impact on my mind.

I glanced at our young ones and was keenly disappointed to see their lack of interest. I knew at that moment that poverty not endured does not affect the privileged, and that the younger al Sa'ud generation had fallen under the enfeebling influence of great wealth.

Plainly, the children were bored at the thought of the Bedouin seed from which they had sprung.

Abdullah was playing a game of backgammon with Sara's oldest son, while the smallest children were cavorting with some small cars and trucks Assad had brought back from his last trip to London.

Recalling the face of my loving mother and her poignant stories of the wonderful grandparents I had never known, my palms itched with the desire to slap the unresponsive faces of the descendants of those tender souls who had been dead for so very long. I looked around for someone to pounce upon, and just as I reached over to pinch the skin on Abdullah's arm, my eyes met Sara's, and she mouthed the word "*Ihram*".

Once again, I had failed to remember where I was going! Thinking, too late, I will perform my rituals once again when I reach my home in Jeddah, my thoughts strayed back to the past, and tears came without warning at the thought of the hardy and brave ancestors we would see no more. Sara gave me a gentle smile of forgiveness, and I knew that my dearest sister knew my thoughts and forgave me my transgression.

Struck by the memory of an apt proverb, "*Only our own eyes will cry for us,*" I was saddened at my family's ability to discard the memory of those who had come before us. I cried out in a forceful voice, "Those who seem dead to you are alive to me!"

My family looked at me in astonishment, all except for Kareem, who failed to control a fit of laughter. I glared at him as he wiped his wet eyes with a tissue and mumbled something to Asad that I tried to hear but could not, regarding the woman he had wed.

To calm my emotions, I turned my attention to my two daughters, and saw that they, at least, had heard something of what I had said.

Maha, preferring Europe and America over anything Saudi Arabian, was of little comfort. She had ignored my boastful commentary on our family history, and now began to complain bitterly about the terminal, dismayed that anyone would have designed an airport terminal as a tent!

"Why dig up the past?" she muttered with a tinge of dismay in her voice. "It *is* the twentieth century, you know."

Amani, though, was entranced by the spotlights mounted on the support pylons. They gave an amazing view of the striking engineering wonder, and she gave a squeal of delight.

Showing off his familiarity with the terminal, Abdullah glanced at his youngest sister and casually remarked that at the present time the fabric roof of the tent covered the world's largest space, though there were plans in motion to cover a larger space in the city of Madinah.

Amani, my most sensitive child, squeezed my hand and smiled sweetly, saying, "Mummy, thanks for bringing us here."

I gave my daughter a happy look. All was not lost. Who could have known that a journey made with such virtuous thought and the desire to praise God for the return of my eldest daughter's lucidity would have long-lasting significance for my youngest child, Amani, and enduringly disastrous consequences for her mother and father?

Chapter Five:
Amani

"Makkah, 'the blessed', known as Umm Al Qurrah, 'Mother of Cities', is the spot toward which every believer faces five times a day in prayer. For millions of Muslims, it is the goal of a lifetime to travel to Makkah for Haj. The city is strictly banned to non-Muslims, but nonbelievers feel the keen disappointment of what they are missing and want to know what lies within. As a Saudi, I have been personally selected by God to protect the true faith that got its start in the holiest city in the world that is located in my country."
—The explanation given to the author by an elderly Saudi Bedouin of why Saudi Arabians are the chosen people of God.

During the joyous occasion of Amani's birth, my sister Sara joined me in the pangs of delivery, giving birth to her second child, a daughter whom she and her husband, Asad, gave the name Nashwa, meaning ecstasy. While Amani has brought bliss into our lives, Nashwa is a loud and obnoxious girl, and has often introduced havoc into Sara and Asad's happy home.

Many times I have secretly questioned Kareem about the fearful possibility that Amani was the true child of Sara and Asad, while Nashwa was of our blood, for

Nashwa's character is remarkably similar to mine. Amani, moreover, bears a startling resemblance to her Auntie Sara, whom she favors in both lovely countenance and calm spirit. Could the staff at the hospital have accidentally mistaken our two daughters? Our children were born eleven hours apart, but Sara and I occupied adjoining royal suites. Infant confusion seemed likely to my mind. Many times over the years, Kareem has attempted to push away my fears, quoting meaningless statistics showing that such mix-ups rarely occur, but each time I gaze on my perfect child, I dread the thought that she belongs to another.

Amani, an absorbed and melancholy spirit, always treasured books more than toys, and from an early age was an enthusiastic student of art and language. Unlike her older sister Maha, Amani, for the most part, created little turbulence and instead generated tranquility and affection in our home.

While Amani's sensitive soul had penetrated more deeply into my heart than that of her two older siblings, I nevertheless should have been alerted to the shadowed tenacity in her complex temperament. My daughter's alarming penchant for animals caused open conflict with other members of our family. Her youthful devotion to all living creatures clashed with the Saudi male's love of hunting and killing all creatures that inhabit our land. While Abdullah and his father gleefully joined other royal cousins in desert hunts, machine gunning gazelles and rabbits by the light of huge spotlights mounted on specially equipped Jeeps and open trucks, Amani crept into her father's hunting room, hiding ammunition, successfully dismantling weapons, and tossing expensive firearms into the garbage. Because of Amani's intense love of animals, she was willing to forgo her strong desire for family harmony.

This humane but troubling trait showed up at an early age. Owing to Amani's fervor, our home was overrun with stray beasts of many species, sizes, and colors.

Most Arabs, unlike many Westerners, feel little devotion for animals, and starving and injured cats and dogs run wild on our city streets. Since the early 1980s there has been an active government policy in Saudi Arabia of collecting strays and abandoning these creatures in the desert to die slow and painful deaths. Yet many animals do outwit their slayers and manage to find a safe haven with those of tender nature.

While I appreciated and sympathized with Amani's pressing compulsion to protect abused animals, Kareem and others in our home were greatly distressed that our property had become a sanctuary for strays. Not content with the mere act of saving their lives, Amani pampered these abandoned creatures as if they were rare and expensive breeds, and when they died, the animals were buried with solemn funeral rites in our garden. The surviving strays she had trained to be lap pets joined the family on our grounds and in our home.

Many times it seemed to me that Amani cared more for animals than she did for members of her own family, but I am a mother who has difficulty punishing or restraining her young, and Amani was allowed her one unfortunate idiosyncrasy.

Kareem employed two young men from Thailand to clean and disinfect after the animals and to train the dogs in obedience. We even took the extreme action of building our own small petting zoo on the grounds, equipping the facility with spacious caged areas and purchasing numerous breeds of exotic animals in the hope that Amani's personal menagerie would satisfy her need to collect and coddle large numbers of animals. Next to the petting zoo area, Kareem had a sizable area walled off for Amani's strays. He commanded his daughter to restrict those animals to that special section of the yard. But after Amani had shed many tears, Kareem reluctantly agreed that she could select her ten favorite cats and dogs, which would be allowed inside her section of our home and given free access to the general grounds area.

In spite of these efforts, our daughter remained alert to street strays, and these creatures invariably found their way to our door.

Once Kareem came home to a strange sight. Three Filipina men who worked for our neighbors were caught in the act of delivering five cats in a bag to one of the Thai zookeepers. Confronting the Filipinos, who were frightened into silence, Kareem was handed a flyer that stated our household would reward the bearer SR 100 for each stray cat or puppy. Kareem flew into a fit of wild anger. After he threatened the Thai employees with termination, they confessed to Kareem that Amani had instructed them to attach the reward flyers to the walls of neighboring palaces and villas. In addition, the two men had been told to roam the neighborhood streets, abducting cats and dogs, and to bring them to Amani. Our daughter had sworn the two men to secrecy, and since Kareem had employed them to work directly for our daughter, they had kept her confidence.

Kareem forced a head count of strays, and when he discovered that he was feeding over forty cats and twelve dogs, he slumped to the ground in a daze. After a long period, without a glance at his family, my husband came to his feet and, not speaking a word, left our home. We heard the wheels of his automobile spin as he left the neighborhood. He was away for two days and three nights. I later learned that Kareem had been visiting his parents during this time. I heard from gossipy servants that Kareem told his startled parents he must have a few days' respite from the complex women in his life, or he would be forced to commit us all to an institution.

While Kareem was away, I decided I must find some manner of dulling my daughter's extreme sensitivity to animals. I made many strange discoveries that had previously gone undetected. The forty cats were dining on fresh fish from the Red Sea, while the twelve dogs were treated to gourmet meats from an expensive Australian-supplied butcher shop. Amani had been appropriating money from the weekly funds that are deposited in a small cash box in the kitchen, money that our servants used for our personal shopping. Our household expenses are so enormous that our bookkeeper had failed to notice the sum taken by our daughter to be used for her animals. When I discovered that Amani was using large amounts of money to purchase caged birds just in order to free them, I seriously threatened my child with visits to a psychiatrist, and for a while she became less involved with the animal kingdom.

I distinctly recall one dramatic occasion that involved my brother, Ali. In the past, Ali had made a point of complaining about Amani's pets. He would grumble to me that no self-respecting Muslim could enter my home for fear that the animals roaming at will would create a need for purification. Ali's unmistakable dislike of animals evidently made an impression on the psyches of Amani's greatly loved creatures, since the dogs generally made themselves scarce and hid in the bushes until my brother passed through the garden.

There was one particular incident that stands out in my mind. Ali dropped by our palace for a brief visit and had just entered the garden gate, when he stopped to order one of our servants to wash his car while he was visiting. While he was speaking, one of Amani's favorite dogs, Napoleon, chose to lift his leg on Ali's freshly laundered thobe. Ali, a vain man who is proud of his handsome and impeccable appearance, became speechless with rage. He kicked the poor creature brutally before Amani could rush to Napoleon's rescue. My daughter was so infuriated that she flung herself on her uncle, beating him on his arms and chest with her fists.

Urinated upon by a dog and physically assaulted by his niece, Ali lost no time in leaving our home, shrieking to the smirking servants that not only was his sister completely mad, but she had given birth to demented children who preferred beasts over humans for companionship.

From that moment, Amani hated her Uncle Ali with the same intensity that I had hated my unfeeling brother as a young girl.

In the Muslim faith, a dog is considered impure, and that fact was a factor in Ali's extreme anger and disgust. In the Islamic faith, if a dog drinks out of any container, it should be washed seven times, the first of which should be in water mixed with dust.

Ali is my only brother, and in spite of our continued explosive differences, he chooses to maintain a relationship with my family. Kareem forced Amani to telephone and apologize to her uncle, but the episode with Napoleon kept Ali away from our home for over two months. When he finally recovered from his anger and embarrassment, Ali returned for a visit, calling ahead to insist that our servants shut away Napoleon.

I was apprehensive about Amani's anger, which I knew was thinly veiled, and was pleased with my daughter when she entered the sitting room on the day of Ali's visit, playing hostess and offering her uncle a glass of freshly squeezed grapefruit Juice.

With an expression of relief over the forgotten incident, Ali said that he happened to be quite thirsty.

Noting the similarities between Sara and Amani, I beamed with motherly pride when my beautiful child graciously handed Ali a glass of juice and a plate of almond cookies. Her demeanor was above reproach. I gave her a happy smile, thinking to buy her a special present the next time that I went shopping.

Ali smiled his approval and commented that Amani would, one day, make some lucky man very happy. It was only after Ali left that I discovered Amani in her bedroom, laughing so loudly that the servants came from all around to learn the cause of her merriment.

Amani told an amazed audience that her uncle had drunk his juice out of a glass that had been licked clean by her entourage of stray pets! My daughter had filled the glass with cool water for her beasts prior to pouring juice for her uncle! Not only that, but she had given the recovered Napoleon a few licks on the cookies before serving them to Ali!

The servants grinned with satisfaction, for Ali is not a popular man with them.

While I tried to appear stern, my lips paid no heed, and my face trembled as I struggled to control my laughter. Giving up the charade of parental guidance, I held my daughter in my arms and roared uncontrollably.

For the first time in her life, Amani exhibited traits that led me to hope she was a child born of my body after all.

I know now that I should have scolded my child for a deed that would have caused Ali a heart attack had he known the truth, but I could barely control my glee. When I laughingly confided the story to Kareem, he had such a look of sheer horror at my amusement, that I knew my husband feared for the sanity of his loved ones.

Kareem's patience snapped at my revelation.

Seething with Muslim anger at the prank and disturbed by Amani's preoccupation with animals, he declared that the large number of animals in our home was ruining his life, and he insisted that we sit down with our daughter and have a frank discussion about her ridiculous obsession.

Before I could respond, my husband spoke into the house intercom and instructed Amani to come into our living quarters immediately.

Together, Kareem and I waited for Amani in the sitting area that is attached to our master bedroom.

Amani's black eyes sparkled with interest as she swept with sprightly grace into the room.

Before I could diffuse the situation, Kareem bluntly asked, "Amani, tell me, what is your object in life?"

Amani, with childlike serenity, replied without hesitation, "To save all the animals from man."

"Saving animals is nothing more than a pampered passion of rich Europeans and Americans," Kareem angrily responded. He looked at me as if I were to blame and said, "Sultana, I thought your child would be more intelligent."

Amani's eyes began to tear, and she asked to leave the room.

Uncomfortable with female tears, my husband thought better of his sarcastic tactics. Kareem tempered his approach and spoke with perfect seriousness. "And, Amani, after you save all the animals, of what consequence will you be to yourself, or to your family?"

Amani squeezed her lips together and looked off into space. Without responding, she gradually came back into our world. Unable to formulate her thoughts, she looked at her father and shrugged her shoulders.

Remaining wisely uncritical of her great love of animals, Kareem clarified the need for greater purpose in human life, to create and inspire those of our own kind.

He reminded Amani that she could perform good deeds for four-legged beasts while still influencing civilization. He added, "Advancing civilization is the responsibility of those who are mistreated in a society, for only out of discontent with imperfection does mankind seek to better the society in which he lives."

Amani scoffed at his message. She raised her voice and asked her father the obvious question, "In Saudi Arabia? What can a female do that will make a difference in this country?"

My daughter looked at me and waited for my expected agreement.

Just as I was about to argue with Kareem, he interrupted me and, to my astonishment, pointed me out to our daughter and said that I, as an unheard female in Saudi Arabia, had not reconciled myself to the life of a royal idler, but that I had become educated and was utilizing my knowledge to further women's causes. He continued by saying that one day women's roles would develop, and our influence would be felt outside the home.

Dumbfounded at Kareem's words, I could add little to the conversation. Never before had my husband acknowledged the righteousness of my vision of freedom for women.

After a discussion of more than an hour, Amani promised her father that she would look beyond her furry friends and find a second, equally challenging purpose in her life.

As affectionate a child as ever lived, Amani kissed each of us good night, and said that she had much thinking to do. As she was closing our bedroom door, she turned back and, giving us a wonderful smile, said, "I love you, Dada, and, Mummy, you too," bringing back to mind the innocent girl our youngest daughter still was.

Thrilled at what he declared a huge success, Kareem held me in his arms and spoke of his dreams for his daughters, as well as his son, saying that if it were up to him, "All the ridiculous restrictions placed upon the heads of women would disappear, just like magic." Kareem snapped his fingers in the air and gave me a tender look.

Cynically I thought that there is nothing like a beloved daughter to induce a man to clamor for adjustments in an unfair world.

Longing for unaccustomed peace in a household of three lively children, I welcomed the idea of the peaceful family life that Kareem promised would come, now that Amani would surely get over her love affair with the world of animals.

Shortly afterward, the Gulf War began, followed by the culmination of Maha's mental instability. During this stressful period, a stymied and solitary Amani had no one to help her search for a more fitting, fresh objective in life.

Now, retracing Amani's pattern of obsession with causes that held her interest, I, a woman schooled in philosophy, which is the critical study of fundamental beliefs, should have recognized that my youngest child possessed the traits often connected with those we deem fanatics, frightening people who eagerly embrace extremist convictions.

Perceiving the resolute earnestness of my daughter, I now reproach myself for initiating an impressionable and mentally confused child into that most religious occasion, Haj. For Amani was only fourteen years old, the time of maximum adolescent upheaval.

During our pilgrimage to Makkah, by one of the strangest transformations in our family history, Kareem and I observed our daughter Amani emerge almost overnight from her dormant religious faith and embrace Islamic beliefs with unnerving intensity. I was nothing more than a mother tending her child, offering her the foundation of her heritage, but it was as if Amani's mind were caught by a higher vision, a secret that was in herself, too intimate to reveal to her mother or father.

The morning after our arrival in Jeddah, we made the short drive in an air-conditioned limousine from that Red Sea city to the holiest city of Islam, the city of the Prophet Mohammed, Makkah. I was thrilled to find myself at the Haj with my most beloved family members in attendance. I tried to concentrate on my prayers but found myself peering out the car window, thinking of ancient times when enormous numbers of the faithful had come by camel caravan or trekked barefoot over rugged and rocky terrain in the eager quest to fulfill one of the five pillars of the Islamic faith.

I wanted desperately to share my thoughts with Kareem and my children, but I saw that each of them was busy contemplating God and his or her relationship with Him. Maha's eyes were closed, while Abdullah was fingering his prayer beads. Kareem seemed glassy-eyed, and I hoped he was not reliving his youthful nightmare of being trampled to death on this day. I leaned close and stared, but my husband studiously avoided my eyes. Amani was caught up in her own solitary meditations, and I thought that my daughter's face seemed afire.

Satisfied, I smiled and patted her hand, thinking that I had accomplished much good in bringing my family together for the holy event.

The ancient city of Makkah is the most beautiful sight for a Muslim's eyes. The city is enclosed by the Valley of Abraham and surrounded by mountain ranges to the east, west, and south. The landscape is rugged, consisting mainly of granite.

I chanted, "Here I am, O God! Here I am!" Outside the Holy Mosque of Makkah, a specially appointed official guide greeted us. He would be our Imam, or minister, during our prayers. Sara and I remained with our daughters, while Kareem and Asad walked away with our sons. As we climbed the marble steps of the Holy Mosque, we could hear other worshippers praying. As everyone did, we slipped off our shoes before entering the mosque.

All Muslims know that the Prophet always moved with the right side of his body, therefore I carefully entered the courtyard of the Holy Mosque by stepping through the Gate of Peace with my right foot first.

Crowds were rushing through all seven gates that open into the Mosque courtyard. There were many pilgrims sitting in the area, most were reading quietly.

That's when the call to prayer was heard. Sara and I, with our daughters, lined up in a row behind the men to give our prayers. Although I am of the royal family, I know that in the eyes of God, I am the same as the poorest Muslim. As soon as our prayers were completed, we walked toward the Kaaba. The Kaaba is located in the centre of the Mosque. Our Koran tells us that "The first house of God that was built for people is the one in Makkah. In a corner of the Kaaba is the Black Stone. The Black Stone had been honored by Prophet Mohammed. We are taught that Prophet Mohammed helped to place it in the Kaaba.

That's when my sister and I, along with our daughters, began to walk around the Kaaba. It is imperative to keep the Kaaba to our left as we chant, "God is most Great. O God, grant us good in this work and good in the hereafter, and protect us from the torment of the fires in hell."

Much to my surprise I saw that Amani was weeping. Through her cries, I heard her ask God to assist her in divorcing herself from the world of royal luxuries, to help her be better equipped to stamp out human wickedness.

She pleaded with God to swallow up all the sins of mankind and to cure the ills of the world. Amani was having a religious experience. Her eyes were red, but she ignored my touch of love, tenderly given as we left the area to continue our walk to the Station of Ibrahim, which is also located in the Holy Mosque. I watched Amani even as I performed further prostrations.

Soon we left to walk to the Well of Zamzam, and the Mas'a, or what is known as the Running Place. My family has built an air-conditioned gallery so that pilgrims would not suffer sunstroke in the hot Saudi desert. Men run but that would be considered taboo for women, so we walk. I drank the waters of the Zamzam from a water tap covered by a marble vault. Just as we were about to depart the waters of Zamzam, we heard a loud commotion sweeping through the crowd of pilgrims.

Curious, I walked toward a group of Muslim women from Indonesia and asked them in the English language if they knew the source of the excitement.

One of them replied, "Yes!" Three men had fallen and been trampled upon, and they had heard that two of the men had died! I could not catch my breath! I could think of nothing but my husband! Kareem! Had his nightmare come true, after all?

I ran back to my sister and our daughters, my eyes wild with terror, my incoherent words making no sense. Sara grabbed my shoulders and demanded to know what was the trouble.

"Kareem! I have heard some men have been trampled. I fear for Kareem's life!"

Thinking that I had seen his body, my daughters began to moan, and Sara raised her voice, demanding to know why I thought one of the dead men might be Kareem.

I told Sara, "A dream! Kareem suffered a dream

that he would be crushed at Haj! Now, some men have been trampled to death in the area where he was last seen."

Sara, like me, has learned there is much in life that is not for our understanding, that unexplained forces move through our lives. She was concerned, though in control of her emotions.

Just as we were about to split into three groups to search for our men, we saw that two stretchers with bodies covered in white sheets were being carried through the crowd. I ran as fast as I could and, screaming, ripped the sheets from the bodies of the dead, first one and then the other.

The four hospital workers from Makkah stood frozen to the spot, not knowing what to expect next from this woman who was clearly deranged.

Praise Allah! Neither of the dead men was Kareem! Both were old, and it was easy to see how they could have been pushed to their deaths.

I held the sheet in my hand and stood over the body of one man, crying out in great relief that I did not know him. I was standing in that position just as Kareem, Asad, and our sons followed the sounds of the shouting women to see what calamity had occurred.

Kareem could not believe what he was seeing. It appeared to my husband that his wife was laughing with joy at the sight of a man dead. He pushed through the crowd and caught me by my wrists, pulling me from the scene.

"Sultana! Have you gone quite mad?" Sara quickly explained what I had feared, and Kareem's angry look softened. Embarrassed, he had to explain the fearful nightmare he had described to his wife.

The atmosphere was electric with emotion. The crowd began to mumble and look menacingly in my direc-

tion, as the wives of the two dead men realized their tragedy and learned that I had laughed like a hyena at the
deaths of their husbands.

We hurriedly left the area, while Asad revealed our
identity to some guards. With the protection of the
guards, Asad gave a gift of SR 3,000 to each of the families
and told them we were of the royal family. He quickly explained my fear of Kareem's dream and pacified the angry
crowd.

After we escaped the scene, my family began to
laugh nervously, and later, as time erased the shame of my
conduct, the situation became a hilarious event that has
entertained them on more than one occasion.

Our rituals were completed for the first day of Haj.
We then returned to our palace in Jeddah, which is situated on the waters of the Red Sea. During the drive, in an
attempt to put the experience of the trampled men out of
our minds, each of us shared our profound experiences of
the day. Only Amani was strangely quiet and withdrawn.

I thought to myself that there was something perplexing about my youngest child's demeanor.

The feeling of impending doom would not leave
me, and once we were back in our home, I followed Kareem around until I could focus my thoughts and
articulate what was in my heart and on my mind. I accompanied him from the entrance hall to our bedroom
and out onto the balcony, then back into the bedroom and
into his library.

An abyss divided our moods. Looking at me in exasperation, Kareem finally asked, "Sultana, what can I do
for you?"

Unsure of what my concerns were, I had difficulty
expressing myself. "Have you noticed your daughter

Amani today?" I asked. "Amani is worrying me. I feel that a strange mood is oppressing our daughter. I do not like it."

In a weary tone, my husband insisted, "Sultana, cease to view danger where there is none. She is at Haj. Do you not believe that all pilgrims are engrossed in special thought?" He paused and then added in a malicious tone, "Other than you, Sultana." Kareem then stood silent, but he gave me a withering look that spoke clearly of his desire for solitude. Irritated, I left Kareem in his library. I searched for Maha, but she had retired to her bedroom and was sleeping. Abdullah was not around. He had gone with his Auntie Sara to their villa. I felt terribly alone in the world.

I decided that I would go to the source of my worry. I walked to Amani's bedroom, and when I heard the mumbling of her voice, I put my ear to the door and tried to understand the words she was saying. My daughter was praying, and her voice pleaded with God with an urgency that awakened my memory of another I had eavesdropped upon from behind a locked door. Suddenly the memory of that other voice in another time reminded me why I was so tormented with anxiety. Lawand! Amani was praying with thesame sort of isolated longing I had often heard from the locked room of her cousin Lawand!

The atmosphere that had surrounded Amani from the moment of our participation in the first ritual of the day had seemed vaguely familiar. Now, on this day, Lawand's insanity had re-emerged in the chilling intensity of Amani's eyes.

I told myself that Amani was going the way of her cousin Lawand.

While still a teenager, Lawand, who was a first cousin of Kareem on his father's side of the family, had attended school in Geneva, Switzerland. Her parents' decision to send her abroad for schooling proved a grievous mistake. While in Geneva, Lawand disgraced her family by becoming involved with several young men. In addition to her sexual involvements, Lawand became addicted to cocaine. While moving secretly out of her room one evening, Lawand was captured by the headmistress, who called her father in Saudi Arabia, demanding that he come and collect his wayward child.

When the family found out about their daughter's activities, Lawand's father and two brothers flew to Geneva and took the girl to a Swiss drug rehabilitation center. Six months later, when her treatment was completed, she was brought back to Saudi Arabia. The family was exhausted with shame and fury, and as punishment they decided to confine Lawand to a small apartment in their home until they were satisfied that she had realized her reckless offense to Muslim life.

When I heard the verdict, I could think of little but Sameera, the best friend of my sister Tahani. Sameera had been a brilliant and beautiful young woman when she was deprived of her freedom so long ago and forced into the dark prison of the woman's room. While Lawand would one day secure her freedom, it seemed that only death would free Sameera from her incarceration.

Within my limited sphere of expectations, I found myself thinking that Lawand was fortunate her father was not the unfeeling sort who could confine his daughter to life imprisonment, or to death by stoning, and I experienced sad relief instead of passionate anger.

How fortunate is the human being who has no memories, for memories often remold the victim of oppression into the image of their oppressor. With terrifying seriousness, I listened as the men of my family mouthed the law of obedience, saying that the peaceful structure of our conservative society rested upon the perfect obedience of children to their parents and wives to their husbands. Without that obedience, anarchy would rule the day. The men of my family firmly stated that Lawand's punishment was fair.

I visited the family on many occasions, listening with profound sympathy to the grief of Lawand's mother and her sisters. Often, the women of the family spoke with Lawand through the locked door. Initially, Lawand begged for forgiveness and pleaded with her mother to set her free.

Sara and I smuggled notes of encouragement to our cousin, advising her to recall the wisdom of silence and to read the books and play the games female members of the family placed through the small opening that had been constructed for the delivery of food and for emptying the pail containing bodily wastes. But Lawand had little interest in occupying her time with quiet pursuits.

After several weeks of confinement, Lawand returned to God and began to pray, declaring that she had seen the error of her ways and swearing to her parents that she would never again commit a single wrong.

Taking great pity on her daughter, Lawand's mother beseeched her husband to set the child free, saying that she felt certain Lawand would now return to the pious life.

Lawand's father suspected his daughter of deceit, since he had told her that her confinement would end when her mind once again embraced the proper thoughts of a believing Muslim.

Before long, Lawand prayed all her waking moments, failing even to respond to our worried voices. I could easily see that Lawand was hallucinating, for she spoke to God in her prayers on an equal basis, shouting that she would represent him on earth, teaching his followers a new moral code of which only she, Lawand, had knowledge.

After one particular visit, when Lawand's mother and I over-heard her madly rejoicing in the confines of her room, I told Kareem that I was certain Lawand had lost her mind.

Kareem spoke with his father, who in turn visited his brother's home. As the eldest brother of Lawand's father, Kareem's father had authority over the family. On my father-in-law's advice, Lawand's father opened the locked door and released his daughter from her prison. Lawand would now be allowed to rejoin her family in a normal life.

Lawand's eleven-week confinement had ended, but the family tragedy ripened rapidly. During the course of her prison sentence, Lawand had disciplined herself to ascetic austerity, and came out of her imprisonment seething with Islamic fervor, claiming that a new day had dawned for Islam.

On the day of her release, Lawand informed her family that all Muslims must denounce luxury and vice, and promptly pounced upon her two sisters for wearing kohl [black powder] on their eyes, rouge on their cheeks, and fingernail polish on their nails. After she made her sisters cower on the sofa, Lawand ripped an expensive necklace from her mother's neck and rushed to throw the precious stones down the kitchen drain. The women of the house could barely restrain her, and the family disturbance resulted in various minor injuries. Lawand was given a shot by one of the palace physicians and a prescription for drugs to calm her mind.

Violence hid its face for a while, but nevertheless survived, and from time to time Lawand would lash out with blunt passion, directing abuse at whoever was handy.

After she ripped Sara's gold earrings from my sister's ears, shouting that to see such gleaming finery hurt the eyes of God, I thought to protect myself by purchasing a small canister of Mace while I was on holiday in the United States. I hid the item in my luggage, even from the eyes of Kareem, and began to carry it in a small bag when I visited Lawand's home.

As is my disastrous misfortune, Lawand selected an afternoon when I was paying a visit to demonstrate her renewed religious fervor.

Lawand, her mother, two sisters, and I were having a pleasant chat while sipping tea, eating pastries, and discussing my last trip to America when Lawand suddenly became restless, her eyes flashing about, seeking some affront to God.

In her temporarily disordered state, she began to criticize her mother's choice of clothing, which Lawand stated was much too immodest for a believing Muslim. Fascinated, I watched as Lawand carefully folded her table napkin and very courteously covered her mother's neck with the fabric. Then, without warning, Lawand began to curse. She made a sudden wild leap in the air, twisting her body in midair to face me.

I saw that Lawand was eyeing my new pearl necklace, and remembered too late Kareem's warning that I should not wear jewelry in her home.

Lawand's pale ascetic face, twisted in passionate and divine conviction, awed me, and I felt the acute danger that she posed. I quickly dug in my small bag and brought out the Mace, warning my cousin that she should quit the room or sit down immediately, or I would be forced to defend myself.

Lawand's mother began to scream and to tug on her mad daughter's sleeve. I braced myself for an attack when Lawand pushed her pawing mother from her side and rushed at me, forcing me into a small corner between a lamp and a chair.

The worst was yet to come. Sara, who had agreed to meet me at Lawand's home, entered the villa at that exact moment. I saw that she held her youngest child in her arms.

Sara's jaw dropped when she saw that Lawand had cornered her youngest sister between a chair and a lamp, and that I was threatening Lawand with some kind of an object.

Knowing Lawand's weakness, Sara quickly regained her calm and subtly attempted to persuade Lawand to stop her foolishness. For a short moment Lawand, with feline deception, pretended to submit to Sara's wisdom. She dropped her aggressive stance and began to rub her hands together in a nervous manner.

Doubting her sincerity, I yelled for Sara to take her baby and run from the room. At the sound of my excited voice, Lawand swung about and then, with all the fury of one who is insane, bounded toward me with outstretched hands, making for my pearl necklace.

I squeezed the Mace container with both hands and Lawand dropped to her knees. In the back of my mind, I remembered reading that it takes double power to disable the insane, so in my excitement, I emptied the container and maced not only Lawand, but her mother and one sister, who had come to Lawand's aid.

Lawand recovered from the Mace attack rapidly, but had lost her will to fight.

Lawand's mother and sister required immediate medical attention. The Pakistani physician summoned to treat the women had difficulty maintaining his professional seriousness, when informed that one royal princess had maced three other princesses who were members of her family.

Her father finally realized that his daughter needed long-term professional attention, which she received in

France, enjoying a full recovery within a year's time.

Everyone in Kareem's family thought I had acted with too much haste, but I refused to let myself be crucified for defending myself against a woman who had lost her mind, and I told them so. Indignant, I added that instead of criticism, I deserved their appreciation for my deed, for the event had led to Lawand's recovery.

While there is a tendency among some to dismiss my actions as those of a female of excitable emotion, I am a woman of deadly seriousness when it comes to women's issues.

A wise man was once asked what was the most difficult truth in life to uncover. His reply was "to know thyself." While others might harbor doubt, I know my own character. Undeniably, I have been endowed with an overabundance of spontaneity, and it is from this exuberance that I gain my power to do battle against those in command of females in my land. And I can claim some degree of success in bending the bonds of tradition.

Now, remembering Lawand's temporary and unhinged obsession with unhealthy fundamentalist fervor, I attached great significance to my daughter's extreme infatuation with our religion.

While I believe in and honor the God of Mohammed, it is my contemplative interpretation that the masses of humanity who are engaging in loving, struggling, suffering, and enjoying are living life as God intended. I have no desire for my child to turn her back on the rich complexity of life and reaffirm her future through the harsh asceticism of a militant interpretation of our religion.

I ran to my husband and said in a rush of words, "Amani is praying!"

Kareem, who was quietly reading the Koran,

looked at me as though I had finally lost all reason. *"Praying?"* he asked, his voice tinged with disbelief at my extreme reaction to another's communication with God.

"Yes!" I cried. "She is exhausting herself with prayer." I insisted, "Come! See for yourself!"

Kareem laid his Koran on his desk and, with an expression of incredulity, humored his wife by following me from the room.

As we entered the hallway leading to Amani's door, we could hear the sound of her voice, rising and falling with the intensity of her words.

Kareem left my side and burst into Amani's room. Our daughter turned, displaying a face lined with pain and haggard with sorrow.

Kareem spoke softly. "Amani, it is time for you to take a small rest. Go to bed. Now. Your mother will wake you in an hour for the evening meal."

Amani's expression appeared stricken, and she did not speak. But still bound to Kareem's influence, she lay across the bed, fully dressed, and closed her eyes.

I could see my child's lips as they continued to move in silent prayer, uttering words that were not meant for my ears.

Kareem and I quietly left the room. Drinking coffee in our sitting room, Kareem confessed that he had a small degree of concern but was skeptical of my exaggerated fear that Amani was sinking into a medieval passion, darkened with thoughts of sin, suffering, and hell. He sat quietly for a short while and then announced that my apprehension was directly linked to Lawand's unhinged denunciations of human wickedness. He told me that Amani's religious revival did not result from insanity, but was essentially linked with the overpowering joy of Haj.

"You will see," he promised, "once we have returned to the normal routine of life, Amani will lapse again into the habit of accumulating wandering beasts, and her religious fanaticism will soon be forgotten." Kareem smiled and asked a small favor. "Sultana, please, allow Amani some peace to turn from her daily problems to a oneness with God. It is a duty of all Muslims."

With a grimace, I nodded my head in agreement. Somewhat relieved, I hoped that Kareem was right.

Still, not leaving such an important matter to chance, in my prayers that evening I indulged in long hours of pleading with God that Amani would once again be the child she had been prior to our attending Haj.

I suffered nightmares throughout the night: I dreamed that my daughter left our home to join an extremist religious organization in Amman, Jordan, that doused gasoline on the clothing of working Muslim women, setting afire and burning to death those whom they deemed nonbelievers.

Chapter Six:
Haj

"Arab lands will now go the way of Iran. Egypt will not be the first to fall, nevertheless it shall fall. The women will be the first to suffer loss of human rights. We women were offered our rights as human beings first by Nasser then by Sadat. The courts have already struck down the humane law giving women the right to divorce husbands who take second wives. Egyptian women cringe to think of what is yet to come, often joking that soon we shall share the unfortunate fate of our Saudi sisters."
—Comments of an Egyptian feminist pilgrim as spoken to Sara Al Sa'ud during the Haj of 1990.

I believed that God must have heard my stirring appeal, for the following morning Amani seemed her usual self. It was as if sleep had erased the apotheosis of human suffering I had witnessed on my daughter's face the day before. She giggled and joked with her sister, Maha, as they ate their breakfast of fresh yogurt and melon and munched on pieces of kibbeh left over from our evening meal.

Our driver delivered us to the Valley of Mina,

which is approximately six miles north of Makkah. We would spend the night in Mina, in an air-conditioned tent Kareem had arranged. By sleeping in the Valley of Mina, our family would be ready for an early morning. The children seemed quite excited at the prospect, since we had never before slept in the valley.

Along the way, we passed what seemed to be an endless line of buses, all transporting pilgrims. Many thousands of others were slowly walking the six-mile journey from Makkah to the Valley of Mina.

Thinking that Amani had returned to normal, I once again found myself glad to be part of this wonderful gathering of the faithful, and I happily looked forward to the last days of Haj.

It was while we were in the Valley of Mina that Kareem met with an old friend from youthful days spent in England. The man, Yousif, was from Egypt. One moment Kareem was standing by my side, and the next he was heartily embracing a man none of us had ever seen.

Looking at the man from a distance, I saw that he had a long, slightly curving nose, projecting cheekbones, and a curly beard. What most caught my attention, however, was the indisputable and concentrated scorn that blazed in his eyes when his gaze fell upon the females in Kareem's family.

Kareem called out the man's name in a loud voice, and I remembered hearing of this person from my husband. Thinking back, I recalled some of what Kareem had told me about this particular acquaintance. During the years of our married life, each time we had visited our villa in Cairo, Kareem's memories of his Egyptian schoolmate had been stirred. Each time, he planned to look up his old friend. And on each occasion the fullness of our family life had prevented his doing so.

Now, after a quick view of the man, I was glad Kareem's plans had never materialized, for I felt myself instantly in conflict with this malevolent character who, to my eye, was conspicuous in his dislike for women.

I wondered what had produced such changes in the man's life, for I distinctly recalled Kareem having told me Yousif had such attractive manners that women found it hard to resist him and he never slept alone.

Kareem and Yousif had known each other during their student days, when they were both living in a land not their own. While in London, Yousif was a carefree, happy individual who was interested in little more than merrymaking with Western women in gambling casinos. Kareem said he was brilliant, with little need to study his lessons, and that was a good thing, for Yousif introduced Kareem to a different girlfriend each week. In spite of Yousif's insatiable lust for female company, Kareem had predicted a great future for his friend in the legal and political system of Egypt, for Yousif had a quick mind and a pleasing manner.

Yousif graduated from law school one year ahead of Kareem, and they had not seen each other since that time.

As Yousif and Kareem began to share their news, my daughters and I stayed in the background, which is our way when the man is not of our family, but we could overhear all that Kareem and Yousif were saying.

Apparently Yousif had changed radically from his years as a student, for after a short conversation, it was evident that he and my husband no longer enjoyed much in common.

Yousif was strangely reticent regarding his career, and when Kareem pressed him on his profession, he would say little more than that he had changed from the youth of Kareem's memory and had become more attached to the traditional ways of Islam.

Yousif proudly told Kareem that since they last met he had married and divorced one woman, who had given him two sons, and had married a second woman, fathering five sons in that union. The man delighted in boasting about the joys of having seven sons. Yousif also mentioned that he had full custody of the first two children, and that the boys had been forcibly taken from the influence of his first wife, a modern woman who insisted upon working outside of the home. She, Yousif said, with ill-concealed disgust, was a teacher with new ideas about women and their station in life.

Yousif spat on the ground when he mentioned his first wife's name, and said, "Praise to God, Egypt is returning to the teachings of the Koran. Egyptians will soon have the law of Prophet Mohammed ruling their lives, rather than the unsettling system of secular law that encourages our women to come out of purdah."

At this bit of information, I began to come to life and was about to intrude on their conversation and tell the man some of my thoughts, when I was struck dumb by further revelations from Kareem's friend.

Yousif proudly told Kareem that his greatest blessing from God was that neither of his marriages had been cursed with the birth of daughters, and that truly, women were the source of all sin . If a man had to waste his energies in guarding women, Yousif said, he had little time for performing other, more important duties in life.

Without waiting for Kareem's response to these shocking comments, Yousif launched into the story of a man he had met while in Makkah. He said that the man was an Indian Muslim and that this Muslim was planning to remain in Saudi Arabia because there was a warrant out for his arrest in India. The authorities in India had discovered two days after his departure for Saudi Arabia that he and his wife had murdered their baby daughter by pouring scalding water down the child's throat.

Yousif asked for Kareem's opinion on the matter, but before my husband could speak, he resumed his loud, rude speech and said that he, himself, thought that the man should not be punished, since he was the father of four daughters and had desired a son to the point of madness. While Yousif acknowledged that the Prophet had not condoned such practice, he thought the authorities should not intervene on a private matter that had harmed no one but the baby girl.

Yousif wondered if Kareem could offer assistance obtaining a work visa for the man, and possibly give him a job in Saudi Arabia so he would not have to return to his country and face trial.

Yousif had not bothered to discover the sex of Kareem's children, and Kareem had begun to breathe heavily. Knowing Kareem's thoughts on such matters, I thought that my husband might strike his old friend and fling him to the ground.

The back of Kareem's neck turned red, so I knew that my husband blushed in anger. I decided that he had eyes in the back of his head, for he motioned with his hand for me to stay away. Kareem curtly informed his old friend that he, himself, had been blessed with two beautiful daughters and one son, and that he loved his daughters as he did his son.

A man with thick skin, Yousif gave his condolences to Kareem, saying that it was too unfortunate he was the father of daughters. Without taking a moment to breathe, Yousif then began to argue the benefits of sons, and wondered why my husband did not take another wife. Kareem could, after all, allow me to keep the daughters, and he could raise our son.

Kareem responded with the calm of a man who is very angry by reminding Yousif of the teachings of Mohammed. "Yousif," he asked, "you say you are a practicing and good Muslim. If so, do you not recall the words of the blessed Prophet when a man entered the mosque and approached the Prophet?"

I knew the story well, since I have always quoted the fairness of the Prophet with regard to women, when fighting the extremists in my land.

Yousif listened with a blank face, and it was evident to my eyes that he was a man who had no interest in the words of the Prophet if those words did not agree with his own thoughts on life.

Kareem plunged ahead, a man intent on making his point by using intellect, and the teachings of a man anointed by God to spread his word, instead of by resorting to brute force. Frankly, I desired to see Yousif beaten and bloodied, but I did have a moment of pride when Kareem spoke with the passion of a muezzin reminding the faithful to come to prayer, as he told the true story of Prophet Mohammed's reminder to all fathers about the equal value of their children, regardless of sex.

A man entered the mosque and approached the Prophet. He sat down and began to talk. After some time, the man's two children, a boy and a girl, followed their father into the mosque. The boy came in first, and received much praise and a loving kiss from his father. The boy settled on the man's lap, while the man continued talking to the Prophet.

Sometime later, the man's daughter arrived at the mosque. When she approached her father, he did not kiss her or put her on his lap, as he had done with his son. Instead, he motioned for the little girl to sit in front of him, and went on talking to the Prophet.

The Prophet was greatly concerned when he saw this. Why, he asked, do you not treat these children equally? Why did you not kiss your daughter as you kissed your son, and let her, also, sit on your lap?

The man felt ashamed when he heard the Prophet say those words. He understood that he had acted in an improper manner toward his two children.

Sons and daughters are both gifts of God, the Prophet reminded him. Both are equally great gifts, and so they should always be treated equally.

Kareem glared at Yousif, his expression seeming to say, now, what do you have to say to that!

This Yousif fellow was a rude man. Ignoring Kareem's obvious discomfort and the message of the Prophet's words, he started his tirade against women once again. Seeing that he had not won over Kareem to his way of thinking, he concluded his efforts by reminding my husband of the breakdown of the family unit in Western countries, stating, "God has assigned a specific duty for men and for women. Women are created for procreation, nothing else. Kareem, come now, who can deny that by nature all women are exhibitionists? This tendency cannot be changed, but it is a man's duty to keep her away from all men, otherwise, she will squander her beauty and give her charms to any man who asks..."

Furious, Kareem turned his back and walked away from his friend. His face was an ugly mask as he led his women from the scene. In a loud voice he said to me, "That Yousif has become a dangerous man!"

I glanced back at Yousif. Never have I witnessed such evil in a man's face.

Kareem called his brother-in-law Mohammed on

his portable telephone and asked him to make some delicate inquiries about Yousif's activities, telling Mohammed that the man was extremely radical and possibly an instigator of violence.

Within hours, Mohammed returned Kareem's call and said that Kareem was correct, that the man was a skilled lawyer whose clients were members of the Gamaa Al Islamiya, an Egyptian Islamic extremist group formed in the early 1980s that was responsible for militant violence in Egypt.

Kareem was astonished. Yousif represented men who were attempting to overthrow the Egyptian secular government. The Egyptian internal security authorities had told Mohammed that there had never been charges lodged against the man, but when in Egypt, he was kept under careful surveillance. Mohammed added that he had placed Saudi Security around Yousif to ensure that he did not cause problems while in Saudi Arabia.

A little less than a year later, Kareem was saddened but not surprised at the news that Yousif had been arrested in Assiut, in southern Egypt, as a principal leader of the Muslim extremist group. While watching a news program, Kareem spotted Yousif's face—his old friend was looking out on the world from a cage. Kareem followed his case closely and seemed somewhat relieved that Yousif had not been sentenced to death, while I thought the world was a more dangerous place with such men among the living and would have welcomed his demise.

In spite of the fact that we were at Haj and knew we should not concentrate on worldly matters, the man Yousif had made such an impression on our daughters' moods that Kareem thought it best to talk the matter through and give Amani and Maha the comforting knowledge that men like Yousif were only a passing phase in a long Islamic history.

After the dinner hour, our family sat and discussed the man Yousif and what he represented in the Muslim world.

We asked each of the children their thoughts on what they had heard that day.

Abdullah was the first to speak. Our son was plainly disturbed, saying that Islam was on the move and that it would affect each of our lives, for the extremist groups were calling for the downfall of the Saudi monarchy. He envisioned Saudi Arabia going the way of Iran, with a man like Khomeini leading our country. Abdullah predicted that his generation of al Sa'uds would live out their lives on the French Riviera, and such a thought was distressing to him.

After hearing what the man had to say about females and their value, Maha was spitting mad and wanted her father to have Yousif arrested and charged as a spy. She thought she would like to see him beheaded, even if it was on trumped-up offenses.

Amani was reflective and said that the Arabic love of all things Western was allowing men such as Yousif to gain power in Muslim countries.

Kareem and I looked at each other, neither of us liking our youngest child's turn of thought.

Maha pinched her sister, accusing her of supporting the man's words.

Amani denied the charge but said that she did consider the possibility that life was more simple when women's roles were more defined and not open for discussion and change. She mentioned that in the Bedouin life prior to the building of cities, men and women were not so confused as they were today.

It was as I had feared! My daughter's thoughts were taking her back in time. She seemed to be losing pride in her femaleness, and I wondered what I could do to reinforce her sense of worth as a modern woman in an advancing civilization.

Abdullah did not understand and began to laugh, asking Amani if she longed for the time when female babies were buried in the sand! It was not too late to take up the practice, he said, Yousif could introduce us to a man who had recently killed his own daughter!

Knowing Amani's delicate mental state, Kareem gave his son a stern look and said that the matter was no joke, that the evil practice was a terrible problem in India, Pakistan, and China. Kareem told us he had recently read an article in a foreign newspaper that quoted startling statistics. Tens of millions of females were missing in those lands, and no one seemed particularly interested in finding out what had happened to them.

My husband felt so strongly about the matter that he insisted upon discussing further the evil practice of infanticide by telling our children a story I was not aware he knew in such detail.

The children moaned and said they were too old for stories from their father, but my husband insisted, saying that while statistics made little impact on our emotions, individual tales of horror brought tears to the eyes and generated action on social issues in the world community.

Seeing my husband in a new light, I listened as he told the famous Muslim tale that had been passed down by professional storytellers from the time of Prophet Mohammed.

"Prior to the founding of the Islamic faith by Prophet Mohammed," Kareem said, "there was a tribe in Arabia that practiced the inhuman deed of burying alive their baby daughters in much the same manner that baby girls are murdered today in other countries.

"Qais bin Asim was the chief of this tribe. When

Chief Asim embraced Islam, he confessed a dreadful tale to Prophet Mohammed."

"O Messenger of God! A daughter was born to my wife when I was away from my home on a journey. My wife was fearful that I might bury the child alive, and after nursing her for a few days, sent this child to her sister so that she might be cherished by another. My wife prayed that I might be merciful to the child when the girl became older.

"When I came back home from the journey, I was told that my wife had given birth to a dead child. Thus, the matter was forgotten. During the time, the child remained being loved by her aunt. Once I went out of the house for a whole day, and my wife, thinking I would be out much longer, thought it safe to call her daughter home and enjoy her company for some time in my absence.

"Unexpectedly, I changed my mind and came home earlier. When I entered my home I saw a very beautiful and tidy little girl playing in the house. When I looked at her I suddenly felt a surge of strong and spontaneous love for her within me. My wife sensed my feelings and thought that my blood had called to my own blood and my fatherly love and affection had sprung up naturally for the girl. I asked her, 'Oh, my wife, whose child is this? How charming she is!'

"Then, my wife told me about the truth of the girl. I could not control my joy and eagerly took the girl in my arms. Her mother told her that I was her father and she began loving me dearly, and calling out to me, 'Oh, my father! My father!' At those moments I felt an indescribable pleasure when this girl child put her arms around my neck and showed me affection.

"Days went by in this way and the child remained being nourished by us and was free from any worry or discomfort. But there were times when this girl caught my attention and such thoughts came to my mind: I have to give this girl to another man in marriage. I will have to bear the insult that another man will know my daughter as his wife. How will I be able to face other men, knowing that my honor is ruined when this child is bedded by a man? These thoughts took hold of my mind and I was tortured incessantly. At last these thoughts aroused my indignation and made me devoid of patience with the girl. After some time of thinking, I decided that I had to do away with the stigma of shame and humiliation for me and for my ancestors.

"I decided I had to bury the girl alive. I could not confide this plan to my wife, so I asked her to get the child ready, that I was going to take her to a feast with me. My wife gave the girl a bath, clad her in pretty clothes, and made her ready for the feast. The little girl was excited, bubbling with cheerfulness, believing that she was accompanying her father on a joyful occasion.

"I left the house with the girl. She was leaping with joy and pleasure, holding my hand every now and then, and running ahead of me, prattling to me with squeals of innocent laughter and gaiety.

"By this time I had become blind to the girl, and was impatient to get rid of her as soon as possible. The poor child was unaware of my sinister intentions and followed me merrily.

"At last I stopped at a lonely spot and began to dig into the ground. The innocent girl was surprised to see me doing this and asked repeatedly, 'Father, why are you digging in the earth?'

"I paid no attention to her questions. She could not know that I was digging a pit to bury my own beautiful daughter with my own hands.

"While digging in the earth, dust and sand fell upon my feet and clothes. My lovely daughter would clean the dust from my feet and clothes while saying, 'Father, you are spoiling your clothes!'

"I was like a deaf person and did not look at her, and pretended that I heard nothing she said. I continued my task and finally had dug a pit large enough to serve my purpose.

"I grabbed my daughter and threw her into the pit, and began to fill the pit with great haste. The poor girl was looking at me with frightened eyes. She began to cry frantically and screamed, 'My dear father, what is this? I have done no wrong! Father, please, do not hide me in the ground!'"

"I kept on doing my work like a deaf, dumb, and blind person without paying any attention to her pleadings and entreaties.

"O Great Prophet of God! I was too heartless to have pity on my own child! On the contrary, after burying her alive, I heaved a huge sigh of relief and came back satisfied that I had saved my honor and pride from humiliation."

When Prophet Mohammed heard this heartrending story about an innocent girl, the Holy Prophet could not control himself and tears fell upon his cheeks. He asked the Chief of the Tribe of Asim, "This is too cruel! How can one, who does not pity others, expect to be pitied by the Almighty God?"

Kareem looked into the faces of his children. "Prophet Mohammed, upon hearing this story, became very gloomy, and he related another story that was similar in its horror."

A man came to Mohammed and told him that he had once been very ignorant. He said that he had no knowledge and no guidance until the Prophet came and made God's wishes known.

This man said, "O Messenger of God! We worshiped idols and killed our children with our own hands. I once had a little and very charming daughter. When I would call her she would run into my arms laughing with joy and pleasure. One day I called this girl to me, and she readily came. I asked her to follow me, and she did. I walked too rapidly, and this girl came running with her small steps. There was a deep well at a short distance from my home. When I reached this well, I stopped and the child came to the well, trotting after me. I caught hold of that child by the hand and threw her into the well. The poor child cried and called out for me to save her. 'Father' was the last word on the child's lips."

When the man finished his story, the Prophet wept for a long time, and the tears were so plentiful that they wet his beard.

"Our ignorance about females was washed away by the shedding of his tears, and today it is considered a vile and cruel act for a man to bury alive, to throw down into wells, or to harm his female children."

I hugged each of my daughters. In our hearts, it was as if the blessed Prophet himself were near us, and it seemed as if the tragic tale of the two young girls had occurred in the present and not centuries prior to our existence. Who could doubt that our Prophet had done much to abolish unjust practices and cruel customs? He had been born in an evil time, when pagan gods were worshiped, when men took hundreds of wives, and the practice of infanticide was common. Prophet Mohammed had great difficulty in abolishing theseevil practices, and what he could not abolish, he restricted.

I told my family that in my opinion, the traditions

remaining from that era and not the Koran were what kept us women in bondage. Few people know the facts that the Koran does not call for veiling, nor the restrictions women endure in the Muslim world. It is the traditions passed down that so hinder us from moving forward.

A lively discussion ensued as to why the position of women was one of subjection to men, with Maha insulting her brother Abdullah by pointing out that her scores in school topped his in every subject.

Just as Abdullah opened his mouth to respond, I warned my children not to make the conversation personal.

Then I brought up the obvious, that the physical vulnerabilities of a woman can be traced to that most important of human accomplishments, the absorption of her strength in carrying, nursing, and rearing children. I have always known that this one fact doomed females to a subordinate status in all societies. Instead of attaining honor for being the producer of life, we are penalized. To my mind, this fact is the scandal of civilization.

Abdullah, whose favorite instructor at school was a Lebanese philosophy professor, showed off his knowledge by giving us a history lesson on women's slow climb from the beginning of life until the present moment. Women had been nothing more than beasts of burden in the earlier days, tending to the children, gathering wood for the fire, cooking the meals, making the clothes and boots, and working as pack animals when the tribes were on the march. The men, Abdullah said, risked themselves in the capture of the game, and their reward for providing the tribe with meat was to rest the remainder of the time.

Teasing his sisters, Abdullah flexed his muscles and said that brute force kept men at the fore, and if his sisters were truly interested in equality, they should work out with his weights in our exercise studio, rather than reading books in their spare time.

Kareem had to restrain our daughters, to keep them from piling on top of their brother. Maha dodged her father's arms and gave a kick to Abdullah's private parts, and Kareem and I both were astonished at her knowledge of his weakest area.

I smiled at the antics of my children, but nevertheless my heart was gloomy as I thought of how we women had suffered from the moment of creation. From the beginning of time, we were used as slaves to do the work, and now that practice continued in many countries of the world. In my own country, women are considered nothing more than objects of beauty, sexual toys for the enjoyment of our men.

I have personal knowledge that women are the equal of men in endurance, resourcefulness, and courage, but I am ahead of my time in the backward land of Arabia.

Kareem became quiet. Then he broke the silence and said that he was remembering his old friend Yousif, and the wrongful path he had chosen.

I became pleased that Kareem had witnessed Yousif's disintegration as a civilized man, for it was as if by recognizing the evil that sprouts and take holds in society when such men gain power, my husband finally became what I wanted him to be.

Kareem mulled over his thoughts. "Sultana, you know, it is unsuccessful men such as Yousif who mold the myth that women are the root of all evil. I know now that although this inaccurate opinion of women is attractive to men, it creates a paralyzing disillusionment that only forms a hateful barrier between the two sexes."

Kareem looked at his son and said, "Abdullah, I hope you will never accept such obstinate resistance to the worth of women. It will be up to your generation to abandon the subjugation of women. I am sad to say that the men of my generation have given new form to women's oppression."

I could only imagine what my daughters were thinking, but Maha seemed bewildered and angry that she had been born into a society so reluctant to adjust to social change, while Amani, so recently immersed in her consoling faith, appeared burdened by the traditional sanctions that favor the subjugation of women.

Weary of men such as Yousif and of the life they envision for women—all of whom they consider wicked and therefore strive to control—I could not reconcile myself to the dark years ahead when women would be forced to protect themselves from the growing movement of the extremists who called so loudly for their banishment from normal life.

As I prepared myself for bed, I felt that the sparkle had gone from the occasion of Haj. This, in spite of Kareem's newfound philosophy that spoke of enlightened liberation within the confines of our family.

The following morning our faces were drawn from our late evening. Silent throughout our morning meal, we prepared ourselves for the most important day of Haj.

We were driven five miles north to the hill of Arafat. This was the place where Prophet Mohammed had delivered his final sermon. Four months later he was dead.

Disheartened, I barely moved my lips as I uttered the words of the Prophet, "You have to appear before your God, who shall demand from you an account of all your actions. Know that all Muslims are brothers. You are one brotherhood, no man shall take from his brother unless by his free consent. Keep yourselves from injustice. Let him who is present tell this to him who is absent. It may be that he who is told this afterward may remember it better than he who has now heard it."

Walking up the steep slope of Mount Arafat, I cried, "Here I am, O God! Here I am!" This is the day when God erases all of our sins and confers his forgiveness.

For many long hours my family and I, with the other pilgrims, stood in the heat of the desert. We prayed and read from the Koran. My daughters, like many other pilgrims, held umbrellas over their heads for shade, but I felt the need to suffer the effects of a baking sun, as a testimony of my faith. Many men and women were fainting all around us. Sunstroke vans were on hand to transport them on stretchers.

As the sun was setting went to the area between Mount Arafat and Mina. Abdullah and Kareem gathered small stones for the following morning's rituals, and without family communication—for each of us showed signs of physical weariness—we rested dearly in order to prepare ourselves for the final day of Haj.

The last morning we chanted, "In the name of God Almighty I do this, and in hatred of the devil and his pretense! God is Great!" Everyone then began casting seven sets of the small stones gathered by Kareem and Abdullah. There are stone pillars there symbolizing the devil.

Cleansed of our sins we then traveled to the plain of Mina. There we found sheep, goats, and camels being butchered to commemorate Ibrahim's willingness to sacrifice his beloved son to God. Butchers were walking among the crowds of people, giving their prices to butcher an animal. Once paid, those butchers would hold the animal, facing its head toward the Kaaba at the Holy Mosque. Then they would loudly pray, "God is Great!" Instantly they would slit the animal's throat so that all the blood would drain out.

Hearing the cries of the poor beasts and watching the blood run freely, poor Amani screamed as one insane and dropped to the ground in a faint. Kareem and Abdullah carried her to one of the small trailers that are set about for the faint of heart and the weak.

They soon returned, saying that Amani was still crying, paralyzed with grief at what she deemed to be the senseless slaughter of many beasts.

Kareem gave me an I-told-you-so look. I felt some small degree of happiness that a recognizable part of Amani's personality had survived intact and hoped that Kareem was right in his assessment that once we departed Makkah our daughter would be her old self.

As we watched the violent activity, I reminded myself that it was an important ritual, that the animals are sacrificed to remind the pilgrims of the lessons they have learned at Haj: sacrifice, obedience to God, mercy to all men, and faith.

The four days of celebration now began in earnest. I knew that Muslims all over the world were joining us, their hearts sad because they were not in Makkah, too. We cut small locks of our hair to signify the end of our pilgrimage. We rushed to change our plain clothes for more colorful attire. Our men slipped on white cotton thobes.

The feasting began in the afternoon. Amani was still pale but had recovered sufficiently to join in the festivities, though she refused to partake of any meat.

Our family gathered at our tent, and we exchanged small gifts and congratulated each other. We said our prayers before sitting to eat our meal of lamb with rice.

What remained of our feast was given to the poor. We soon left to travel a short distance to our palace in Jeddah where we would continue to celebrate. From this time own our children were now entitled to place the honored title of Hajji before their first names, for they had fulfilled the fifth pillar of Islam. I felt a smile cross my face, knowing that we had pleased God by doing Haj.

Now, I prayed for God to please me by releasing my daughter Amani from the fundamentalist leanings that seemed to grip her soul. I knew that mental instability could lend sanctity to the most extreme doctrine. I did not want my daughter sacrificed to the militant ideals, so common to many religions, which I had struggled diligently against from the moment of understanding.

It was not to be. Whether I had pleased God or not, his decision concerning my daughter failed to please me.

The trip to Makkah would later prove to be both a blessing and a misfortune for my family. While Kareem and I grew closer than we had been since the first few years of our marriage, and Maha and Abdullah sought to live the lives of responsible citizens, Amani became a gloomy recluse.

Chapter Seven:
Extremist

*My deepest fears were realized. Let us imagine a desert
country lying in absolute darkness with many living things
swarming blindly about in it.*
—BUDDHA

Haj was completed and summer was upon us. The
hot desert air had disturbed us little during our pilgrimage
to Makkah, for our minds were on other, more important
matters connected to our spiritual oneness with God.

From Makkah we traveled to our palace in Jeddah,
thinking to return to Riyadh the following day. It was not
to be. While I was organizing the palace staff for our departure, Kareem entered the room and said that he had
canceled our flight, for he had been informed by the air
traffic controllers that there was a particularly turbulent
sandstorm moving from the Rub Al Khali desert toward
the city of Riyadh. Even without the effects of a sandstorm, nearly four thousand tons of sand routinely settle
on Riyadh every month. Wanting to avoid the terrible
sandstorm that would soon assault our capital, dumping
sand that stings the eyes, fills the pores, and covers every-

thing, I was pleased that we would remain in Jeddah despite the fact that Jeddah's humidity is more oppressive than the dry desert heat of Riyadh.

Abdullah and Maha were excited to be postponing our return to Riyadh and their normal routines for a few more days. Our two eldest children began to plead with us to take a small holiday while in Jeddah. I looked at my husband and smiled. But the smile faded from my face when I noticed that Amani was sitting off to herself in the corner of the room, her nose in the pages of the Koran. Amani was quickly becoming a glum ascetic and seemed unconcerned as to where she might be. It appeared to me that my youngest child had raised barriers against her normal desire for harmless fun, for in the past nothing thrilled Amani more than to swim in the lapping, warm waters of the Red Sea.

Determined to avoid becoming even further depressed by Amani's activities, I nodded my head, yes, in response to Kareem's questioning eyes. So, in spite of the humidity and the heat waves that were dancing in the air, Kareem and I decided to remain in Jeddah an additional two weeks, for we could see that our two eldest children were sorely tempted by the blue mirror of the Red Sea waters, which we could view from our palace walls.

I was not displeased at the idea, for I, like many members of the royal family, prefer the lively port city of Jeddah to the staid atmosphere of Riyadh. Thinking that I would take my daughters shopping in the modern shopping malls of Jeddah and entertain family friends who lived in the city, the holiday loomed pleasantly in my mind. Had not Amani chosen this time to expand the growing gap between herself and her family, it would have been a perfect time in an otherwise imperfect life.

I was down on my knees in the long corridor that connected the various wings of the palace when Maha made the discovery that her mother was attempting to overhear the voice of her sister, Amani, through a crack in the doorway leading into the Turkish baths and indoor garden area.

"Mummy! What are you doing?" Maha called out in a loud, laughing voice, even as I tried to wave her away with my hand.

Inside the room, Amani stopped speaking, and I heard my daughter's determined footsteps as she made her way toward me. I made a desperate attempt to spring to my feet so that I could move away from the door, but my pointed shoe heel caught in the hem of my long dress. I was struggling to free myself when Amani flung the door open and stood staring down at her obviously guilty mother.

I was unnerved by my daughter's accusing face, for her piercing eyes and tight lips made it plain that she clearly understood the situation.

Unable to acknowledge my despicable deed, I began to rub my fingers against some red threads that were worked into the hall carpet, and with what I hoped was a lilt to my voice, I began to lie with the intensity of one who knows her listeners see through her lie.

"Amani. I thought you were in your room, darling." I exclaimed. I returned my gaze to the carpet, seriously studying the red threads. "Sweet daughters, have either of you noticed the red stains on this carpet?"

Neither of my girls responded.

With a frown, I gave the red threads a few more rubs, and with my shoe heel still caught in my dress, I stood up hunched over and limped down the corridor. Short on explanation, I mumbled, "The servants have become quite lax. I fear that the stain is permanent."

Amani, unable to allow me the pleasure of believing that my small lie had been convincing, spoke to my back. "Mummy. This carpet is not stained. Those are red roses woven into the pattern."

Maha could not restrain herself, and I heard her as she began to giggle.

Amani called out, "Mummy, if you wish to hear my words, you are most welcome. Please, come into the room where I am speaking." The door leading into the garden room slammed with a thunderous clap.

Tears formed in my eyes, and I rushed to my bedroom. I could not bear to look at my beautiful daughter, for since we had returned from Makkah, she had begun to clothe herself from head to toe in black, even going so far as to wear thick black hosiery and long black gloves. In the privacy of our home, only her face remained uncovered, as my child wrapped her beautiful black hair in a stiff black head covering that reminded me of something a goat-herding Yemen woman might wear. When Amani ventured outside our palace walls, she added a veil of thick black fabric that hindered her vision, even though the religious officials of Jeddah were much more relaxed in pursuing women with unveiled faces than were those of Riyadh. Our desert capital is known throughout the Muslim world for its diligent morals committees, which are composed solely of angry-faced men who harass innocent women on the city streets.

Nothing I could say or do could persuade my daughter to dress more comfortably than in the heavy black cloak, veil, and head-dress that strike most Muslim believers in other Islamic lands as nothing less than ridiculous.

I could not control my sobs. At great risk to my happiness, I had battled most of my life for my daughters to have the right to wear the thinnest of veils, and now my dear child dismissed my small victory as if it had no value.

And that was not the worst. Not content with her newfound faith, Amani felt the zeal of the missionary to convert others to her new way of thinking. Today, Amani had invited her closest friends, along with four of her younger cousins, to our home to hear her read from the Koran and speak about her interpretation of the Prophet's words, which sounded distressingly like the interpretation I had so often heard from the government's Committee for Commendation of Virtue and Prevention of Vice.

The intonation of Amani's childlike voice was ringing in my head as I closed the doors to my private quarters and lay crossways on the bed, wondering how I was going to tackle this latest crisis of motherhood.

While eavesdropping, I had overheard Amani as she read from the holy Koran:

> Do ye build a landmark
> on every high place
> to amuse yourselves?
> And, do ye get for yourselves
> fine buildings in the hope
> of living therein forever?
> and when ye exert
> your strong hand
> do ye do it like men
> of absolute power?
> Now fear God and obey me
> And follow not the bidding
> of those who are extravagant,
> and make mischief in the land,
> and mend not their ways.

My knees shaking, I had listened in horror as Amani stressed the Saudi royal family's similarity to the ostentatious sinners in the verse of the Koran.

"Look around you. Witness the wealth of the home from which I speak. A palace fit for a god could be no finer. Are we not disregarding the very words of God in embracing the opulence of costly indulgence that no human eyes are fit to see?"

Amani's voice went soft, as if she were speaking in a whisper, but I had closed my eyes and leaned closer, listening with great care. I could barely hear Amani's words. "Each of us must banish extravagance from our lives. I will set the first example. The jewels I have received from the wealth of my family name, I will give to the poor. If you believe in the God of Mohammed, you too must follow my example."

I did not hear the audience's response to their leader's outlandish demand, for at that moment, my eldest daughter, Maha, had made my unwelcome presence known.

Now, remembering Amani's promise to divest herself of her jewels, I pushed myself from the bed and hurried to my daughter's bedroom. There, I opened the safe she shared with her sister and removed a large quantity of expensive necklaces, bracelets, earrings, and rings, locking those items into the safe in Kareem's office. I had taken Maha's jewelry along with Amani's, for who knew what offense Amani might commit in her state of religious upheaval.

I knew that the total value of Amani's jewelry alone was well into the millions of dollars, and it had been given to her by those who loved her and desired economic security for her future. I promised myself that if Amani genuinely wanted to provide for the poor, then money would be given to her for that purpose.

Feeling depressed and unappreciated for our generosity, I remembered the millions of riyals Kareem and I had quietly donated over the years to the poor of the world. In addition to the required zakah liability, the percentage of our annual income not needed for our daily living expenses, Kareem and I contribute an extra 15 percent of our income for purposes of education and medical care to various Muslim countries less fortunate than Saudi Arabia. Never have we forgotten the words of the Prophet: *"If you give alms openly, that is well, but if you give them to the needy in private, it is even better for you, and will atone for some of your bad deeds. Allah is aware of all you do."*

Thinking of the funds we had provided to build medical clinics, schools, and private dwellings in the poorest of Muslim lands, I felt the keen desire to remind Amani of the enormity of the financial contributions made by her parents. Had my child discounted our charitable activities as meaningless? Or was her true desire to turn our family into beggars, like those who benefited from our great wealth?

Returning to my bed, I lay quiet for over two hours, thinking thoughts, discarding wild ideas, not knowing how to do battle with a force that is higher than any man.

Darkness had fallen over my room when Kareem came home from his Jeddah offices.

"Sultana. Are you ill?" Kareem switched on several lamps and walked to my bed, peering down at my face with concern.

"Your face is flushed. Do you have a fever?"

I did not answer my husband's questions. Instead, I took a deep, tortured breath. "Kareem, one of your flesh and blood is plotting the overthrow of the monarchy."

Kareem's face turned from pale brown to bright red in a matter of seconds. "What?"

I feebly waved my hand in the air. "Amani. Today, our daughter held a meeting of young princesses and good friends. I accidentally overheard her speaking. She is using the Koran to turn her youthful cousins and acquaintances against the leadership of our family."

Kareem clicked his tongue in the Arab manner that denotes disbelief. He laughed. "You are crazy, Sultana. Amani is the least likely of our children to incite violence."

I shook my head. "No more. Religion has strengthened our child. She is beginning to resemble a hungry lion rather than a gentle lamb." I repeated to Kareem what I had overheard.

Kareem made a face. "Sultana. Believe me when I say this latest passion is nothing more than a passing phase. Ignore her. Soon she will tire of her excesses."

It was clear that Kareem himself was tired of the topic of Amani's religious conversion. I had talked of little else during the past week. Amani's passionate embrace of all things extreme in our religion tortured her mother, while her father dismissed his daughter's fervor with a joke and a prediction that it would be short-lived.

I realized that Kareem and I would not share and resolve this latest crisis together as we had in Maha's case. I felt the fight go out of my body. For the first moment since giving birth to Abdullah so many years before, I grew weary of motherhood, and wondered how many more generations of women could be enticed to burden themselves with the solitary and thankless procreation, nourishing, and guidance of the human race.

With a rasping sound in my throat, I cried out to my husband, "How lonely is the life of a woman!"

Fearing that I would react in an extreme manner to my grief, Kareem patted me tenderly on my back, and sweetly asked if I would like my dinner served to me privately in our quarters. He said he would take the evening meal alone with our children, if that were the case.

With a sigh of martyrdom, I decided not to stay alone. I had been in solitude for many hours, and I did not want to give Amani the idea that her mother was sulking. I pushed myself off the bed and told my husband I would freshen myself for dinner and see him downstairs.

Kareem and I met in the small family sitting room, and since we were an hour early for dinner, I asked him to go with me on a stroll in the Turkish bath and garden area.

Remembering the evening we had shared before, Kareem thought I was feeling romantic, and his eyes caressed my face with tenderness.

I returned his smile, but in reality I wanted to examine the garden area and see what evidence, if any, my child had left of her religious meeting with her friends and royal cousins.

We entered a large, beautiful courtyard that had been designed by a famous Italian fashion designer. Over the years, many of our royal cousins had attempted unsuccessfully to copy the loveliness of our unique "Turkish room." A flowing waterfall situated in the back of the room emptied clear water into a large circular pool inhabited by many exotic fish. A stone path circled the pool, and beautiful flowers, tenderly cared for by the staff of gardeners, lined the walkway. Two raised sitting areas were located to the left and to the right. Lush green foliage imported from Thailand was draped over the rattan furnishings, which were covered in pastel cushions. Glass-topped tables were set about the sitting areas, and it was a most pleasant spot for our family to enjoy morning or evening coffee.

The walls were made of special tinted glass, but the greenery was so abundant and dense that it shaded us from the hot rays of the sun. A stone pathway, carved with the faces of various wild animals, led around the waterfall. I felt sad as I walked on the face of a giraffe, for I remembered that Kareem had had the stones specially carved for Amani, as a surprise to our animal-worshiping child.

The walkway took us to the Turkish bath area. Our home in Cairo had such a room, and I had requested the Italian designer to study that design and duplicate it at our palace in Jeddah.

The Turkish bathhouse contained four baths, each one in a different style and size. Steps led to each bath, and over one of the larger baths was an arched bridge made of stone. The water gave off a steam that I watched rise and dissipate into the cool air.

My family had enjoyed many wonderful times in the Turkish baths, and Kareem and I, just the evening before, prior to our night of romance, had soothed ourselves by enjoying a lengthy steam bath.

There was nothing I could see to indicate that Amani had held a religious meeting in our home. Yet my head still thundered with the words I had overheard. I desperately wanted Kareem to acknowledge the seriousness of Amani's new passion, for our daughter was now speaking of her desire to insist to authorities that she be appointed as a female imam, a woman who would minister to other women's religious needs. While I wanted my daughter to live the life of a good Muslim, I had no desire for her to further the bondage of women under the strictest interpretation of the traditions that so hobbled females in our land.

Sensing correctly that Kareem was not burdened by Amani's passionate embrace of all that I had fought against since an early age, I thought to remind him of where such religious passion could lead, for I knew that my husband was sensitive to the subject of the al Sa'uds' legitimate claim to the throne and the wealth and privilege that accompanied our envied position.

Knowing my husband's world was firmly centered in a fashionable life of luxury, which could hardly be afforded without the vast wealth of the Saudi oil fields, I swept my hand across the lovely setting of the Turkish bath. "This," I said to Kareem, "is what our daughter believes is a great sin, to enjoy what God has seen fit to provide our family."

My husband made no response.

I pressed him further. "Kareem, we must take action. Or do you want your own flesh and blood to lead the revolt that will bring down the house of al Sa'ud?"

Kareem, still not believing his daughter capable of serious mischief, refused to further analyze Amani's disenchantment with our royal status, saying only that our daughter should be left to her consoling faith, even if it was against her mother's obstinate resistance.

Holding me tightly by my shoulders, Kareem forbade me to mention the subject again, making a ridiculous statement. "Sultana," he said, "I decided long ago that each of us must respect the other's delusions, or there will be no peace in our home. Now, darling, drop this disagreeable subject."

After days of soul-searching, I finally reached the understanding that I was not to blame for my daughter's new direction in life. I decided that Amani's zeal for a cause was a direct result of Saudi Arabia's horrendous poverty, which had been relieved by sudden and enormous wealth. To get to the heart of the matter, I had to go back in time.

Many people, Muslims and Christians alike, despise Saudis for their unearned wealth. Yet, few bother to understand the wretched poverty endured by all Saudi

Arabians until the mid 1970s. I highly resent this hasty analysis of our current situation.

Many years passed after the actual discovery of oil under the sand of the desert before our people benefited from the riches guaranteed by the oil production that had been organized by American companies. In the beginning, King Abdul Aziz, my grandfather and the founder of Saudi Arabia, trusted the smooth-talking men who made false promises, not understanding that the deals they struck put millions into the pockets of the Americans and paltry sums into the coffers of Saudi Arabia. Only when the American oil companies were forced to be fair did they behave in a principled manner.

Thus, due to the disproportionate method of dividing the proceeds from the oil wealth, it took many years for the Bedouin tents of the desert to be replaced by luxurious villas and palaces. Meanwhile, the people of Saudi Arabia suffered greatly. Infant mortality in Saudi Arabia was among the highest in the world, for there was no money, doctors, or hospitals to treat the sick. The Saudi diet consisted of dates, camel milk, and goat and camel meat.

I can remember seeing the desperate look in the eyes of one of the wealthiest men in the kingdom as he shared the horrifying tale of his early years. A brilliant and highly respected man of business, he spent the first fifteen years of his life going from door to door in the mud-hut village of Riyadh, in an attempt to sell small bags of goat's milk. He was the man of the family at age seven, for his father had died of a slight infection received when he cut himself with his sword while slaughtering a camel for the Haj feast. The infection had turned to gangrene, and his father had left the living with screams of great pain rending the air.

As was the custom of the day, the young boy's

mother was wed to a surviving brother of his father, a man who had many children of his own. The young boy felt responsible for his five younger siblings. Four of the five children were buried by his own hand, their deaths the result of poor nutrition and lack of medical facilities. His brutish climb to prosperity was a tale of Dickensian horror.

After a youth spent amid dire poverty, it was quite natural that the first Saudi generation to know the power of wealth would pamper their offspring, showering them with all that their money could purchase. While Kareem and I grew to adulthood without knowing need, we understood the vital force of our parents' poverty, which had made a lasting impact during our youth. However, the children born from our generation never knew deprivation, even secondhand, and so did not realize what it really meant to be poor.

Civilization followed a natural course, for concentrated wealth balanced insecurely upon a lost heritage may at any moment be dismissed as of no value. It was only a matter of time until the shaky foundations began to tumble.

The conventions and traditions accepted by past generations were questioned by my generation. The generation that followed mine often, wholly without restraint, followed their animal instincts. This primitive rejection of social order brought forth a natural backlash of religious fanaticism and disdain for extravagant fortunes.

Now, those who are most fanatical are the offspring of my generation. Having never known life without great wealth, and spared any knowledge of the consequences of wrenching poverty, our children and the children of our acquaintances are scornful of our economic ease and are searching for a purpose greater than the accumulation of additional riches.

My child Amani became a leader of a group of women who strive to be even more militant than the men who lead the faithful to overturn the throne claimed by the Al Sa'ud clan.

While Amani sought to save the souls of those she knows as relatives, or claims as friends, she brought forth a confession from her cousin Faten, the child of my brother, Ali, that none of us could ever have imagined.

No man has been haughtier with women than Ali. As a child, he treated his ten sisters with contempt. As a young man living in America, he bedded and casually discarded hundreds of Western women. As a husband, he treated his wives as slaves, caring little about their happiness, careful to wed girls at first puberty so that they knew little of man's nature and accepted his perverse behavior as normal. In addition to four wives, Ali settled one concubine after the other in his home. As a father, he virtually ignored his daughters and showered affection on his sons.

It was only natural that his son Majed, brother of Faten, grew into a sadistic youth who considered women nothing more than sexual objects.

Looking back, I know now that Majed would have been beheaded or shot to death by a firing squad had his crime become common knowledge. Nothing could have saved him from this fate, not even the fact that he is the son of a high-ranking prince, for his sin was without precedent in the al Sa'ud family.

We had returned to our home in Riyadh, where each afternoon after school Amani continued her daily Koran sessions with those relatives who were interested in returning to the times of darkness, when women would remain silent on all aspects of life that did not occur within the confines of their homes.

It was a Wednesday afternoon, and I watched from my bedroom balcony as one after another of my daughter's friends and relatives left our driveway in the safety of their chauffeur-driven limousines. Faten, the daughter of my brother, Ali, was the last to leave, and I thought it odd that she and Amani talked for many long moments, with passionate embraces exchanged on more than one occasion. Sadly, I guessed that Faten, in her desperate unhappiness as the daughter of my unfeeling brother, had fiercely seized the cause my child had offered her.

Desperate to return to a normal relationship with my child, I cautioned myself not to introduce the topic of religion with Amani ever again, but to let God lead her where he wanted her to go. Still, I thought to interest Amani in a game of backgammon or cards, to see if I could focus her mind on something other than her faith.

When I timidly knocked on my daughter's door, there was no response. I heard the sound of weeping and entered her room. I felt irritation sweep through my body, for there sat Amani, holding the Koran in one hand and wiping her tears with the other. While I wanted to shout that religion was not meant to sadden a person, I resisted the urge and knelt at my child's feet. I began to pat her knee and calmly question her on the cause of her grief.

Expecting to hear that she had received some message from God not meant for my ears, I was startled when she replied, "Mummy, I am truly grieved by what I must do!"

Then my child threw herself into my arms and wept as one who has heard the most devastating news.

"Amani! Daughter, what is this?"

"Mummy." A spasm shook her small frame as she sobbed. "A terrible sin has been committed. I have learned a loathsome secret. God has told me to make this sin public."

"What sin?" I shouted, alarmed that Amani had somehow heard of Maha's love relationship with her friend Aisha, knowing that if their affair were made public my daughter and our family would suffer greatly.

Amani looked at me with big eyes. "Faten has revealed a confidence that is troubling her soul. This sin is too terrible to reveal, yet I must."

Relieved that Amani was not speaking of her sister, I speculated on which of the al Sa'ud scandals might be plaguing my child. In a family the size of the al Sa'ud clan, there is much gossip regarding the ungovernable conduct of the young princes and, on rarer occasions, the youthful princesses. Male members of the family will often be featured in foreign newspapers after a great gambling loss or having been caught in a sexual misadventure with a foreign woman. After family holidays in the West, more than one princess has returned to the kingdom expecting an illegitimate child. Rarely is the complete truth revealed, as the various relatives rush to cover the misdeeds of their children to prevent their personal misfortunes from becoming common knowledge throughout the al Sa'ud clan.

Amani blurted out, "Mummy. It is Majed. Majed has committed a sexual sin."

I had difficulty maintaining a serious face. "Majed? Amani, Majed is his father's son." I pulled my daughter's face to mine, warning her, "If you speak of this matter, the men of our family will do nothing more than share a laugh at your expense. Ali is proud of his son's success with foreign women."

Everyone in our family knew that Majed, Ali's second son, participated in foreign activities within our country, attending parties in foreign compounds and dating non-Muslim women from the hospitals and foreign airlines. This kind of activity was generally frowned upon by Muslim families, but Ali thought it a perfect opportunity for his second son to enjoy sexual freedom in a land where such activities are strictly forbidden between people of the Muslim religion.

My heart ached when I saw the seriousness of Amani's expression as she explained further. "No, Mummy. You do not understand. Majed has performed a sexual act without the consent of the woman." I had no idea what my daughter was talking about. "Amani, what do you mean?"

My daughter began to weep once again. Between her convulsive sobs, she asked that I go and find her father, saying that she needed his guidance in her decision about whom to inform of Majed's terrible conduct.

Hurt that Amani desired her father's opinion over my own, I nevertheless went through the house, looking for Kareem. When I finally located him with Abdullah and Maha in the game room, playing a lively game of pool, I felt a twinge of jealousy, thinking to myself that all three of my children preferred their father to their mother. I had to bite my tongue to avoid blurting out Kareem's distressing character flaws in an attempt to redirect my children's devotion.

All three members of my family jumped when I loudly yelled, "Kareem! Amani needs you."

"One moment. It is my turn."

"Kareem. Your daughter is weeping. Come now."

My husband gave me a filthy look. "What have you said to her, Sultana?"

Already testy and now wrongly accused, I used my hand to knock each of the brightly colored pool balls into the holes at the sides of the table. I walked away, unconcerned with the disappointed moans coming from Kareem and Abdullah. "Now," I shouted over my shoulder. "The game has ended. You have won. Now perhaps you can tend to your child."

Kareem was on my heels as we entered Amani's room. The tears had gone from my daughter's eyes, and she had the fixed look of one who has made a decision.

Kareem spoke first. "Amani? Your mother says that you need to tell me something?"

"Father, Majed has to be punished for what he has done. I have read carefully all that is written of such matters, and there is no other way. Punishment must be given to my cousin."

Kareem sat on a chair and crossed his legs. He had a squeezed, funny look on his face, as though for the first moment he realized that Amani had gone too far in her religious quest.

His voice quiet, he asked, "What has Majed done that is so terrible?"

Still an innocent girl, Amani's face turned a bright red. "I am ashamed of what I have to say."

"Just say it," Kareem prodded.

Embarrassed at speaking thus in the presence of a man, even her own father whom she had purposely requested to share the confidence, Amani stared into her lap. Her face was clear and innocent as she told us a tale of evil blackness.

"One evening Majed attended a party at one of the Western compounds. I believe that it was the compound for Lockheed employees. While there, he met an American woman who took an interest in the fact that he was of the royal family. As the evening went on, Majed became drunk, and the woman thought better of her promise to go with him to a friend's apartment. When Majed understood that he had wasted his evening and that there would be no sex that night, he left the compound in an angry mood. On the way to his home, he went to visit a friend, who happened to be in a hospital with minor injuries from a car accident. While at this hospital, Majed became angrier, and in his drunken condition, he slipped from room to room searching for a blonde or foreign woman whom he could coax or pay to have sex.

"It was after midnight, and there were few employees who were not sleeping."

Amani's bottom lip began to tremble, and Kareem had to persuade her to continue. "And...what happened then, Amani?"

The accusation tumbled from my daughter's mouth. "Majed had sex with a woman in the hospital who was a patient, a woman who had been seriously injured and was not conscious."

I could not move. As one who has been turned to stone, I listened as my daughter and my husband continued to speak. Kareem shook his head in disbelief. "Amani. Faten told you that?"

"Yes, Father. And more."

"Amani. No. Faten is imagining this. It cannot be true. It is too sick to be real."

"I knew you would resist the truth," Amani accused. "There is proof."

"Proof? What proof? I would like to know."

"Well, there was a man from Pakistan working in that area of the hospital. He discovered Majed leaving the room, and when he examined the patient, he saw that the sheets on her bed had been disturbed. He followed Majed and threatened to call the authorities. When he was told that Majed was a prince, he demanded money. To quiet him, Majed gave him what he had in his pocket."

"Amani." Kareem, highly dubious, cautioned his daughter. "Watch the words that come from your tongue. Rape. Blackmail. This is too much to believe."

"It is true! It is true! You will see! Now there is going to be trouble." Amani's words rushed, one atop the other, as she tried to convince her father. "Now it has been discovered that the woman who was in a coma, a Christian woman from another land, is with child! Even though she has been in the hospital, unconscious, for six months! She is three months with child! There is a big investigation in that hospital, and Majed fears that his name will be made public in the scandal."

Thinking for the first time that there might be some truth to the story, for the details were many, I began to breathe heavily, wondering how we could avoid this scandal.

Amani tearfully completed her tale of horror. "Faten caught him trying to break open the safe in their father's office in order to steal cash. When she confronted him, Majed confided in his sister that the Pakistani has demanded a lot of money. This man wants one million riyals to remain silent about Majed's royal identity. Majed cannot ask his father for that amount of money without an explanation, and the man is going to name him. Majed has been given one week to come up with the money."

Kareem and I stared at each other, wondering if what we were hearing was the truth.

I recalled terrible words that Majed had once used against Abdullah, ridiculing my son for his refusal to have sex with what Abdullah had claimed was a particularly ugly American, a woman twice my son's age who had been willing to have sex with a young prince for money. Majed had accused Abdullah of being a man who did not like women, saying, "A true man can become excited over a she camel!" I vaguely recalled that Majed had then told Abdullah something about this woman being better looking than the last one he "rode"—a woman who was unconscious and had not known the fun she was missing.

When discussing the incident, we had assumed

that the woman must have been drunk. Now, in light of what Amani was saying, had that woman been unconscious from an injury? Had Ali's son raped a woman who had no ability to speak for herself? The timing of Abdullah's confidence now fit Amani's story. I wanted to ask Kareem about that conversation, for he had been told of the matter by Abdullah and had shared the story with me. From that time Kareem had forbidden Abdullah to accompany his cousin Majed to foreign parties.

Kareem came back to his senses when Amani said, "Majed has to be punished. I will have to tell Wijdan to inform her father of Majed's misdeed."

I heard Kareem grinding his teeth. He, as I, knew that the father of Amani's good friend was a religious man who worked out of the royal mosque. While he bore no special animosity toward members of the royal family, he was a man of religion who followed his conscience. He would be a difficult man to buy off, and if nothing else, would insist on discussing the matter with the religious council and the king. The last thing our familyneeded was for that particular man to be told of the situation.

Besides, I still had hope in my heart that a mistake had been made and Majed was innocent of such unspeakable and indecent behavior.

Kareem instructed his daughter, "Amani, this is no topic for young girls to discuss. I will investigate these charges, and if they are true, I give you my word that Majed will be punished. Now, I must have your promise that you will tell no one what you have just said."

Expecting Amani to disagree, I was pleasantly surprised when my child seemed relieved to discharge the problem to her father. She promised him all that he had asked.

Within three days, Kareem had discovered the ugly truth. Indeed, there was a Christian woman in a local hos-

pital who had suffered a serious head injury in an automobile accident within the kingdom seven months before.
She had been unconscious for that length of time. Now,
the hospital staff and the family of the woman were in a
crisis, for the medical staff at the hospital had discovered
that the woman was four months pregnant. There was an
ongoing inquiry at the hospital to find the guilty party.

Amani's horrifying story was true. Kareem said
that Ali must be told, and asked me to accompany him to
my brother's home. For once in my life, I experienced no
glee regarding my brother's misfortunes.

My stomach churned as we entered the side gate
into the enormous compound that housed Ali's four wives
and seven concubines. As our automobile entered the
gate, I caught sight of many women and numerous children gathered on the portion of the lawn that was made
partially private by green foliage. The children were playing, while the women were gossiping, playing card games,
or knitting.

How strange, I thought, that over the years the
women my brother had wed, along with the concubines
he kept, had developed close and loving relationships. It
was rare for so many women attached to one man to
maintain such a successful and friendly rapport.

I could not imagine sharing Kareem with even one
woman, let alone ten. I thought that perhaps the lack of
love in my brother's temperament had caused the women
to seek friendship and companionship with those of their
own kind. Or perhaps my brother inspired no love at all
from his women, and each one welcomed the intrusion of
another to seduce Ali away from her marriage bed.

That thought brought a smile to my face.

But when I remembered the tragic reason for our
visit, my smile vanished.

Ali was in a jolly mood, and he extended a friendly

welcome to our unexpected and unexplained visit.

After an exchange of amenities, and our third cup of tea, Kareem broke the bad news. It was not an easy exchange, and Ali became distressed as Kareem informed him of what we had learned.

Ali's expression changed from that of a contented man to that of one lost in sorrow. For the first time in my life, I felt sympathy for my brother, recalling words I had often heard spoken by those wiser than I. *"Those whose hands are in the water should not expect happiness from those whose hands are in the fire."*

Ali was a man with his hand in the fire. Majed was summoned, and the boy's arrogant facade cracked when he saw the furious look on his father's face. I wanted to hate the boy, but I remembered an incident that had occurred when I was a child. After being corrected for some minor infraction, Ali once called our mother an ignorant Bedouin and moved to kick her. When my sisters and I begged our mother to beat Ali with a big stick, she sadly responded, "Why blame a young boy for resembling his father?"

Now, just as Ali had resembled our father in character and behavior, Majed was the image of Ali.

Kareem and I left my brother and his son when Ali began to strike Majed with his bare hands.

A week later Ali confided to Kareem that the problem had been "handled." He reported that he had located the Pakistani orderly and had made the man very rich. The Pakistani had invested his money in Canada, and with Ali's assistance would soon receive a passport to that country. Our family would hear no more from that troublemaker, Ali declared.

Shaking his head in bafflement, he told Kareem, "All this disruption, for a woman."

Neither the hospital nor the family of the woman

raped by Majed was ever aware of the truth of the matter, that the guilty party was a royal prince.

Majed was sent away to school in the west. Amani, convinced that no punishment could be worse than banishment from the land of the Prophet, was pacified.

Once again, wealth had absolved the family responsibility for a crime committed.

I suppose I should not have been angry or surprised, for as my brother said, it was only a woman.

It seemed that nothing disturbed the male domination of my country, even when one of their own was guilty of the most heinous crime.

Chapter Eight:
Love Affair

*When love beckons to you, follow him, though his ways are
hard and steep.*
—KAHLIL GIBRAN

Amani and her sister, Maha, woke me from a
pleasant afternoon nap. Through the heavy doors leading
into my private quarters, I could hear my daughters
screaming at one another.

What had Amani done now? I thought to myself as
I quickly dressed. Since Amani's religious conversion, she
liked to tell people what she thought of them, never hesitating to enumerate the immoral actions of her brother
and sister, searching endlessly for a pretext to censure her
siblings.

My son, Abdullah, was loath to fight. Dreading
Amani's incalculable and apparently unappeasable wrath,
Abdullah, more often than not, simply ignored his sister.
On the rare occasions that Amani's demands were simple
to fulfill, he capitulated.

Amani did not find such agreement possible with
Maha. In her older sister, Amani was dealing with a fe-

male whose character was at least as strong as her own, for Maha's violent temper had been apparent from her first breath.

I followed the sound of my daughters' shouts. Several of the servants were standing in the doorway of the kitchen, but they were disinclined to interrupt what to their eyes was lively entertainment.

I had to push my way into the room to arrive just in time. Maha, who is much fiercer than her younger sister, had reacted violently to Amani's latest regulation. As I rushed toward my daughters, I saw that Maha had her younger sister pinned on the floor and was rubbing her face into the pages of the morning newspaper.

It was as I had thought. Just the week before, Amani and her religious group had come to the conclusion that the kingdom's daily newspapers were made holy because their pages contained the word God, the sayings of the Holy Prophet, and verses of the Koran. The committee had decreed that newspapers were not to be walked upon, eaten upon, or thrown into the trash. At the time, Amani had given notice to her family of this religious decision, and now she had evidently apprehended Maha committing an irreverent act, heedless of her noble instruction. The result had been predictable.

I shouted, "Maha! Release your sister!" Spurred on by her anger, Maha seemed not to hear my excited command. I made a futile attempt to pull Maha away from her sister, but my daughter was determined to teach Amani a lesson. Since Maha was stronger than Amani and I together, she was the victor of our three-way struggle.

Red-faced and breathing with great effort, I looked to the servants for assistance, and one of the Egyptian drivers moved quickly to intervene. The man had a lot of strength and was successful in separating my daughters.

One battle always invites another. Verbal insults

replaced physical force. Maha began to curse her baby sister, who was weeping bitter tears while accusing her elder sister of being a non-believer.

I proposed to mediate but could not be heard above the mayhem. I pinched the skin on my daughters' arms until they were silenced. Maha stood in smoldering sullenness. Amani, still on her hands and knees, reached to straighten the pages of the ripped newspaper. My daughter kept her devotions to the end.

The causes for religious fervor are many, and the results are endless. It occurred to me that some people appear at their worst in their religion. Certainly, that was the case with Amani. In the past I had felt both doubtful and hopeful that religion could, in time, soothe rather than incite Amani. But now I felt with dull certainty that such would not be the case.

My patience did not equal my anger, and I led my daughters by their ears into the sitting room. With a firm voice, I called for the servants to leave us to ourselves. I glared at my children, thinking ungallantly that I had made a grievous mistake in inflicting upon the world such troublesome characters.

"The wailing of the newborn infant is nothing more than a siren of warning sung for a mother," I said to my daughters.

My face and glance must have made me look like a madwoman, for my daughters' expressions were stricken. They held a curious respect for their mother's moments of insanity.

Thinking to avoid a second, larger quarrel with three participants rather than two, I closed my eyes and took a deep breath. Once calmed, I told my daughters that each of them would have an opportunity to speak but that there would be no more violence.

Maha burst out, "Too much! Too much! Amani is

driving me insane! She will leave me alone, or..." I could see that Maha was searching through her mind for the worst possible insult, "I will slip into her room and rip up her Koran!"

Amani gasped in horror at the thought. Knowing how spirited and daring Maha could be when she was determined, I forbade my daughter the irreverent act.

Her fury unleashed, Maha continued. "This stupid idea of not discarding old papers! We will be forced to build a large building to store them." She looked at her sister, "You have lost all good sense, Amani!" Maha looked back at me and charged her sister with dictatorship, "Mother, from the moment we departed Haj, Amani no longer feels my equal but my master!"

I agreed completely with Maha. I had seen my daughter's religious beliefs pass, with impressive speed, from confusion to a flourishing vision. Her sense of divine righteousness was producing ridiculous household sanctions that excluded no one.

Just a few days before, she had discovered one of the Filipina gardeners proudly displaying a pair of rubber sandals that had been imprinted with the name of God on their soles.

Instead of granting the anticipated praise for his purchase, Amani shrieked in rage, grabbing the poor fellow's shoes and accusing him of blasphemy, threatening him with severe punishment.

In tears, the young man confessed that he had purchased the shoes in Bahtha, a popular shopping souq located in the downtown district of Riyadh. He thought his Muslim employers would be pleased to see that the name of God was printed on his shoes.

Calling the shoes the work of the devil, Amani called a special meeting of her religious group and stunned them all by revealing the sacrilegious shoes.

Word spread to other religious groups, and pamphlets were distributed in the city, advising people not to buy or to wear such shoes.

The shoes were rather shocking, since Muslims are taught never to walk on any item bearing God's name, even going so far as to be sure our shoes are never left lying soles up, in case that might be some insult to our maker. Yet, Amani's reaction was somewhat dramatic, since the young Filipina was not of our faith and not acquainted with our truths. My daughter was cruel in her angry denunciations.

Since an early age, I have been drawn to the idea of a kindly God, a being that does not find sin in every human delight. I knew with certainty that my child was not acquainted with the God of Mohammed, as taught to me by my loving mother. I sent a questionable prayer to my maker, asking that Amani's gloomy devoutness take a holiday.

My thoughts returned to the present crisis, and I looked upon my daughters.

With Maha's threat of defacing her Koran looming as a real possibility, Amani promised to refrain from inspecting her siblings' habits.

Maha declared that if Amani would only leave her to her own inclinations, however distracting they might be to her sister, she would commit no further violence.

I hoped the truce would stick, but I had my doubts, for Amani was readily moved to judge all before her, never really happy except when making religious war. And Maha was not one to bear timidly the taunts of her sister.

My two daughters, trapped in a family unit, were too volatile a mixture for everlasting peace. I abandoned desolation and yielded to motherly affection. With the deepest love, I embraced each of my daughters.

Maha, always quick to anger and prompt to forgive, gave me a genuine smile of peace. Amani, slow to pardon those she deemed in the wrong, was stiff and did not yield to my affection.

Exhausted by the responsibilities of motherhood, I wistfully observed my girls as they went their separate ways.

All at once, the room was empty of their mad energy, but the resulting quiet was not comforting. I felt edgy, and told myself that I was in need of a stimulant.

I rang the bell for Cora and asked that she bring me a cup of Turkish coffee. Then, without knowing my reason, I abruptly changed my mind and asked instead that she mix me a strong drink of bourbon and cola.

Cora stood openmouthed with surprise. It was the first time I had requested a drink of alcohol during the daylight hours.

"Go on," I demanded.

I sat, reading the newspaper without absorbing the news. I admitted to myself that I was looking forward to my drink with discomfiting anticipation, when Abdullah arrived at home.

Abdullah moved with speed through the door into the hallway. I caught a glimpse of my son's face and did not like what I saw. Accustomed to his gentle character, I knew from his dark expression that he was torn by agony.

I called out, "Abdullah!"

Abdullah strode into the room. Without inquiry, he let loose his anguish.

"Mother! Jafer has fled the kingdom!"

"What?"

"He has run away! With Fouad's daughter, Fayza."

Staggered by confusion and skepticism, I could not speak. With my mouth hanging open, I sat and stared at my son.

Still in his early twenties, Jafer Dalal was a young man admired by all who knew him. He was both handsome and strong, with a serious but kindly countenance bespeaking quiet wisdom and calm strength. He was a charming conversationalist, a gentleman of refinement and courtesy. Jafer was one of but a few young men whom Kareem trusted completely with the women of his family.

Jafer was Abdullah's dearest and most cherished friend.

Often I told Kareem that I would have liked to have known Jafer's parents, for never had a man been better raised. But that could never be, for Jafer's mother died when he was only twelve and his father was killed in the Lebanese civil war when Jafer was seventeen. His one brother, older by four years, had been critically wounded in the Lebanese war and was a permanent resident of a nursing facility located in the south of Lebanon. Orphaned while still a teenager and without any siblings to offer him shelter, Jafer moved from the only home he had ever known and traveled to live with an uncle in Kuwait, who managed some businesses for a wealthy Kuwaiti.

As a Palestinian Sunni Muslim, born and raised in the refugee camps of southern Lebanon, Jafer did not have an easy life.

After the Iraqi invasion of Kuwait, the PLO stood behind Saddam Hussein. It was not surprising that after the war ended there was much resentment by the Kuwaiti citizens towards their large Palestinian population. While Jafer's uncle and his family had remained loyal to their Kuwaiti sponsor and could have remained in Kuwait, there was such a backlash of antagonism toward anyone with Palestinian identification that the Kuwaiti sponsor recommended that the family move to another land. The kindly man did not want such a fine family to risk danger by remaining in Kuwait. "Let a few years pass," he promised, "and the crisis will be over."

This Kuwaiti sponsor co-owned a business with Kareem, and he suggested to my husband that Jafer's uncle would make an excellent employee for a particular job opening in that company's offices in Riyadh.

As there was some bitterness at the time between our king and Yassir Arafat with regard to the Gulf War, there was a political movement in Saudi Arabia to avoid employment of people with Palestinian nationality. As a high-ranking prince, however, Kareem could do as he pleased. On the recommendation of his Kuwaiti partner, he employed Jafer's uncle.

After the man arrived in Riyadh, he became one of Kareem's most trusted employees, assigned difficult tasks and responsible posts. Jafer accompanied his uncle and so impressed my husband that he was given a management position in Kareem's law offices.

From the moment Abdullah was introduced to Jafer, the two young men became fast friends, Abdullah claiming Jafer as the brother he never had.

Jafer came into our lives only two short years ago, yet he quickly became a beloved member of our family.

Conspicuously attractive, Jafer drew much female attention wherever he went in the city. Abdullah claimed that women passed his friend notes of invitation while in hotel restaurants. Once, when Jafer accompanied Abdullah to the King Faisal Hospital and Research Centre to visit a royal cousin who was hospitalized there, three foreign nurses volunteered their telephone numbers to Abdullah's friend after the briefest of conversations.

I thought Jafer wise beyond his years, for it appeared that he lived a life of celibacy in a land that frowned upon illicit relationships between men and women.

Sensing that the young man was lonely and of an age to settle down, Kareem reproached Jafer for his persistent bachelorhood. Making serious offers to introduce Jafer to Lebanese or Palestinian contacts, men who might introduce him to marriageable Muslim women from those countries, Kareem declared that it would be a tragedy if Jafer avoided love, adding that even good men could be ruined by too much virtue.

With a wink in my direction, Kareem mischievously added that all men should experience the pleasures and tribulations of female companionship.

In jest, I made a threatening move toward my husband, for I knew the truth—that Kareem, a happy father, could not fathom a life without children.

Kareem failed in his attempt to provide female company for the young man whom he had grown to respect and love, for Jafer never accepted Kareem's generous invitations.

Abdullah added to the mystery by saying that his friend was polite but firm in refusing all offers of female companionship. I was puzzled but so consumed by the problems presented by my daughters that I thought little more of Jafer's private life.

Looking back, I wondered how we could have thought that a full-blooded, sensual man like Jafer would scorn all that love had to offer?

The truth as to why Jafer had deferred marriage was made known in a most devastating manner that threatened to end in tragedy.

Abdullah, who had loved Jafer with perfect sincerity, now let his grief swell to great proportions. There was something disarmingly childlike about him as he complained, "Jafer never told me about Fayza."

It was the darkest time of Abdullah's young life. My son's disheveled innocence pierced my heart, and it was difficult for me to believe at that moment that he would soon celebrate his twentieth birthday. At that moment Kareem arrived, as angry as Abdullah was sad.

"Abdullah!" he shouted. "You have risked your life and the lives of innocents!"

Kareem told me that when Abdullah was informed of Jafer's disappearance, he became distraught and left Kareem's offices in a dangerous mood. Fearful for his only son's safety, Kareem followed in hot pursuit. My husband claimed that Abdullah drove his automobile through the streets of the city at high speed. Kareem said that at one point Abdullah's car crossed the center lane and forced a line of drivers from the road.

"You could have been killed!" Kareem was so agitated at the possibility that he reached across and slapped our son's face.

The sharp slap shocked and silenced my husband.

Over the years of my children's turbulent growth, I have pinched and slapped all three of them with irresistible pleasure. But never had Kareem struck one of our children! Kareem was as stunned by his action as I, staring down at his offensive hand as though it were not his own.

He embraced his shivering son and apologized, saying that in the course of following Abdullah's reckless path, he had gone out of his mind with worry.

The room was filled with emotion, and it took many moments for the mystery of Jafer and Fayza's hidden romance to be completely revealed.

Fayza was the daughter of Fouad, Kareem's partner in three foreign businesses. Fouad was not of the al Sa'ud family but distantly related by marriage to a daughter of a royal.

Many years before, Fouad was allowed to wed into the royal family, even though he was not from a clan of the Najd (the central area of Saudi Arabia), nor was his tribe particularly close to the al Sa'uds. Generally, al Sa'ud women were wed out of the family only for political or economic reasons. Fouad was from a prosperous Jeddah trading family that had bitterly fought the al Sa'uds during the early days of the formation of the kingdom.

Anxious to forge a bond between his family and the rulers of the land, Fouad offered an immense dowry for Samia, a princess who, we often said in kindness, was spared the distracting handicap of being a great beauty.

No one in the royal family could believe Samia's good fortune, for she was long resigned to remaining a spinster, cruel gossip about her bad skin, small eyes, and bent back having stripped away all marriage possibilities.

Fouad, determined to attach himself to the respected al Sa'ud clan, heard of Samia's lack of beauty through women who knew her family, but his only desire was to marry a woman of many virtues. He had heard the lurid stories told by his female relatives about alluring women who made the most miserable wives because, carefully coiffed and richly garbed, they could think of little besides expensive homes, many servants, and endless jewels.

Fouad knew sound advice when he heard it. Denouncing the lure of beauty, he said that he desired a woman of humor and warmth. The particular princess he sought, while uncongenial to a poet's dream, was one of the more popular royals, well loved for her charm and grace.

Thinking that Fouad was a fool, Samia's family accepted his offer, and a wedding was arranged.

Fouad was well pleased with his wife, for she had a sense of humor, which, Fouad knew, would see them through the tribulations of marriage. His new bride facilitated matters by falling deeply in love with her husband. Theirs was the happiest of unions.

Fouad was a Saudi man who adored his one and only wife and who was the proud father of three sons and one daughter. In one of the stranger quirks of nature, Fouad, a plain-faced man, and Samia, a woman who was pitied for her appearance, produced the most dazzling offspring. Their three sons were strikingly handsome, while their only daughter was a ravishing beauty.

Fayza was the only girl I have ever seen who rivaled Sara's youthful splendor. Stories about her fair complexion, wistful dark eyes, and long coal-black hair stirred the blood of Saudi Arabian men, who could only imagine the girl's physical attractiveness from hearsay.

Fayza had other irresistible qualities. She inherited something of her mother and was a girl of rare, dry wit who often enlivened our female gatherings.

I was sorry that Fayza was older than my son, for I thought Abdullah would have loved her intensely, had he been given the opportunity.

Beautiful, witty, and smart, Fayza was a university student at a women's school in Riyadh. She was in the first courses of predentistry and had aspirations to open a children's dental facility.

Fouad confided that while he wanted his daughter to attain a degree, in reality she would have little need for working skills. He proudly confided to Kareem that at the completion of his daughter's education, Fayza would be married into a wealthy family. Meetings had already been conducted, and Fouad had his pick of three influential families. When his daughter graduated, he would allow her to have supervised meetings with each of the three young men in question, allowing his child to have a say in her future.

When Kareem told me Fouad's plans for Fayza, I felt great joy, thinking how far we had traveled since the days of my yout. None of my sisters had a voice in the choice of their husbands. And, Sara! Who among us could forget the nightmare Sara had endured in her first marriage to an evil man. She was only sixteen when our father forced her to marry a man forty-eight years her senior. The man was very wealthy and had business connections with our family. Sara became hysterical when she heard the news, pleading with our father to have mercy and cancel the wedding. Sadly, not even our mother could reverse his decision. As it turned out, Sara was allowed a divorce after she tried to take her own life. My sister was an innocent girl who knew nothing of men and their sexual appetites, but her husband subjected her to the cruelest of sexual bondage and abuse. It was a tragic union that scarred my sister and almost claimed her life. In my family, I was the only daughter privileged to meet my husband before he became my intimate partner in life. And that decision had resulted from nothing more than the actions of a spirited girl, combined with the determination of a curious suitor.

When I first learned that I would be wed to a royal cousin, I telephoned the sister of that cousin, pretending I had been seriously scarred from a chemical accident. Little in my land is more valued than female beauty. The rumor I purposely started (in order to have my engagement called off) led to a personal meeting with a group of female relatives of that cousin. These women inspected me as if I were a camel in a market, and I reacted in an outrageous manner, snapping and biting until they fled my home. When Kareem heard of my behavior, he insisted upon meeting me. Happily, Kareem and I were attracted to each other, or who knows what else might have occurred.

Now a man raised in the strictest of times was casually speaking of allowing his child the opportunity to take part in the selection of her husband.

How happy I was at the news!

Yet I did not let myself rejoice too long, for I knew that most women in my land still were used as nothing more than political or economic prizes. Nevertheless, I assured myself, each individual battle won would eventually lead to widespread and enormous victory.

And now Fouad's dreams for his daughter's future had come to nothing. His only daughter, a beautiful woman sought by the wealthiest men in my land, had eloped with a penniless Palestinian refugee.

"How did this happen?" I asked my husband.

With their lawyer's minds and information gathered by Samia, Kareem and Fouad had pieced together the drama of the two lovers.

Weeks after Jafer began his work at the firm, Fouad's family came into the office to sign some papers. Fouad had acquired some rather large business interests abroad, and he put some of those businesses in the names of his children.

Jafer was responsible for the clerical aspects of the documents. When Fouad's family arrived, they were ushered into Jafer's office, where the young man was told to obtain the necessary signatures. As our religious customs demand, Samia and her daughter, Fayza, were veiled. Feeling protected in a locked office, in the presence of a trusted employee, both women threw their veils off their faces for the purpose of reading and signing documents.

Now in the midst of the controversy, Samia had

the dimmest recollection that her daughter and Jafer had stared at each other for too long a time. Samia, innocent in her inherent goodness, did not connect her daughter's nervous behavior and crooked signature with the medley of incredible fancies that were playing upon her child.

At the time, Samia listened without hearing and looked without seeing.

The handsome young man, Jafer, offered them tea, and Samia watched her daughter as she gratefully received his attentions, their hands lightly brushing in the innocent exchange of pens and cups of tea. She told her husband that, at the time, she had thought the touches were accidental.

Kareem reported that Fouad had screamed insults, blaming his wife, telling her that all men are by nature villains, and that she, the mother of an innocent girl, should have been more attuned to Jafer's evil nature. Fouad had moaned, claiming that Jafer was nothing more than a man with a poem on his lips and a dagger in his pocket!

Samia could recall nothing more, except that her child had seemed flushed and feverish while in the company of Jafer.

Fayza's personal Filipina maid, Connie, knew many details. She was carefully questioned by Kareem and Fouad. The two men discovered that there was no end to the intrigue of the two lovers, and according to Connie, it was Fouad's daughter, rather than Jafer, who had pursued the affair.

Connie reported that from that first day, Fayza was stricken by a great love, a weakening love that made the girl forget to eat and sleep. Torn between loyalty to her family and desire for Jafer, Fayza confessed to her maid that love was the victor. She would have this man, Jafer, or no man at all.

Connie said that she had never seen a girl so taken by a man.

Knowing the plans of Fayza's parents for their lovely daughter, Connie found herself in an unenviable position. She could not report the truth about her young mistress, yet she knew that she should. Connie swore to Fouad she had reminded Fayza that the daughter of a wealthy Saudi family, with close connections to the al Sa'uds, could not end up with a Palestinian clerk, that such a situation could only lead to misfortune.

Having a tendency to lapse into criticism of our male-dominated society, I thought of where the blame might be placed. Thinking of Saudi Arabia's restrictive social customs, I interrupted Kareem and told him I had come to a conclusion, that Fayza's overreaction to a charming, handsome man made a mockery of our system. My voice thick with frustration, I declared that if men and women could only meet each other under normal circumstances, these delusions of instant love would be more infrequent.

While I do believe that great attractions lead to genuine love, such as had happened with my sister Sara and her husband, Asad, such a happy outcome is rare. When life is filled with harsh social restrictions, when young men and women rarely have the opportunity to enjoy one another's company on ordinary social occasions, spontaneous emotions are quick to rise to the surface, often ending in terrible personal tragedies.

With an irritated look on his face, Kareem said he would quit the room if I insisted on burdening the conversation with my well-known theories about the subjugation of females in the Saudi culture!

Abdullah looked at me with longing, his eyes begging me not to make a scene. For the sake of my son, I agreed to be quiet.

Kareem, subtly pleased, continued to describe the drama. Fayza, telling Connie her heart had been a willing recipient of love, knew that Jafer loved her, too, but that he was vulnerable, in his low position, to her elevated status. She feared that he would never take the initiative.

Fayza boldly called Jafer at his office, asking him to meet with her, promising that her family would never know.

Jafer, while acknowledging to Fayza that no woman had ever affected him as she had, refused the tempting offer, asking the girl what benefit could come from such temporary bliss, for when the relationship ended, unbearable mental torture would be the result of his loss.

Fayza gleefully confided to Connie that Jafer was snared, that she was certain she would soon see him, for their telephone conversations had become hot with passion, Jafer warning her that if he ever had her, he would never give her up. His words were delightful to hear.

Fayza persisted. After two weeks of increasingly intimate telephone conversations, which only served to further their desire, Jafer's resolve weakened. They agreed to meet at the Al Akariya, a large shopping mall in the city of Riyadh.

At last, a veiled Fayza, masquerading as a relative of Jafer, walked beside the man she had sought. The two walked from shop to shop, getting to know one another. They aroused little suspicion, for an Arab man with a veiled woman was a common sight in our city.

Their walking relationship was unnatural, but they were too fearful to seat themselves at a restaurant to share a meal, for they knew that restaurants were the principal target of the active and increasingly familiar morals committees, which harass people of every nationality who live in Saudi Arabia.

Such committees are composed of menacing men who unexpectedly surround and enter eating establishments, demanding identification of the restaurant patrons. If proof is not forthcoming that the men and women sharing a table are husband and wife, brother and sister, or father and daughter, these frightened people will be arrested and escorted to a city jail, with punishment freely given. The legal penalties vary according to the nationality of the "criminal." Muslim offenders can be flogged for their social misconduct, while non-Muslims are jailed or deported.

In the beginning, Jafer and Fayza adjusted their morals to the situation.

Over time, Jafer located an apartment, offered by a sympathetic Lebanese friend, where they could meet in privacy. Since Fayza, as a woman, was not allowed to drive, she was forced to trust a family driver. Knowing that his participation could result in deportation or worse, Fayza lessened his hesitation by offering the man a large sum of money.

Out of this tempting attraction a great love blossomed. The lovers knew that neither one of them could ever love another. Jafer asked Fayza to marry him. Then, just as they were building up their courage to make their love known to their families, a crisis occurred. One of Saudi Arabia's wealthiest men approached Fouad for the privilege of asking the beautiful Fayza to wed his oldest son. Pressure mounted for Fayza to agree. Fouad declared that the perspective bridegroom was matchless.

"How long I have toiled to build a perfect relationship, which my father would so readily destroy." Fayza cried out to Connie.

The desperate lovers made their decision to flee the country. Fouad had been tricked, his honor tarnished, and now he would stop at nothing to find his only daughter. Knowing how difficult it was for females in Saudi Arabia to travel freely, I asked, "How did Fayza manage to leave the kingdom alone?"

"She did not," Kareem replied, "leave alone."

I was pleased to hear that Fayza did not commit the sin of traveling alone. Saudi women are forbidden by our religion to travel without a male member of the family as escort. This particular restriction is taken directly from the words of the Prophet, who said: "She who believes in Allah and the Last Day (meaning the Day of Judgment) must not travel any distance that is normally covered by one day's and one night's traveling unless accompanied by a *mahram*."

A woman's *mahram* is any relative to whom she cannot be married, such as her father, brother, uncle, nephew, stepfather, father-in-law, or son-in-law. She is allowed to travel with her husband as a matter of course.

I discovered that Fayza had talents in the art of treachery. She told her parents she needed some time away from mounting pressures. She hinted to her mother that a positive response would be forthcoming to the marriage proposal if she could only enjoy a small holiday. She thought she would like to visit her cousin, a girl who married a man from Dubai. Could she be rewarded with a weekend before she pledged herself to marriage?

Samia was bedridden with a sprained back, so Fayza's younger brother went along as his sister's required male escort.

Why should anyone be suspicious of Jafer taking his annual holiday during this same period? In their wildest imaginations, no one in the family had linked the young man with Fayza.

Once in the safety of Dubai, removed from the dangers of Saudi Arabia, Fayza outmaneuvered her younger brother, slipping her passport from his travel bag while he was in the shower, and making an ordinary pretense of shopping with other females. Her brother volunteered to drive, dropping them at the Al Ghurair Centre on his way to meet a Saudi friend who was staying at the Chicago Beach Hotel, located on one of the most beautiful beaches in the Emirates.

From the Al Ghurair Centre, a popular shopping area, Fayza whispered to her cousin that she had to seek a toilet but would soon return. Her cousin, intent upon selecting perfume, thought little of the deception, promising Fayza that she would wait for her in the shop.

Fayza was not seen again. To her cousin's horror, she had disappeared.

A frantic search ensued, with Fouad and his wife fearing the worst for their daughter's safety. Had their child been kidnapped, raped, or murdered? While such crimes were rare in the Emirates, violent acts were occasionally committed.

When Connie learned of her well-loved mistress's strange disappearance, she collapsed into a weeping fit and confessed her knowledge of Jafer and Fayza's activities.

A father's love knows no reason. Not believing that his innocent daughter could be so devious, he cast all blame upon Jafer's head.

Neither Kareem nor I had ever heard of Fouad's resorting to abuse or force. He was known to all as a soft-spoken, kindly man. This was not the case during the emotional upheaval he suffered after his daughter's flight with a man. He fired the unfortunate Connie, putting her on the next flight to Manila. Then, in his wild rage, Fouad burst into Kareem's offices and physically assaulted Jafer's uncle. There was a terrible scene, with Fouad threatening the man's life if Fayza was not returned unharmed, still a marriageable virgin.

The police were summoned by a frightened Indian secretary in a neighboring office.

In Saudi Arabia, liability for public disorder falls upon the foreigner, never upon a Saudi. In this case, Fouad was questioned by the police and apologies were made for their interference in a private matter. But had Kareem not been higher in rank and influence than Fouad, Jafer's uncle would have been imprisoned.

Everyone in my family felt saddened by the insoluble problems of human life, and no one knew the appropriate action to take.

Sara and I visited Samia in her home. Muttering that "life without love would be a mistake," I said everything wrong, causing poor Samia's ugly face to grow uglier still, while Sara knew how to express intense feeling in her own quiet way.

Bewildered by her child's rash flight, Samia had difficulty speaking and began to stutter anxious responses to Sara's kind sympathy.

When we departed Samia's home, I asked my sister, "How can the outworn traditions of our society be changed, without painful destruction of the older generation's expectations?"

It is my opinion that marriage brought about by love is most natural and rewarding, while the majority in my land scorn love and look only for respect and companionship after marriage.

How would we Saudi Arabians ever reconcile our differences?

Unable to determine his daughter's whereabouts without professional assistance, Fouad contacted private investigative agencies in France and America. One week after his child disappeared, Fouad discovered that she was in the United States in the state of Nevada, registered in a hotel as Jafer's wife.

The moment the information came to Fouad, he traveled with his three sons to America, vowing to bring Fayza home. He promised his wife that their daughter would not remain with a Palestinian. Caught up in his tyrannical affection, he said that Fayza's death would be preferable to the loss of his personal honor.

This bit of news created a furor in our household.

I bit my nails until my fingers bled.

Abdullah fell into a melancholy mood that threatened his health, sensing that nothing would ever be the same again.

Praying for the souls of the lovers, Amani glumly predicted that her prayers would not be answered, that the lovers had foolishly taken their paradise on earth, and that fires of molten metal would welcome them as they exited this earth.

Abdullah glared at his sister and cuttingly remarked that perhaps Jafer felt Fayza's feminine perfection was worth the quitting of heaven.

Caring deeply for both Jafer and Fayza, Maha became hostile to anyone who criticized the lovers, declaring that no man or government should have authority over true love.

Abdullah and I pleaded with Kareem to make contact with Jafer, to give him a warning to flee. I told Kareem that Fayza's male relatives needed more time to accept the crucial fact that Fayza now belonged with another. Their extreme anger could not prevail; time would ease their rage.

It was not to be. My husband infuriated me, remaining true to the Saudi male policy of accepting any injustice, if that injustice involved a man's obsession with his women or the family honor. Thinking to incite him to action, I insulted Kareem, telling him that I was disappointed to discover I had wed a man who failed to probe the deeper complexities of life, who instead was a dull, unfeeling type that tended to remain on the surface of things.

As I left my husband standing openmouthed in amazement at my attack, I could not resist one final barb. "Kareem, how can you have no conflict between logic and feeling? Are you not human?"

Silently I retreated, but secretly I had Abdullah take action. At my urging, he searched Kareem's office and found the information that had been provided by the investigative services looking for Jafer and Fayza.

Triumphant, we were careful to hide ourselves from Kareem and Amani, making our telephone call during the long evening prayer, knowing that Kareem was in the mosque and Amani locked in her room, facing Makkah, saying her prayers.

With shaking fingers, Abdullah punched the number of the Mirage Hotel in Las Vegas, Nevada, where Jafer and Fayza were known to be registered.

As I watched the brooding face of my beautiful son patiently waiting for the hotel operator to ring the room, I was possessed by the fever a mother has for her children, wishing for Abdullah's pain to leave his body and enter mine.

Jafer answered the telephone.

Abdullah tortured himself trying to find the right words to make Jafer understand that he was in great danger. His friend was dismayed at their rapid discovery but felt secure in his married state. "What can they do now?" he asked Abdullah.

When Abdullah repeated the question to me, I grabbed the telephone from my son's hand. "They can do plenty, Jafer," I yelled. "Fouad's honor has been attacked, his only daughter has vanished with a man not thought suitable! Do not be a fool! You are an Arab, you are aware what reactions such anguish will bring to an Arab father!"

Jafer tried to soothe my fears, claiming that their love would see them through any persecution.

Fayza came to the telephone, speaking softly into the receiver, which Jafer still held in his hand. Fayza's sultry voice told of the wonderful love that had prevailed, in spite of the substantial obstacles placed in its path by the laws of our land.

"Fayza, you are still a youth of twenty and have loosened yourself from our ancient traditions. Your father cannot do this. Fouad is a man of desert mentality, and he can only flow down the main stream. In his mind, you have committed a shocking offense. Leave that place! Meet with the men of your family at a later date."

My pleas for the lovers to vanish made no impact. How weak my words must have seemed to their brave spirits. Courageous, Jafer vowed he would face the fury of Fayza's family.

I returned the telephone to my son, thinking that I had done all I could.

I thought, is it a glory or a disaster that they have no suspicion yet of the extent of their tragedy? I realized the narrow limits of their lovers' vision. Jafer and Fayza were blinded, believing that the strength of their great love could conquer the challenge of her furious and disapproving family.

Fretting in silence, I could only hope that Jafer and Fayza would be able to delay destiny for a while.

It was four days before Fouad returned to the kingdom.

His voice low and uneasy, Kareem called me from his offices and reported that Fouad and his sons had returned from America.

My throat closed around the words I could not ask.

After a dry pause, Kareem added that Fouad had

returned with his daughter but without her husband.

My voice returned. "Is Jafer dead?" I asked, wondering already how we would break the cruel news to Abdullah.

"No. Jafer is not dead," Kareem answered, his voice causing me to doubt his words even as he spoke them.

I was quiet, waiting for the news I was not sure I wanted to hear.

"Sultana, I am coming home. Together, we will tell Abdullah what has happened."

"What happened?" I screamed, thinking that I could not bear to wait for Kareem to make the twenty-five-minute drive from his office to our home.

I heard a click and the line went dead. I told myself that my husband's news must be dreadful, for Kareem, like most Arabs, had a habit of putting aside unpleasant truths until the last possible moment.

Fouad had told my husband little, only that there had been a minor scuffle in Jafer and Fayza's hotel room, and that Jafer had been left unconscious but without serious injury.

Fayza? Naturally, his daughter had been traumatized by the incident and was now at their palace under sedation. Without the influence of Jafer, Fouad believed his daughter would quickly return to her senses.

I looked at Kareem and announced with certainty, "Jafer is dead!"

"Nonsense. They were in America."

Two weeks later we received a telephone call from Jafer, who had returned to Lebanon, and we finally learned the truth of the matter.

Jafer's words to me were, "All is lost." He paused. "Except for my skin, which is safe."

"Abdullah!" I called out. "It is Jafer! Come quickly!"

Kareem, Maha, and I circled Abdullah as he spent

long moments quietly listening to his dearest friend, comforting the caller with reassurances. "What could you do? You had no choice."

With a start, I heard my son say, "I am coming!" stating that he would soon be on his way to Lebanon, that nothing could keep him from his friend's side.

I grabbed Abdullah's arms and began to shake my head no, vigorously.

My feet left the floor as Kareem yanked me from my son's face.

Abdullah put the telephone on hold. With tears running down his face, my son buried his head in his hands and began to weep bitter tears. His words were muffled, difficult to understand. "Jafer is ruined! He is ruined!"

"What is this about Lebanon?" I inquired, too agitated at the thought of Abdullah traveling to that country to consider Jafer's condition.

"Hush, Sultana," Kareem ordered.

Abdullah finally calmed himself and explained how Fouad and his sons had taken Fayza from Jafer.

The telephone call had awakened them in the night. Fayza's father and brothers were in the lobby. "Could they come up, please?" Fouad's tone was civil; Jafer was encouraged and felt no fear of physical assault.

When Jafer opened the door, he felt pleased and smiled.

Fouad and his sons took no time to talk. Provoked by Jafer's smiling face, which he now feared they had mistaken for a smirk, Fayza's brothers set upon him. Caught by surprise, Jafer was no match for four men.

Jafer said he was hit on the head with a heavy object, and blackness overcame him.

Hours later, when he revived, his new bride and her male relatives were gone.

Jafer said he knew all was lost once they had stolen Fayza away from him. He was well aware that it is illegal in Saudi Arabia for a Saudi girl to marry a man who is not a Saudi national. Such a marriage requires royal approval, which is nearly impossible to get. He could receive no legal assistance in claiming Fayza as his own, despite their married state, for their union was not recognized in Saudi Arabia. Had Jafer been a Saudi and Fayza a Palestinian, there would have been no difficulty, for Saudi men can marry whom they wish.

In spite of that knowledge, Jafer flew to London, making a desperate attempt to reenter the kingdom, but was told that his resident's visa was no longer valid.

Jafer, having feared Kareem's scorn, now overcame his fear and asked to speak to my husband. He wondered if Kareem, with his princely status, could help?

Kareem said he could but would not. Now that he knew Jafer was alive, he had no intention of placing him in a position that would ensure his murder. Kareem warned Jafer that Fouad and his sons would certainly kill him if he returned to the kingdom.

Kareem had never said so, but I knew he would never forgive Jafer for his deception. My husband had suffered acute embarrassment because a trusted employee had conquered and stolen the beloved only daughter of his long-time friend and partner. Only his intense love for Abdullah had kept him silent.

Never one to promise more than he could give, Kareem recommended that Jafer try to find a life for himself in Lebanon, now that it seemed the country was finally returning to peace.

"How sad," I said. "It is the end of a magnificent love story. And now Jafer stands alone against an overwhelming power."

Standing quietly to the side of the room, my son

was an unforgettable figure clad in his white *thobe*. He was straight and tall and suddenly looked a man. His face was sad, and with dramatic intensity, Abdullah said no, that was not the case. Jafer would never be alone, for he would not forsake his friend. He was going to visit him in Lebanon.

Kareem and I refused our son permission to travel to that country, but Abdullah seemed not to care and said that he would go nevertheless.

Such a trip would invite a thousand calamities! I was miserable as I prepared myself for bed, plotting to stop my son from his sentimental journey.

I should have known I would fail, for it is impossible to control a son in blossoming manhood. Such youthful vitality does not easily accept defeat.

Chapter Nine:
Abdullah

We will give it unto our children, and they unto their children, and it shall not perish.
—KAHLIL GIBRAN

After the distressing incident with Jafer and Fayza, I suffered a persistent and depressing change, retreating into myself. My son, Abdullah, plotted his trip to Lebanon with such inspired devotion that I came to believe him when he said nothing would hinder the potentially perilous journey.

Kareem cautioned restraint, for he said our son's ardor would cool when the difficulties of travel to Lebanon became more apparent. I grew cross with my husband, and with a voice raised in disbelief asked how he could remain so calm while those to whom we had given life tortured my mind with grief.

With a mysterious half smile, Kareem reminded me that Abdullah's passport was locked in our safe. It would be impossible for our son to leave the kingdom.

For these reasons, my resistance to Abdullah's plan was sporadic, unorganized, and ineffectual. In a matter of days, my once close relationship with my son became one of strained silences.

Everyone who lived in our palace fumed and despaired. While Abdullah packed his suitcases, his sister Amani mourned to see how little she could do to improve the morals of her brother and older sister. Spurred on by her faith, Amani began to spy on our employees. Horrified by what she called the looseness of our staff of sixty servants—for there are many secret romantic encounters among those who serve us—Amani set out with blunt directness to convert our Christian and Hindu servants into the superior Muslim faith.

After a hundred quarrels with my daughter over her inconsiderate and indiscriminate coercion of those who practice a religion different from our own, I finally acknowledged that I had met my match in Amani, who continued to outdistance her mother in sheer perseverance.

I spent many hours in the solitude of my room, mulling over the lives of my children.

When my three offspring were infants, they gave my life great joy and meaning. In the days of their early childhood, only Maha generated chaos, and I had no reason to anticipate peril at every turn. In those pleasurable times, moments of parental happiness vastly overshadowed the dark intervals of my fear and worry over the fates of these small beings to whom I had given life.

Now that my children were nearing adulthood, I came to the frightful conclusion that the only prerequisite to contented motherhood seemed to be a precarious dependence upon chance, for nothing I said or did altered my children's unpredictable behavior.

As one who has enormous difficulty adjusting to failure, I took to my bed, complaining to Kareem that nothing in my life was progressing as I had hoped. My psychological decline came at a time when Kareem's business was quickly expanding. As his free moments were limited, he was ill equipped to console and liberate my soul from melancholy, that mental interloper that had intruded and dismantled my joyful pursuit of happiness.

I felt increasingly alone. Suppressing every display of emotion other than self-pity, I began to sleep poorly and to overeat, gaining unwanted pounds. Continually ignored by those whom I was attempting to manipulate, I became progressively bad-tempered with my family and the servants. I even acquired a disgusting habit of twisting, pulling, and biting on my hair. The length of my hair became shorter, and the thickness became thinner, until Kareem, after noticing my habit, sarcastically commented that he thought I had employed a new and more enthusiastic hairdresser when in reality I was behaving like a child by pulling it out.

I was quick to snap an ugly retort, unfairly accusing Kareem of loving none but himself, which was why I, alone, had to keep watch over our children.

Gently impatient, Kareem got a distant look in his eyes, and I felt as if he left me without leaving the room. When his spirit returned, he said that he had been trying to remember a comforting verse he had once read about the rearing of spirited children. Kareem recited, "*You may give your children love, but not your thoughts, for they have their own thoughts.*"

"Kahlil Gibran," I said.

"What?"

"That verse, it is from *The Prophet*. And it was I who read that particular verse to you while we were awaiting the birth of our firstborn."

Kareem's stern face softened as a smile parted his lips, and I wondered if he was remembering the happy moments so long ago that we had spent with our infant son.

That was not the case, for he complimented me by saying, "Sultana, you are an amazing creature. How can you remember such a thing?"

Kareem had always marveled at my memory, for once I'd read or heard something, my recall never failed in accuracy.

I was pleased with his recognition, but the causes of my discontent were too deep and varied to be so easily dissolved. In a collision with my children, my mad passion had blinded me to my husband's clear and logical mind. With no one else to battle, I continued to snarl at my husband. In contempt I compared Kareem with Nero, the mad fiddler of Rome, blind to disaster even when his kingdom was aflame.

Angered by my repeated insults, Kareem thought better of his solicitous sympathy and left me alone to consider his parting observation, which was not comforting. His spiteful words were, "Sultana, you have it all. Yet, you fear everything and understand nothing. I predict that you will, one day, be committed to an institution built especially for the insane."

I hissed like a snake and Kareem left, not to return for two days.

Shortly after our heated exchange, I was unconsciously twisting my hair with one hand while idly thumbing through one of my many foreign publications when I read an article in an American magazine that told of a rare disease that strikes females only, causing women to pull their hair out until they become completely bald. Once bald, those unfortunate women then progress pulling out and eating their eyebrows, eyelashes, and body hair.

I let go of my hair. Did I have that disease? I ran to view my image in the mirror, and to search through my scalp for bald spots. My hair did seem thin. Now I was truly worried, for I had never cured myself of vanity and had no inclination to be bald! Besides, in the Muslim religion, it is forbidden for a woman to be bald.

Time proved that I did not have the disease, for unlike the women in the article, my attachment to beauty helped me to quickly cure myself of the habit.

Despite retaining my hair, I feared that I had lost my passion for life, and I told myself that if my debilitating depression was not conquered, my old age would be premature and triumphant. Feeling sorry for myself, I imagined that I would suffer a slow death through the gradual diminution of my senses.

I was saved from my self-destructive behavior by my dearest sister.

Sara, a contemplative genius, was sensitive to my dulled lust for life, and she began to spend many hours by my side, humoring me with her undivided attention. Sara understood my feelings perfectly and knew that worry over Abdullah and Amani now ruled my life.

My sister looked upon me with great pity when I tearfully told her, "Sara, if I had to live my life over again, I do not believe that I could survive it."

Sara's mouth curved upward in a half smile as she wryly observed, "Sultana, few of our family would survive if you were to live your life again."

Our laughter filled the room.

My sister was so dear. Sara was not without problems of her own. She herself was burdened with an unruly child, yet she came to my aid at a time of great need. While four of my sister's five children strove for perfection, Nashwa, Sara's teenage daughter, born on the same day as Amani, relished controversy.

In strictest confidence, Sara told me to be thankful that Amani had attached herself to religion, for Sara had the opposite problem with Nashwa. Her daughter was wildly attracted to members of the opposite sex, and twice Asad had discovered her meeting Saudi teenage boys in a music shop at a shopping center in the city.

Tears streamed down Sara's face as she confided in me that her daughter flirted outrageously with every male who entered their palace grounds. In a voice filled with disbelief, she said that the week before, Nashwa had begun an explicit sexual conversation with two of the younger Filipina drivers. One of Nashwa's brothers had overheard the conversation, and when confronted, Nashwa boldly acknowledged her action, stating that she had to do *something* to interrupt the monotony of life in Saudi Arabia.

Asad had been forced to fire the young drivers and to employ older Muslim men from Egypt who would respect the Muslim way: to ignore the willful women of the house.

Just that morning, Sara had overheard her daughter speaking with a female friend on the telephone. The two girls were discussing in great detail the pleasing physique of the girl's eldest brother. It seemed to Sara that Nashwa had a crush on this boy, and now my sister had to reconsider or regulate her daughter's visits to that home.

Sara's face was drawn with worry over the outcome of Nashwa's loose morals and unbecoming conduct, saying she had often heard that one of nature's oversights was that beauty and virtue often arrive in separate packages. Nashwa, my sister said, was an innocent-faced beauty who was sadly lacking in virtue.

I had to agree that my difficulties with Amani paled in comparison with my sister's problems with Nashwa. There was some consolation in the knowledge that Amani's piety had the approval of the religious authorities, while Nashwa's activities could embroil Sara and

Asad in that never-ending web of the Saudi religious and legal system.

I was once again overtaken by the thought that Nashwa was my true child, while Amani must be attached by blood to Sara. I thought to ask Sara about the matter, but had a moment of anxiety that an actual exchange of daughters might result from my baseless speculation. I reminded myself that in my country it is better to wrestle with a persistent religious fanatic than with a young girl habituated to sexual stimulus.

In an effort to raise my sister's spirits, I told her that too often when dealing with our children, we parents see little but the defects. I thought to mention some of Nashwa's good traits, but could find nothing to say.

Sara and I were still for a time, looking at each other. We knew instinctively that we understood each other perfectly.

With her daughter in mind, my sister began to ponder the progress of civilization. Our children had been sheltered from all worldly concerns, lavished with creature comforts, provided with intelligent pursuits and moral guidance, yet the careful organization of their lives had made little impact on their development.

Sara said she had come to the conclusion that human character was linked to nothing more than genetics, and that her children might as well have grown like weeds instead of meticulously tended plants. "Besides," she said with a laugh, "the radicals of one age become the reactionaries of the next, so who knows the eventual outcome of our offspring?"

Since it always lightens one's burdens to be reminded of another's troubles, even if that person is one greatly loved, I began to feel more cheerful than I had in days.

I laughed and agreed with my sister, saying that

the seeds we planted had not all flowered. Thinking that all of life is in God's hands anyway, I promised myself I would worry no longer.

Sara went to inquire about her youngest children, who were playing in our palace playground, which is located next to Amani's petting zoo, while I promised to bathe and dress myself for a visit to Fayza. Neither Sara nor I had seen the poor girl since she was forced to return to the kingdom, though we had heard, with some surprise, that she had recovered and was now seeing close friends and relatives.

Enjoying uncommon peace for the first time in days, I was unprepared for a shocking telephone call from my husband. His voice was alarmingly intense. "Sultana, go to the safe and locate Abdullah's passport."

"Why?" I asked.

Kareem told me to shut up and do as he said.

Thinking the worst, I dropped the telephone receiver to the floor and ran rapidly into my husband's home office, which is located on the first floor in our home. My hands refused to cooperate with my memory, and it required three attempts to open the combination safe.

My husband kept his passport in his office safe, while mine and the children's were kept at home.

My fingers riffled through the various documents and papers.

Abdullah's passport was missing!

I was then struck with the horrible realization that I could account for only two out of four passports. Looking closely, I saw that Maha's passport had disappeared along with that of her brother.

What was going on? How had this happened? No one, other than Kareem and I, knew the combination of this particular safe.

"No!" I said to myself when I could not find the special papers of permission Kareem had signed for the women of his family to travel outside the kingdom without the company of a male member of our family.

I was confused. Was Maha traveling alone? Or did she and her brother flee the kingdom together?

The private telephone in Kareem's office began to ring.

My husband had tired of waiting. When I picked up the receiver, he shouted, "Sultana! What is going on?"

I told Kareem of my unsettling discovery.

"And the dollars?"

I had not thought to look for the large amount of money we kept in dollars in our safe for the purpose of fleeing the kingdom should a religious revolution ever grip our land. It was money we hoped we would never be forced to use to bribe safe exit from our country.

I opened the large drawer at the top of the safe. It was as Kareem had expected. The money was no longer there! As our fears of unrest in Arab lands had grown, the money had increased. Abdullah had taken over a million dollars in cash from his parents' safe. Had my son lost all his good sense?

"The dollars have disappeared," I glumly reported.

"Go, see if Maha is at school. I am on the way to the airport."

I cried out, "Hurry!" I knew that my son was on his way to Lebanon. But how was Maha involved in this? Surely Abdullah was not taking his sister with him to a land still filled with danger, for there were problems still, even after the civil war ceased. I was lightheaded with fear and confusion.

"I will try to call you from the car. Now. Do as I say. Find Maha!"

I fetched a simple dress and hastily pulled it over

my head. Reaching for my *abaaya*, veil, and *shayla*, I threw on my outer garments as I ran through the house, calling out for my sister Sara to accompany me to Maha's school. I yelled at Cora to find Mousa, the youngest of our Egyptian drivers, a man who, I knew from past experience, could be urged to break the city speed limit.

Maha's school was fifteen minutes by automobile from our palace, but we arrived in ten minutes. Along the route, I told Sara what little I knew of the situation.

Maha's face turned crimson red as I burst into her classroom, calling her name. Seeking the face of my child, I hovered over her desk and said, "Maha! You are here!"

Maha pushed my arms from her neck, exclaiming, "Where did you think I was?"

The seventeen girls in Maha's history class were taking notes while listening to a male instructor, who appeared on a large television screen in the center of the room. The lesson was being given via video, since it is forbidden in Saudi Arabia for a male professor to come into personal contact with female students.

I quickly told the headmistress that I needed my daughter to return to our home. Without a hint of curiosity about my unusual behavior, she calmly instructed Maha to gather her books. She asked if Maha would be away for longer than a week. Since I did not know, I said that she would. The supervisor said in that case she would have Maha's instructors save my daughter's lessons for her return.

"Mother! What is going on?" Maha wanted to know as we settled ourselves in the car.

"I feared that you were with Abdullah."

"Abdullah?"

Maha, only seventeen years old at the time, was a junior at a girls' high school. My son, at age nineteen, was supposed to be at his university, an institution that girls did not attend. Maha looked at me in astonishment. "Mother, you are behaving like a crazy person." She looked at Sara for confirmation. "Auntie, what is wrong?"

Sara explained the mystery of the passports, saying that we could not understand why Abdullah had taken hers.

My sister's eyes met mine across the head of my daughter. Sara's thoughts matched mine perfectly.

"Fayza!" We uttered her name in unison.

I told the driver to take us to the home of Fouad and Samia. "Quickly!"

Abdullah's plans ran clear through my mind. My son had taken Maha's passport for Jafer's wife, Fayza! Abdullah had plotted her rescue. It was Fayza who was traveling on Maha's passport. Fayza was going to Lebanon with my son, not Maha! With her face veiled, it is possible for a Saudi woman to travel abroad using the passport of another.

When Maha understood the significance of her brother's deed, she pleaded for us to return to our home.

"Mother! Let them go!"

It was a difficult moment. If I made no move to notify Fayza's parents, I was an accomplice to my son's unwelcome intrusion into another man's private affairs. If I was the cause of Fayza's continued separation from the man she loved enough to wed, I could never again claim to battle for the rights of women in my land.

Sara and I stared at each other for many moments. Sara's eyes were clear and penetrating, and I knew that my sister was reliving the horrible sexual abuse she had endured in her own first marriage. Had our mother not revolted against our father, risking a divorce and possible permanent separation from her own precious children, Sara would have remained in sexual bondage to a man she hated, never knowing the wonderful love she now shared with Asad.

My decision was the result of the intolerance and sever restraints suffered by the women of my land. Wanting to live up to the best, and not the worst in my ancestry, I instructed Mousa, "Take us home."

Maha laughed and kissed me time and again, crushing me against the seat of the automobile.

Sara's eyes grew luminous. My sister smiled and squeezed my hand, saying, "Sultana, do not worry, you have made the correct decision."

Mousa's eyes grew unnaturally wide, and his mouth opened and closed, reminding me of a bird that had become overheated in the desert sun. His face grew darker in color, and I could see that he violently disagreed with this turn of events.

I spoke in French, a language he did not understand. "Look at the driver's face," I told my sister and my child. "He does not approve."

"What man in this country would approve a woman's right to choose her husband?" Maha wanted to know. "Tell me one! And...and...I will wed him!"

I looked back upon the events of that day and felt a rush of recognition. My heavy spirit had at last achieved tranquility, for I understood that my daughter shared the blood of one who was enlightened, yet had no knowledge of his liberation.

"Abdullah," I answered quietly. "Your brother. My son. Abdullah is such a man."

In happy silence I stared at my daughter's face, but was imprisoned in my past. I saw the form of my firstborn as he lay in his mother's arms. The emotions I felt on the day of his birth returned to me in a flash, such a rush of joy that by its nature must be brief. I had wondered then if my newborn son would uphold and thereby reinforce the harsh rules pertaining to females in my land. I had prayed that such would not be the case, but that he would influence our country's history in an agreeable manner and help to bring change to the rigid social customs of Saudi Arabia.

It was difficult to judge Abdullah's actions calmly, but in an honest appraisal of his activities, I knew that my deepest desire had been realized. A male child born of my womb would remodel the land of my birth.

How brave was my bold son!

No longer caring about Mousa's reaction, I spoke in Arabic, reminding Sara and Maha that the men of Kareem's generation had once sounded the voice of reason when it came to their women, but that this voice had been silenced by their clash with the militant men of religion. Grieving over the timid men of our age, I no longer looked to them for relief.

But hope was not lost, so long as we women of Arabia gave birth to men such as Abdullah.

I told Maha and Sara what I knew to be the truth, that my beloved son was a prince who would one day use all his power and influence to enhance the status of Saudi women.

Renewed by my son's brave act, I talked of nothing else the remainder of the trip home, scandalizing Mousa with my frank discussion of complete freedom for all women, even for his own wife, whom he forced to live with his parents in a small village in Egypt while he worked in Saudi Arabia.

Kareem was impatiently awaiting my return. He did not seem surprised that I expressed great happiness, and I imagined that he supposed my change of mood was linked to the safe recovery of our daughter. Never did he know that my happiness was linked to our son and the fact that Abdullah had turned his back upon injustice, and his face to a free life for all people.

Maha was a bit frightened by the intensity of her father's blazing eyes, and she mentioned some small task that required her time.

Sara gathered her children and went home to Asad, whispering in my ear that I should call her as soon as possible.

I could hear Amani's voice in the background, rising and falling with the sounds of her deeply felt communication with God.

Finally, I was alone with my husband.

I thought that Kareem's face was hardened by the oppressive weight of his discovery, and I was unprepared for his ruthless accusations.

He declared his feelings without questioning his wife. "Sultana, your scent is on Fayza's flight."

For a short moment, I was silenced by his insinuation. As one whose anger runs to extremes, I appeared at my worst when I struck out at Kareem's arm with my fist.

Well acquainted with my passions, Kareem was prepared. He sidestepped, avoiding the blow.

Over the years, Kareem had disciplined his reactions so that he appeared moderate, always making me appear the worse in our conflicts. Today was no exception. "Sultana. This is no time to fight. Our son and Fayza have fled the kingdom." My husband grabbed me. "You must tell me their travel plans."

All my denials failed to convince Kareem that while our son might have inherited my talent for brilliant deception, I had no hand in his present action.

Like the town thief who is not believed when a loaf of bread is stolen, my past reached into the present, and a frightening avalanche of accusations flamed out against an innocent woman.

I was paying a dear price for my militant past.

I thought Kareem's conduct as a husband might

have been more loyal, and I told him so.

Kareem asked how he could believe me. He said he had married a woman who was half angel and half devil, and the devil in me often ruled the angel, and when it came to issues that concerned women's lives, I could not speak without lying and could not act without treachery!

Angrier than I have ever been—for what human endures false censure with grace—I spat at Kareem's feet and left the room, promising never again to enter a conversation with the man to whom I was wed.

Kareem thought it best to bury his doubts, for he was concerned that without my assistance, he might not succeed in finding his son or in returning Fouad's daughter. Kareem said that if he were in the wrong he was sorry, and that I must save our son from committing an offense that would further entangle him in another man's personal affairs.

Suspecting his true motives, I refused to answer his request for forgiveness, squeezing my eyes shut so I did not have to view his face, and motioning with my hand for him to go away.

As soon as the door slammed, my pleasure at revenge faded.

Where was my son? Was he safe?

For five days there was no peace in our home, for Kareem and I had no diplomatic communication. Amani prayed and wept, while Maha sang love songs and celebrated Fayza's escape.

Is anything in life more sweet than success?

With a singleness of purpose, Fayza evaded the snares that had been prepared for her and was reunited with the man she loved.

I could never have anticipated the reaction of

Fouad and Samia to Fayza's desperate flight. Prepared for Kareem to be forced to use his position as protection for our only son, I was pleasantly surprised by Fouad's meek acceptance of his daughter's behavior.

On the fifth day after their disappearance, Abdullah called us from Cyprus, the small island nation located close to the shores of Lebanon. Abdullah had no fear of our reaction and declared firmly, against our protests, that he had administered justice, not vengeance, by bringing Jafer and Fayza together.

My breath left my body when Abdullah confided that Fayza had telephoned her parents an hour before, and that Fouad and Samia had left their anger behind them and wanted nothing more than a second opportunity to welcome Jafer as their son. Fouad told his child that if she and Jafer would not turn their backs on her family, he promised he would not "step in the same raging river twice."

How true it is that humanity refuses compromise during prosperity, and reaches out for arbitration when weak. Swayed by the fear of never seeing their beautiful daughter again, Fouad and Samia had come to the conclusion that they would accept her marriage to someone beneath them in wealth and status.

Being of a suspicious nature, I thought perhaps it was a trick to ensnare Jafer in a land where he had no rights. Once in Saudi Arabia, he could be imprisoned on the slightest pretense, if that was Fouad's wish.

Fayza's parents did not confirm my pessimism.

That day, Fouad and his family flew to Greece and met Jafer and Fayza in a golden land where men had been civilized from an early age. Thoughts more bitter than death were put to rest, and Jafer and Fayza at last found happiness in the family unit that had once challenged the legitimacy of their marriage.

Special permission was obtained for Fayza to wed a Muslim from another land, and a second, more festive wedding was held in a hotel in Cairo, Egypt.

Kareem and I traveled there with our two daughters to join our son for the occasion.

Jafer and Fayza insisted that male and female guests come together for a reception at the Mena House Hotel. Their great love even made a dour Kareem smile, although he was a prince ashamed that his son had interfered in his friend's private life. Kareem's tension was relieved when Fouad confessed that there could have been no other ending, for long before Abdullah had rescued Fayza, his daughter's extreme misery had led him and his wife to the knowledge that she must be rejoined with Jafer. Fayza's grief could not be ignored. Fouad assured my embarrassed husband that they, themselves, had been on the brink of parental surrender the day she had fled.

Kareem and I watched as Fouad grasped Jafer and Fayza as if they were one. From the look on Jafer's shining face as he watched his wife, it was clear that he loved her more madly than ever.

How pleased I was! A Saudi woman was happily wed to one forbidden.

I whispered in Kareem's ear, "See, every straight line can be forced into a curve!"

A family tragedy was transformed into a scene of great harmony.

Later that evening, from the courtyard at our Cairo villa, Kareem and I watched the loveliness of the Egyptian sky.

My husband surprised me with a heartfelt apology. Hovering nebulously between shame and love, Kareem promised that he would not prejudge me again, that Abdullah had told him I was not privy to his plot to free Fayza. It had been Kareem who had given our son the combination to our safe. In the excitement of the moment Kareem had forgotten!

Then, as though it were an afterthought, Kareem reached into his pocket and brought out the largest diamond I had ever seen. The stone was hung on a golden chain. My husband tenderly fastened the necklace around my neck, and I felt his lips as they brushed my shoulder.

A few years ago, I had hated the bitter emptiness of my married life. Just the month before I had hungrily sought the meaning of life. The moment was a breeding ground for all sorts of emotions—affection, regret, and, most of all, confusion. Was Kareem that rare phenomenon, a Saudi husband who was gentle, virile, practical, and intelligent? Had I been wrong in my assessment of his character? How could a Saudi man be the answer to my happiness when I had fought against Saudi men all my life?

I had once heard that a miser is never satisfied with his money, nor a wise man with his knowledge. Was I a woman who would never know fulfillment? That possibility was frightening.

Another thought came to my mind, an Arab proverb, "*If your husband is made of honey, do not consume him.*"

I looked at Kareem in a new light. Remembering the numerous insults I had inflicted upon him, I prayed that God would shorten my tongue and increase my powers of reason.

I smiled at my husband. Suddenly I felt many wounds heal—injuries suffered because of Kareem's conduct earlier in our marriage.

For some reason, my scars could scarcely be detected.

Chapter Ten:
Fatma

Something was dead in each of us
And what was dead was Hope.
—OSCAR WILDE

The following afternoon, Kareem and I were sitting together with our children on the veranda at our villa in Cairo. An immaculate flower garden encircled the large covered porch, and the sweet scent of roses and honeysuckle permeated the air, bringing to mind the wealthy British presence that had once occupied the unwelcoming city. My husband and I were savoring the coolness of the spacious and shaded area, for there was not a hint of an afternoon breeze, and the concrete structures of the populous city had retained the oppressive heat of the day, dulling the senses of Cairo's eight million occupants.

Our three children whispered among themselves, claiming that we had once again been forgotten by "Forgetful Fatma," as they often called our Egyptian housekeeper when she was out of earshot.

I warned my children not to make fun, that Fatma was no longer young and her feet had difficulty moving her abundant body. Still, I stifled a smile, thinking that the children were probably right in their assessment of the situation. Fatma had more than likely begun some new chore, entirely forgetting her employers as they waited impatiently for a cool drink. Fatma was absentminded and did have a consistent inability to remember why she left one room to go into another. Many times Kareem had complained, saying that Fatma should be let go and a younger, more energetic woman hired in her stead, but I resisted his urgings because the woman was dependable and had always displayed a genuine love for my three children.

Kareem accused me of being unable to part with Fatma's lively tales of Cairo scandals. But that was not the case.

Fatma has been employed as our permanent, live-in housekeeper since we purchased the villa many years before. Abdullah was only two years old at the time she came into our lives, and our girls were not yet born, so Fatma was a constant in their young lives.

Just as I pushed myself from my chair to go and remind her of our earlier request, I heard the familiar scraping of her loose sandals as they struck the marble floor of the interior hallway leading to the veranda.

I looked at Kareem, and he gave an irritated shake of his head. My husband had no understanding of why he should be inconvenienced by the aging of a servant.

Feeling mischievous, I said, "My husband, do not forget that God is watching you."

Kareem tartly replied, "Sultana, do not concern yourself with my relationship to God."

The children thought we might slip into an argument and ruin the afternoon, so Amani wrapped her arms around her father's neck, while Maha began to rub my shoulders and begged me not to lose my temper.

I felt too good to fight and said so. About that time, my attention was drawn to Fatma. Recalling the graceful and slim woman of years past, my eyes affectionately followed her heavy figure as she painstakingly opened the double glass doors that led from the villa onto the veranda. Fatma was enormous and had great difficulty balancing the tray stacked with crystal glasses and a matching crystal decanter filled with freshly squeezed lemonade.

Like many Egyptian women, Fatma had struggled with a weight problem from the moment she bore her first child. With each new addition to her family, she had grown larger and larger, until a childish Abdullah had fearfully questioned me, asking how Fatma's skin could continue to hold her figure together.

Slowed by her weight, Fatma took many moments to walk the few steps from the doorway to the table of white-painted rattan. Abdullah jumped to his feet and took the tray from her, insisting that he would serve the family.

Kareem and I exchanged glances, and I saw that my husband bit the inside of his lip to keep from protesting. Ever since he was young, Abdullah was easily affected by the suffering that comes so often undeserved to mankind. I felt proud of my son's sensitivity, but I knew that his father had no desire for him to do the work of servants.

To distract Kareem, I asked Abdullah to tell us more about his experiences in Lebanon, for since we had met him in Cairo, we had enjoyed little private time to hear of his adventure. I remembered that in Kareem's youth, he had spent many happy times in the beautiful city of Beirut, where large numbers of the Saudi royal family had gone for rest and relaxation before the days of the mad and senseless war that had nearly destroyed the once lovely land of Lebanon.

Abdullah saw hope where Kareem said there was none. Abdullah said that he had been impressed by the Lebanese spirit, marveling that the Lebanese people had not only survived, but had endured a most vicious civil war with their optimism intact, refusing to acknowledge that they could not surpass their brilliant past. Abdullah thought that given half the chance, the Lebanese would once again rise to claim an exalted place in the Arab world.

Abdullah paused and looked at his father. He wondered if Kareem might be interested in investing money in that country.

Kareem rewarded Abdullah with an approving smile. My husband is a man who seeks economic opportunity at every chance, and our son's previous lack of interest in such matters had always been a weight on his mind. But Kareem's smile quickly vanished when Abdullah added that the infrastructure of Lebanon was almost completely in ruins and that there were many good causes to which Kareem could donate funds.

I almost dissolved in laughter when I saw Kareem's face. He sat up straight and tried to show some interest, but my husband had difficulty concealing his desperation; he looked at his son as if seeing him for the first time.

I knew that my husband had not yet recovered from Abdullah's proud announcement that he had donated the bulk of the one million dollars he had taken from our safe to the hospital that housed Jafer's older brother. My husband had no heart to reprimand his son for such a good deed and had gazed at Abdullah with sad affection, in spite of his dismay at losing one million dollars.

Kareem confessed to me later that in his mind donating money to Lebanon was equivalent to tossing good money after bad, for who knew when the guns of destruction would once again flame across the Lebanese sky. Let the Lebanese show that they were serious about peace, and Kareem would look into the possibility of assisting his fellow Arabs.

Abdullah had been stricken by the lack of facilities at the institution that housed Jafer's brother, and now he spoke again of that place. He said that he could not forget the wretched condition of the war-wounded who lived in the hospital. Abdullah's eyes welled with tears as he told of men and women without limbs, confined to small rooms, for there were no prostheses or wheel-chairs. Abdullah had discovered men tied to wooden tables, men who had no movement in their bodies, men stoically accepting the idea of a life devoid of any pleasure.

Abdullah said he had learned a tragic truth, that a large number of the Lebanese wounded had no surviving family members to provide funds for their care.

In anguish, he asked, "Does the world neither know nor care about the damage done to that country?"

I reminded Abdullah of a happy thought, that Jafer's brother had been luckier than most, since Jafer had routinely sent money for his medical expenses. But even his situation was bleak when compared to the advanced health care facilities our oil wealth guaranteed the inhabitants of Saudi Arabia. Jafer's brother would now enjoy the latest treatment available, for Fouad had insisted upon taking his son-in-law's brother home with them to live as one of his family.

Now our son wanted his father to distribute more of his personal wealth for the needy of Lebanon. Abdullah thought that a new hospital supplied with the latest equipment would be an auspicious beginning.

I leaned forward, interested to hear my husband's

reply, for I knew it was painful for Kareem to refuse any wish of his beloved son.

Kareem had closed his eyes in concentration and was beginning to rub his forehead with his hand when without warning our family gathering was interrupted by a most pathetic howling.

Baffled, we looked at each other and then realized that the strange noise was coming from inside our villa and that the sound was made by Fatma!

A look of relief flashed across Kareem's face, for his son's interest had been diverted. Abdullah was the first to move inside. My daughters and I quickly followed, leaving Kareem alone on the veranda.

My first thought was that Fatma had burned herself, for she was standing over the kitchen stove, frying beef and onions for our dinner. But I quickly saw that her weeping had not interrupted her cooking, for she continued to stir the ingredients in the pan and seemed not to realize that her wails had penetrated the stone walls of the villa.

"Fatma! What is the problem?" Abdullah asked.

Like the voice of doom, Fatma replied, "Oh, Abdullah! The female most blessed is she that has never been born! Next to her in happiness is the female who dies in infancy!"

Bereaved to madness, Fatma began to thump her chest.

Maha grabbed the wooden stirring spoon from her hand, while Amani began to console the poor woman with soothing sounds and comforting words.

Abdullah gave me a questioning look with his brown eyes.

I shrugged, as confused as he. I had no thought other than that Fatma's husband might have divorced her and taken a younger wife, though they had seemed a well-satisfied couple in the past. Fatma's husband, Abdul, doubled as our gardener and family chauffeur, and the couple had often said they considered themselves fortunate to work for wealthy people who paid a good wage and who were rarely in the country. They were guaranteed plenty of free time to spend with their children, who lived in an apartment in Cairo with Abdul's mother. Yet, I knew that by law Egyptian men, like Saudi men, have full power over their women, and it was not unusual for an old man to take a second wife, or even to divorce his first wife and take a younger, more attractive woman into his home.

The experiences of my life have taught me that men are generally at the root of female grief. Thinking of Fatma's bitter words of female misfortune, I imagined a man as their cause, for nothing is more demoralizing to a woman of Fatma's age than to be abandoned by a husband of many years.

Abdullah, Amani, and I led Fatma to a chair in the sitting room, while Maha tended to her unfinished tasks.

Fatma moaned as she walked, holding her hand on the top of her head, like someone trying to stop the pain.

Wanting to get to the cause of her grief, I waved my children from the room and asked her point-blank, "Fatma, has Abdul divorced you?"

Fatma raised her head and looked at me, her languid eyes blinking at my question. She repeated my words, "Abdul? Divorce me?" She then smiled, but only with her lips. "That old man? Let him try! I will crack his bald head like an egg and fry his brains on the sidewalk."

I had to struggle to keep from laughing aloud, for in the past, Kareem had often commented that in his opinion Abdul lived in fear of his wife, and that there was at least one married woman in the Arab world who had no need of feminine advice from me.

Abdul was half Fatma's size, and once Kareem had

come upon the couple unexpectedly and had seen with his own eyes Fatma strike her husband on the back with a large board.

I asked, "Then, if it is not Abdul, what is the problem?"

Fatma's heavily wrinkled face fell, and she became lost in her own morose thoughts. She sighed so heavily that I knew her sadness had a heartfelt source, and I asked myself with dismay what could be the cause of her anguish.

"Fatma?" I reminded her of my presence.

Suddenly her face turned bright red, and Fatma's despair burst forth.

"It is my granddaughter Alhaan. Her father is an evil being, a donkey of a man, that Nasser. I would kill him with my bare hands if my daughter would allow it! But no! She says she and her family must live their lives as they see fit."

Fatma's eyes flashed with anger, and her huge bosom heaved with indignation. "My own daughter demands that I stay out of her family matters!" She looked at me aghast and asked, "Can you imagine that? To have no say in my own granddaughter's life?"

Feeling utterly bewildered, I asked, "What has Nasser done to his child? To your granddaughter?"

Surely, I thought to myself, if the mother of the child has no objections, the harm to the child must not exist.

"That Nasser! He is from a small village. What does he know?"

I drew back in surprise as Fatma spat upon our newly carpeted floor.

Fatma was talking in every direction, cursing Nasser, crying out for her daughter, and begging God to help her grandchild.

I lost my patience and, raising my voice, demanded to know. "Fatma! Tell me, now! What happened to your granddaughter?"

Disconsolate and at a loss, Fatma tightly squeezed my hand and said, "Tonight. Tonight they will make Al-haan into a woman. They have an appointment with the barber at nine o'clock. This ritual I do not believe is necessary. None of my daughters were so treated. It is that Nasser! Can you help me, mistress, please...?"

The past surged up in my mind. How well I remembered the horrible story told to me by my oldest sister, Nura, when she too had been made into a woman.

Kareem and I had not yet wed, and I was young, only sixteen years old. My mother had recently died, and Nura, as the eldest daughter, was instructed to answer my questions regarding female circumcision. I had not known until that time that Nura and our two sisters closest to her in age had endured the horrific rite, and as a result had been subjected to lifelong pain and suffering.

In Saudi Arabia's not so distant past, circumcision of women had not been infrequent, with each tribe following a different custom. Just this past year, I had read a book my son had purchased while in London. The book was titled *The Empty Quarter*, by St. John Philby, a respected British desert explorer. With assistance from my grandfather, Abdul Aziz Al Sa'ud, the founder and first king of Saudi Arabia, St. John Philby had carried out extensive explorations in Arabia in the 1930s.

I had taken the book from my son's room and derived great pleasure from reading this man's history of the Arab tribes that make up the population of Saudi Arabia, until I came across a section of the book that told of the Englishman's findings concerning female circumcision. I had imagined the brutalization of my own sisters and had cringed and cried out when reading about a conversation

Philby had documented with the Arab men of the desert:

But his strong subject was sex, and he loved to poke fun at Salih by dilating on Manasir practice in the matter of female circumcision. "Take it from me," he said, "they let their women come to puberty with clitoris intact, and when a girl is to be married, they make a feast for her circumcision a month or two before the wedding. It is only then that they circumcise them and not at birth as do the other tribes— Qahtan and Murra, Bani Hajir, ay, and 'Ajman. Thus their women grow up more lustful than others, and fine women they are too and that hot! But then they remove everything, making them as smooth as smooth, to cool their ardor without reducing their desire. The girls are dealt with in their tents by women who know their business, and get a dollar or so for the job. They are expert with the scissors, the razor, and the needle, which are all used for the operation."

I could not help wondering at this information. It struck me as strange that men thought of complete women as lustful, yet condoned the barbaric procedures performed on these women in order to "cool their ardor." From my own readings, I had learned that female circumcision caused women to dread any intimacy with their husbands, and I came to the conclusion that there is no rational thought or pattern when it comes to the mutilation of females.

My grandfather, Abdul Aziz al Sa'ud, was a man who was ahead of his time, and he looked for better ways in all matters. Coming from the Najd, he did not believe in the circumcision of women, or in the flaying circumcision of men, which was as terrifying as female circumcision.

In the flaying circumcision of men, the skin is removed from the navel down to the inside of a man's legs. On witnessing such brutality, our first king forbade the practice. But in spite of my grandfather's decree, the old ways died slowly, and people were willing to risk punishment to carry on with what they had been taught by the ones who came before them.

While some tribes forbade circumcision of their women altogether, others excised the hood of the clitoris only. The cutting of the hood of the clitoris is the least common method, and is the only procedure that is analogous to male circumcision.

Then, there were those poor women who belonged to tribes in Arabia that removed all of the clitoris, along with the labia minora. This is the most common method of female circumcision and is comparable to removing the head of a man's penis. My own mother paid no heed to the new ruling, and three of her daughters were subjected to the cruel practice of female circumcision. The remainder of the women in our family had been spared the rite of circumcision due to the intervention of a Western physician and the insistence of my father to my mother that circumcision of females was nothing more than a pagan practice that must be stopped. Strangely enough, it is the women in Muslim countries who insist upon the circumcision of their female offspring, fearing that their daughters will otherwise be scorned for being different, resulting in husbandless futures. On this one topic regarding female sexuality, educated men have advanced beyond their women.

There is another, more atrocious and dangerous method of female circumcision, named the pharaonic circumcision. I could scarcely imagine the pain experienced by the women who received the pharaonic circumcision. This process is the most extreme, and after the rite is completed, a girl is left without a clitoris, labia minora, or labia majora. If such a procedure were done on a male, it would involve amputation of the penis and the scrotum around the testicles.

How barbarous were these old customs that still lingered in our present day! In Saudi Arabia, much had been accomplished to eradicate the tradition, and most women of my land are no longer subjected to this terrible experience. The men of my own family had forbade the pagan tradition, but still some families of African descent who lived in Arabia were prepared to risk punishment rather than forgo the rite, swearing that nothing other than the reduction of female pleasure will preserve female chastity.

I had known that the practice of female circumcision was thought to have begun along the Nile Valley, and I had speculated in my mind that the barbaric ritual might end where it had begun. Yet, many women in Egypt and throughout the continent of Africa were still subjected to this most inhumane ritual.

Over the years, as my own family no longer practiced this rite, I had been successful in pushing the thought of female mutilation from my mind.

Now Fatma tugged on my arm. Her imploring gesture brought me back into the present. With great sadness, I recalled the face of the young girl, Alhaan, for she had visited her grandmother in our villa on many occasions. She was a pretty child and had seemed bright and happy. I created a vivid mental image of the girl being led to the barber, undressed by her mother, with small legs spread before the man with the sharp razor.

I recoiled in horror. In disbelief, I wondered how the mother of that girl could condone such evil inflicted on her beautiful daughter? Yet, I knew that many mothers were allowing such intolerable practices, for it is estimated by world health organizations that female genital mutilation has affected between 80 and 100 million women worldwide. So much pain inflicted on little girls!

With hope in her voice, Fatma examined my face

carefully and asked, "Mistress, can you save my grand-daughter?"

I moved my head slowly and heavily. "What can I do, Fatma, that you can not? I am not of your family. My interference would be resented."

"You are a princess. My daughter, she has respect for someone who is a princess."

I had learned long ago that those who have no wealth believe that money has provided wisdom along with economic freedom, but this was a matter of deeply ingrained culture. Instinctively, I knew that Fatma's daughter would not welcome my intrusion.

I waved my arms helplessly. "What can I do, Fatma? Since I reached the age of understanding, I have wanted female freedom from such practices." My voice fell low, along with my spirits. "Now, it seems that the world is becoming darker and darker for those of our sex."

Fatma remained silent, and a sorrowful look came into her black eyes.

"If I could, I would help your granddaughter. But I have no authority to voice my opinion."

Fatma looked disappointed but spoke words without reproach. "I understand, mistress." She stared at me from half-closed lids. "But I beg you to come with me. To try."

Surprised at Fatma's stubbornness, I felt my resolve melting away. I felt a shiver run through my body and asked in a weak voice, "Where does your daughter live?"

Fatma's thick lips exploded with her excited reply, "Very close, not more than a short ride in an automobile. If we leave now, we can arrive before Nasser comes home from work."

I summoned all my courage and stood. I told myself that in spite of almost certain failure, I must make an effort. I knew that I would be forced to lie to my husband, or he would forbid me to go. "Fatma, go and get your things. And say not a word to anyone of this matter."

"Yes, mistress! I know it is God's will that you help me!"

I watched her as she hurried away, moving faster than I could ever remember. Despite our vastly different worlds, the two of us had become comrades fighting for the same cause. By the time I combed out my hair, applied lipstick, and located my handbag, I had decided to tell Kareem that Fatma had just that morning learned her daughter was ill with a rare female disorder. But her daughter had refused treatment, saying that if it was God's will that she die, she would not reverse his decision by accepting treatment from any man. Fatma had pleaded with me to go and convince her daughter that she must fight to live for the sake of her own children. To be more convincing, I would complain that I did not want to go, but how could I forgive myself if the woman died and I had made no effort. It was a weak scenario, but Kareem shied away from female problems and would more than likely grumble but make no move to stop me.

As it turned out, I was not forced to tell such a wild tale, for Abdullah said that his father had received a telephone call while I was speaking with Fatma. Kareem had asked Abdullah to tell me that he was going to join one of his royal cousins in a Cairo casino and would not be home until later that evening. I knew my husband wanted to put time and distance between himself and his son's earlier request to donate millions of dollars to a failing Lebanese economy, and I had a sense that his excuse to leave our home was as dishonest as the lie I had been prepared to tell. Kareem shares a common trait with most Arabs. My husband cannot say no, but would rather speak a small lie and disappear from the sight of the one who requires an answer.

"Good!" I muttered under my breath. Kareem's discomfort at being around his son had come at an opportune time.

After advising me of his father's message, Abdullah turned his attention back to the television set, and I saw that he was mesmerized, watching an Egyptian soap opera that was greatly favored by Arabs from many lands. I noticed that Amani's lips had formed a disapproving pout. My daughter was not pleased at her brother's selection, for that particular show was not allowed in Saudi Arabia because of its many scenes that hinted of sexual impropriety.

"Abdullah, I need you to drive me to the home of Fatma's daughter. Can you come?"

My son looked for any opportunity to drive the new white Mercedes Kareem had purchased and shipped into the country for our Cairo home. I knew from past experience that Kareem would have taken the older Mercedes into the busy district of downtown Cairo, since he greatly feared the taxi drivers in that teeming city.

Abdullah flicked the remote button shutting off the television set and gallantly leapt to his feet. "I will get the car."

The Cairo streets were crowded with vehicles of every description, and the traffic was almost at a standstill. Pedestrians threaded in and out of the traffic. People hung onto the sides of buses already packed with humanity; they clung precariously to the doorways or windows as if it were the most natural way in the world to travel.

As our car inched through the city streets, I gazed in amazement at the mass of people who had descended on the city of the Pharaohs and shuddered, for it was easy to see that Cairo could not continue to exist as it was.

Abdullah interrupted my thoughts, asking me the

point of our errand.

I swore him to secrecy. When I told him of Fatma's source of sorrow, a flash of anger swept over my son's face.

Abdullah said that he had heard of such things but had thought such tales were exaggerated. "Is it really true?" he asked. "Are such things done to young girls?"

I thought to tell him about his Auntie Nura but reconsidered, for it was such a private matter, and I knew my sister would be keenly ashamed if my son knew of her mutilation. Instead, I told him the history of female circumcision.

While my son was pleased that the custom was ending in our own land, he felt sickened that so many women still suffered unnecessary pain.

We were silent the rest of the trip, each of us awash in our own thoughts of the evening's business.

Fatma's daughter lived in a small alley that branched off from a main shopping road in the city of Cairo. Abdullah paid a shop owner for the privilege of parking our car on the sidewalk in front of his clothing shop and promised the happy man a generous bonus if he would ensure that no damage occurred while we were away.

Abdullah guided Fatma and me, hands on our backs, as we weaved through the pedestrian traffic and entered the alleyway that led to our destination. The alley was too small for automobiles, so we walked down the middle of the stone-paved street. Strong cooking odors drifted around us as we passed a number of cafés specializing in Arabic dishes.

Abdullah and I exchanged many glances, for we had never visited the poorer sections of Cairo. The close living quarters and the poverty of the inhabitants were a shock to us both.

Fatma's daughter lived in a three-story building at the center of the alleyway. The building faced the neighborhood mosque, which looked worn and was in urgent need of repair. The bottom floor housed a bakery, while the two top floors were rented out as apartments. Fatma pointed up and said that her daughter, Elham, lived on the top floor. Incredibly, Elham must have been looking down at the crowd from the flat-roofed building, for she recognized her mother, and began to yell Fatma's name, which we could barely hear over the loud noise of city life.

Abdullah did not know that in this particular family women were permitted to meet men not of their family (in Egypt the custom varies from family to family) and told me that he would wait in a small café we had passed that served *shawarma* sandwiches, which are thin slices of lamb that has been turned and cooked on a split and placed into a piece of Arabic bread, with tomato, mint, and onion for added taste. *Shawarma* sandwiches were a big favorite of all my children, and Abdullah said that he was becoming hungry.

Elham and three of her four daughters met us on the stairwell, all four speaking at once, demanding to know if there had been some illness or tragedy in the family.

My first thought was that Elham looked identical to a young Fatma.

She gazed at me in fascination when Fatma introduced me as her employer, a princess from Saudi Arabia, for I had never met this particular child, even though I had met most of Fatma's children and grandchildren. I grew extremely conscious of my showy jewelry, for in my haste, I had not remembered to remove my large diamond earrings or my opulent wedding ring, which I realized were more than conspicuous in such poor surroundings.

Elham's youngest daughter, a girl of only six, was slapped by her mother as she rubbed her small fingers across the stone in my ring.

At Elham's insistence, we were led into her small sitting room, and she left us for a short time to go and boil water for tea. Fatma had two granddaughters in her lap and a third at her feet. Alhaan was nowhere to be seen.

I examined my surroundings and could see that Elham lived a simple life. I tried not to stare at the threadbare floor coverings and the torn slipcovers, for I did not want my attention to be misunderstood. There was an open brazier in the middle of the room, and a square table pushed against the wall was piled with religious books. A small gas lamp hung down from the ceiling, and I wondered if the apartment was not supplied with electricity. I noticed that Elham's apartment was spotless, and it was evident that she was a proud woman who took great trouble keeping the dust and bugs out of her simple home.

Elham soon returned, serving sweet tea and small almond cookies she said she had baked herself for the family celebration they were having that evening. She mentioned to her mother that Alhaan was excited over the event and was on the rooftop, reading the Koran and quietly preparing herself for the most important day in her life.

The atmosphere remained cheerful until that moment, as Fatma brought up the topic on our minds, pleading with her daughter to cancel the planned ritual, to spare her child great pain and suffering.

Fatma talked in a rush and, seeing that she was making no dent in her daughter's determination, pointed to me and said that if Elham would not listen to her own mother, perhaps she would pay heed to a woman who had been educated by bright minds, a woman who had learned from respected physicians that the mutilation of girls was not encouraged by our religion and was nothing more than a custom with no basis or meaning in modern life.

The tension built, and though Elham was polite and listened to my thoughts on the matter, I could see that the lines of her face were set and her eyes were glazed over with stubborn determination. Knowing from Fatma's confidences that the family was religious, I shared my knowledge of religious thought, saying that nothing in the Koran spoke of such matters, and that if God had considered it a necessity for women to be circumcised, then surely He would have given that message to Prophet Mohammed when He revealed His wisdom to His messenger.

Elham admitted that while female circumcision is not mentioned in the Koran, the practice was founded upon the customs of the Prophet so that it had become Sunna, or tradition for all Muslims. She reminded me of a well-known *hadith*, or tradition, addressed but not recorded in the Koran. This *hadith* says that Prophet Mohammed one day told Um Attiya, a matron who was excising a girl, "Reduce but do not destroy."

It was this tradition that Elham and her husband were going to follow regarding female circumcision, and nothing I could say would alter their decision.

We discussed the issue until I could see the light begin to leave the room. Sundown was approaching. I knew that Nasser would return soon, and I had no desire to confront the man of the house over such a delicate matter. I made some small mention that it was time for me to return to my children.

Fatma, sensing failure, began to wail and slap at her cheeks until her face was completely reddened.

A look of distress flickered in Elham's eyes at her mother's grief, but she said that the decision had been reached by her husband and that she agreed with his thinking. All four of her daughters would undergo the rite of circumcision when they reached the proper age.

I could see that Elham wished for my departure. Understanding that I could do nothing to erase the frightening shadow cast over the lives of the female children of this home, I stood and said my farewells.

With quiet self-assurance, Elham's eyes met mine, and she politely bade me good-bye. "You have honored my home with your presence, Princess Sultana. Please, come again another day for a longer visit."

Against her daughter's wishes, Fatma insisted upon staying for the ceremony, saying that if the evil deed was going to be done, she wanted to supervise the barber's work to make sure he cut nothing more than the tip of her granddaughter's clitoris.

I submitted to the inevitable, leaving Elham's home without accomplishing my goal. My feet felt leaden as I walked down the long staircase. In an effort to give myself time to calm my nerves, I stood immobile on the steps and recited aloud a verse from the Koran, *"You cannot lead aright whomever you wish, it is God who leads whomever He wishes."*

My son was waiting, sitting at a small table in the front of the café. His questioning gaze followed me as I made my way to his side.

My son peered at me expectantly. "So?" he asked.

I shook my head. "No. There is nothing to be done." Abdullah's face clouded as I admitted my failure.

"Come," I said, "let us return home." I glanced over my shoulder as we left the small alley, gazing into the night. Elham's home had melted into the darkness as though it had never existed.

When my son began to talk, I urged silence with the press of my hand against his lips.

I was unable to control my weeping. Without

speaking, my son drove his sobbing mother home. As soon as I arrived back at our villa, I called out for my astonished daughters to abandon their current activities and pack their belongings. Our family would leave Cairo as soon as their father returned from the casino.

I whispered to Abdullah that the city I had loved since childhood was in danger of losing my affection, though I hoped our evening's experience would not result in my vigorous dislike of everything Egyptian.

Abdullah's eyes flashed with understanding, and I was gratified to see that my son appreciated the reasoning behind my words.

Kareem soon arrived with the odor of alcohol spread about him, which brought on a sudden and prolonged prayer from Amani for God to look past her father's sinful acts and restore Kareem to the status of heaven's most favored. In the context of her plea, Amani began to describe the burning agony of hell that awaited members of her family.

Already in a foul mood, I quickly wearied of Amani's enthusiastic fanaticism. I was incensed that she would take it to the point where she spoke critically of her family. I told her in no uncertain terms that I had not yet received notification that God had appointed my daughter to the sacred role of frightening mankind into decency.

I reached across to pinch the skin on her face, but Kareem grabbed my hand and held it tight to his chest, ordering Amani to leave our presence, suggesting that she complete her prayers in the privacy of her room.

Kareem then became noisy in the irritating manner of a drunkard, saying that he had often observed my inability to control my destructive temper, and he thought the time had come to teach me a useful lesson.

We looked at each other for a time. Kareem stood still, waiting for my response. His lips were curled with contempt, and it was easy to see that he was in a rare mood to fight.

I quickly scanned the room for a weapon with which to bang my husband's head, for I am a woman who meets threats with violence, but Kareem knows me well and placed himself between me and the brass pot I had decided to use against him.

The will to battle left my body in a rush, for there are times when I can think reasonably, and Kareem is twice my size. Without a weapon, I am at a notable disadvantage and once disarmed can be quickly overcome. Besides, it was best not to escalate our disagreement into a brawl, for past experience had taught me the impossibility of winning an argument with a drunken Kareem. But my thoughts were filled with scorn, and I had difficulty remembering why I had ever loved Kareem in the first place.

Wishing to avoid a useless confrontation, I knew that I must recapture the favored position.

I laughed, and said to Kareem, "Look at you! You resemble an elephant who is threatening an ant!" I then smiled at my husband and said that I was more than pleased he had returned early, that I yearned for his companionship at a time of great sorrow.

Kareem was not at his mental prime and was easily bested. Bewildered for a short moment by my change in tactics, he eased into my trap and became overly remorseful for his unthinking words, patting my shoulder, offering apologies, and wondering why his dear wife was distressed.

I looked at my watch and saw that it was nearly nine o'clock. Half insane with the knowledge that the innocent child, Alhaan, would soon undergo female mutilation, I instantly forgot all thoughts of myself, and with tremendous sadness told my husband that there is no loveliness in life for women and that in my mind it would be advantageous for all females to die.

Kareem could not fathom the reasoning behind my dark ideas. He asked, was my life not perfect? Was there anything I desired that my husband did not provide?

Knowing that my main source of distress is the social injustice directed toward women, he reminded me that together we had ensured that in our home, our daughters felt little of the prejudice that exists against females in our land. What more could one man do, he wondered, than to guard those he loved.

Kareem smiled sweetly and tenderly brushed my lips with his fingers.

I had a quick thought that Kareem *was* endowed with a winsome charm that atoned for his less admirable traits.

Unsure how to address the ambiguous issue of my general dissatisfaction with the status of women, Kareem announced that it was my inescapable destiny to be born in Saudi Arabia, and in the end women must accept the limits imposed by our culture. My husband reminded me that God knew all things, and His purpose in planting my feet in Saudi soil had not been made known to those bound on earth.

My emotions in a whirl, I once again felt dislike for Kareem, regretting that all men could not be turned into women and live in our limited and often cruel world long enough to attain understanding. I wanted to rage at my husband's distance from my knowledge of the pain that women endure.

How can woman bind man to the grief that walks the earth and settles at the feet of each woman by turn? Sensing the futility of longing for men to suffer women's position in society, while women enjoyed the status of male rank, I told myself that I was too keyed up to be capable of a normal conversation and suggested to my husband that we go to sleep early, then rise refreshed to a day of new thoughts.

Because he follows a set pattern of fighting and then sleep after alcoholic drinking, Kareem agreed and willingly prepared himself for bed, while I located the children and gave instructions for them to eat their evening meal without us and to be available with bags packed to depart Cairo in the morning.

By the time I returned to our quarters, my husband had begun to breathe the deep, peaceful rhythms of one already at rest.

With my mind in conflict between my own rebellious thoughts and Elham's traditional beliefs, I considered what Kareem had said, that I was a woman at odds with my fate. Yet, in spite of my second-class status, I knew that I could never yield to meek acceptance of female circumcision.

Before falling into a troubled and unsatisfying sleep, I vowed to myself that my fury over the fate of girls such as Alhaan would outlive the barbaric custom that had aroused it.

Chapter Eleven:
Monte Carlo

"To call women the weaker sex is a libel; it is man's injustice to women. You will guard your wife's honor and be not her master, but her true friend. Let not either of you regard another as the object of his or her lust."
—MAHATMA GANDHI

Fatma's face was distorted with an effort to appear cheery as she bade us a good morning. She had been hard at work in the kitchen when the family awakened and seemed distraught at our abrupt announcement that we were departing Cairo and traveling to Monte Carlo that very morning. There, on the French Riviera, we would join three of my sisters and their families who were on holiday in the small principality of Monaco.

I had already imagined the scene of her granddaughter's circumcision and knew that the tragic evening did not lend itself to words. Still, I maneuvered a quiet moment away from my family to inquire about Alhaan's safety.

With clasped hands and a steely glint in her eyes that reflected her lingering anger, Fatma said that the child had not fared well. On her son-in-law's instruction, the barber had removed all of the girl's clitoris, along with her labia minora. Fatma said that special compresses had to be made to stop the flow of blood.

Feeling undeserved guilt that I had been unable to prevent Alhaan's brutalization, I asked in alarm, "Do you fear further complications?"

Fatma tried to relax her expression when she saw that my eyes were filling with tears and realized that I was becoming distraught.

"Mistress"—she hugged my neck as she spoke—"the deed is done. Now we must live with it. You did all that you could. I bless you for your love of another who is not of your own blood. Take comfort from my belief that Alhaan will recover."

I could find no words to speak. Fatma turned me loose and her eyes met mine. Our gazes stayed fixed on one another for a long time. Neither of us looked away or moved, and I felt a great love surging from Fatma to me.

Fatma moistened her lips before she continued. "Princess Sultana, you entered my dreams last evening, and now I feel that I must convey the message of the dream."

I held my breath, afraid of what I might be told, thinking that I had never fared well in supernatural predictions.

Fatma gazed at me with sad affection. "Mistress, you are surrounded with life's possessions, yet you appear empty. This discontent comes from having the heart of a child in the body of a woman. Such a combination will bring great difficulties to one's soul. Neither you nor any other child of God can resolve all of mankind's problems. I was told to tell you that it is not shameful to bow to reality and that you should allow the lust for conflict to cool in your veins."

My mother's face appeared to me as a dark dream

of disconnected memories. There was no doubt in my mind that my mother was using the form of the earthbound Fatma to communicate with her youngest child. Fatma's words were just the sort of advice my mother had often given me in the days of my childhood. When I was young, her words of wisdom were unclear and seemed to have no connection to me. Now that I was an adult, that was no longer the case.

I had known then, even as a child, that when my mother understood that she was dying, her only regret in passing from earth was that she was leaving my intense character without a firm guide. Her fears had been that I would react to adult controversy in the same hasty manner I had confronted problems when I was a child, when I had no goal but success, embroiling myself in one conflict after another.

My beloved mother was communicating with me!

I felt a warm glow throughout my body and felt calmer than I had in days. My memories were no longer obscure, and I keenly felt my mother's divine presence.

I had no explanation to give for the sudden whimpering I heard arise from my throat, or for the sobbing and incoherent woman who threw herself into Fatma's strong arms, a woman who still felt as a child, longing with all her heart to have but one short moment with the one who had given her life.

I cried out to a sympathetic Fatma, "How blessed are those who still have their mothers!"

When leaving the city of Cairo, I could not help thinking of the gloomy fate awaiting many young girls in the country of Egypt. I whispered to my son that such tragic events make Egyptian life less bright and cheerful than is fitting in such a country.

Late that afternoon, our private plane landed at the Nice-Cote International Airport in southern France. The husbands of my three sisters had leased a large villa in the hills above Monaco, which they had assured Kareem was a short drive from the airport. Asad had arranged for three limousines to meet our plane and transport our family and baggage from the airport to the villa.

Actually, at one time the villa had been a palace belonging to a French aristocrat and had over sixty rooms, so there was more than enough space for our combined families. None of my sisters was married to a man who had taken more than one wife, so our group of eight adults and sixteen children was unusually small for an Arab gathering of four families.

There are three highways going from Nice to Monaco, but none of us wanted to travel the coastal road, or the Inferieure Corniche, which is generally traffic-packed. The Moyenne Corniche is the middle road, and the Grande Corniche is the high road.

I expressed a desire to take the Moyenne, since I knew it was the best of the three and had wonderful views of the coastline.

Kareem disagreed, saying that our daughters should choose the road we would travel.

I pinched the flesh on his leg, indicating that his idea was not sound, but he continued to ask their opinions.

As I knew they would, Maha and Amani began an immediate squabble, each of them insisting upon a different route.

I whispered to Kareem, "I told you so."

Our daughters have never reached agreement on any issue, regardless of the subject, since the time they learned to speak. I admitted to myself that nothing in our lives had been simple since I had given birth to three children.

The driver settled their argument by saying that a truck loaded with eggs had suffered a mishap, and the Moyenne was temporarily blocked. Since two of the three roads were congested with traffic, he suggested that we take the Grande.

Like the baby she is, Amani pouted, but Maha and Abdullah were joyful, pointing out various interesting sights they had not remembered from our last trip to Monaco over three years before.

The Grande Corniche was built by Napoleon, and he had his builders follow the route of the ancient Roman road. The drive took us along the southern slope of the Alpes Maritimes, and the scenery was spectacular.

I mentioned that after the uninspired brown and beige shades of desert countries, the lush greenery of Europe was restful to my eyes.

Amani took my comment as a slur upon the home of the Prophet, whereupon Kareem lost his patience and asked his daughter *please* to omit religious interpretations of the simplest social remark.

I thought to myself that my own precious daughter was becoming thoroughly unlikable. My love for her flowed as strongly as ever, but there were moments when I suffered extreme distaste for Amani's overbearing attitude.

Pleased that my family's confined journey was coming to an end, I was happy to see my sisters Sara, Tahani, and Nura, when our car pulled up the circular driveway to the front of the villa. How welcome it made me feel that the three of them had evidently been eagerly waiting by the door for our arrival.

My pleasure was short-lived.

"Reema has been hospitalized!" Nura announced as soon as we had completed our greetings and my three children had gone to seek out their cousins.

"What?" I responded, trying to imagine what ill-ness had struck the fifth sister in age in our family.

"She has been injured," Sara volunteered, while ex-changing a meaningful look with Nura.

"Yes?" My voice was so low that the sound barely left my throat. I had a sudden fear of an automobile acci-dent, for traffic accidents are a main source of death in Saudi Arabia, where many young boys recklessly race their vehicles through the streets.

My sisters and I stood without speaking, awk-wardly facing one another. I moved my weight from foot to foot, waiting for someone to enlighten me about my sister's condition.

Kareem and Asad stood to the side, watching but not speaking.

When no one spoke, my stomach churned. Was my sister dead, and was there no one in my family with the nerve to tell me?

Finally I asked weakly, "Is her injury serious?"

"It appears that it is not life-threatening," Nura stated.

The Arab manner of avoiding bad news is madden-ing! I felt the urge to scream, for someone to tell me all that there was to know, to release me from the agony of attempting to force small bits of information from my re-luctant sisters.

"What has happened?" I demanded. "Anything is easier to accept than this torturing doubt!"

My sisters looked at one another strangely. Surely, Reema was dead!

"Let us go inside," Asad suggested as he placed a tender hand on Sara's arm. "I will have tea prepared."

I followed Sara into the villa, taking no notice of the rooms as we passed them by. I was thinking of poor

Reema. The fifth daughter in our family had always inspired family sympathy. From the date of her birth, Reema had not been blessed with obvious skills or beauty. While my sister was not born with a face scarred or misaligned, there had been nothing in her appearance to bring forth envy from other young mothers.

Nura had once confided that Reema was the only daughter whom our mother had felt no need to protect with the blue stone that was believed to ward off evil spirits, for who would wish the evil eye upon an infant so displeasing in appearance?

In addition, as a young girl Reema had been cursed with a heavy figure that brought her cruel taunts from unfeeling children.

Of my nine sisters, Sara is the most beautiful. Of the remainder of our female family members, four sisters are notably pretty, three are appealing, another is elegant and graceful, while Reema lacks a single mark of beauty. In a family of ten daughters, Reema was the unattractive sister who failed to excel in school or in games. Her one outstanding accomplishment was her ability to duplicate our mother's cooking skills, improvising delectable Arabic and French dishes that did nothing to help her expanding figure.

Living in a country where nothing is more admired than female beauty, Reema was not esteemed.

Once we had settled ourselves in the sitting room, Kareem and Asad left us to go and arrange tea. As the door was closing, I heard Asad speaking in a low voice to my husband, and knew that Kareem had discovered Reema's fate before her own sister.

"I must know the truth. Tell me. Is Reema dead?"

"No," Nura responded. Yet, my sister's gloomy face reflected the seriousness of the situation.

"She was attacked by Saleem," Tahani finally said.

I felt cold all over. "Truly?" I asked.

With tremendous emotion, Nura added, "Our dear sister was viciously attacked by her own husband."

"Why would Saleem want to hurt Reema?" I wondered. "Surely, she gave him no motive!"

Like many unattractive people, Reema had always been pleasing in character, striving to make all around her feel delightful and gay, as if her joyful countenance could outwit nature, eliciting admiration from those in her company.

Saleem? My memory of Reema's husband flashed through my mind. Saleem, like Reema, was not blessed with physical beauty. But he was known to be a most quiet and gentle man. As we often say in the Arab world, "*Every pot has its cover.*" Saleem was considered a perfect partner for Reema, and their union seemed to suit them. His violent action was completely unexpected and out of character.

I put to Nura the most logical possibility, "Did Saleem lose his mind? Is that why he assaulted Reema?"

I was not prepared for what I heard.

Approximately a year before, Reema had confessed to her oldest sister, Nura, that a dark secret was consuming the light in her life. Reema said that her dear husband was undergoing a bizarre personality change that had begun with a strange restlessness and dissatisfaction. Suddenly the blackest melancholy overcame the formerly contented Saleem. Where he had once been well pleased with his home, he was now irritable, finding endless fault with his wife and four children. He no longer expressed an interest in his work, and for many days he would remain in bed until mid-afternoon. Saleem was caught in the tyranny of his own emotions, which prevented the entire family from living a normal life.

While Reema's attachment to Saleem had increased during the years of their married life, Saleem coldly told his wife that he had never loved her, that as a matter of fact he had never known love at all, and had married Reema for no reason other than to gain prestige from her family name.

Reema confronted Saleem's unreasonable hostility with faithful love and genuine concern. Reema told Nura that she feared Saleem must have a brain tumor, or at least be suffering from a chemical imbalance. Why else would a man so radically change, when there had been no trauma in his life.

Reema pleaded with her husband to seek medical attention. But instead of looking to professional help for his misery, Saleem dwelt on his unhappiness. Saleem, a man who rarely drank alcohol, began to drink with increasing frequency. When drinking, he would be come violent toward Reema and the eldest of their daughters.

Reema told Nura that she feared she would soon be divorced and separated from her two youngest sons, for Saleem had threatened to liberate himself from Reema, insisting that this was the only way to free himself from his unhappiness.

Nura was helpless at giving advice, for no one in our family could approach Saleem's family without creating tension. His family had recently requested that one of Nura's daughters be wed to their youngest son. The engagement did not materialize because Ahmed and Nura had already arranged a different groom for their child. Saleem's family had held themselves at a distance since that time, taking offense where none was intended.

Nura said that while Saleem slowly pulled himself together so that he began to function at work, his contempt for Reema only grew more intense. Saleem began to take frequent trips to the Far East, and Reema knew from some of the brochures she found in her husband's belongings that these trips were not of a business nature. Saleem was participating in sexual junkets to Bangkok and Manila.

Just the month before, Reema went to Nura's home with a bruised face and a horrifying story. Our sister had discovered her husband in bed with one of the Sri Lankan maids. When she protested, Saleem went at her with his fists and threatened Reema with the loss of her children if she dared open her mouth to anyone in his family. Saleem's family was known to be devout and religious, and they would have expressed great shame at his conduct, though they would have been helpless to change his mood.

While it is true that many Saudi men turn to secret pleasures with women to whom they are not wed, none of the females in our family had married a man so insensitive as to flaunt sexual relations with a servant in his own home.

Reema, perplexed and not sure where to turn, went to a Egyptian woman known for her religious wisdom. She asked that the woman put in writing the answer to the question: *Does Islam permit a man to have sexual intercourse with his maidservant without marrying her?* Surely, her husband would heed a religious ruling, if she brought it to him in writing. To go against the teachings of the Koran would be unthinkable in the mind of our pious sister!

Nura said that Reema had confessed she was going to confront Saleem with the ruling. Nura had cautioned our sister, concerned that Saleem no longer enjoyed total sanity.

I asked if Nura recalled the words of the ruling.

She replied that she had taken a copy for herself and filed it with her other religious material. Who knew what other woman might have need of the information at a later date?

Nura said that to the best of her memory "the woman wrote that Islam does not allow a sexual relationship between a master and a servant. The idea was outrageous, and only through marriage could a sexual relationship exist in Islam."

The woman acknowledged that what happens in actual life is not always sanctioned by Islam and that there were many cases in the kingdom that had been brought to her attention involving a master forcing his servant to yield to his wishes, exploiting her inferior position to get cheap fulfillment of carnal desire. The woman stated that such a relationship was illicit and led to the three evils expressly forbidden by Islam. The evils of which she spoke are: "Any relationship which adversely affects the moral fabric of society, or leads to promiscuity, or affects the rights of any individual. In Islam, the only lawful way to have sexual intercourse is through marriage."

Reema's courage in seeking an outside opinion caused me some surprise, for she was meek in nature.

"Was this information the cause of Saleem's attack?" I asked my sisters.

Nura answered in the negative.

"Then?"

Sara began to weep and left the room, saying that she could not bear to hear the details again. Tahani rose to follow her, but Asad was standing near the door. I caught a glimpse of him wrapping his arms around his wife as he led her to a private corner.

Tahani returned and sat by my side, and began nervously to pat the top of my hand.

I thought to myself that I was being prepared for a distressing account.

"The physician would not tell us the full details, but Father and Ali went to his office and were told the truth of the matter, for Saleem finally confessed to the physician what exactly had happened to Reema.

"It seems that Saleem had just returned from a short trip to Bangkok and had smuggled in pornographic videotapes. After a night of drinking and viewing the tapes, Saleem wanted to have sex with his wife, although he had not displayed affectionate interest in Reema for some time.

"When Saleem awakened Reema in the middle of the night for sex, he was told that she was having her monthly period."

With half-shut eyes, Nura leaned back on the sofa.

Like all Muslims, I know that the Koran forbids sexual relations during a woman's menstrual cycle. The Koran clearly states: *"They ask, concerning women's courses, respond: they are a hurt and a pollution, keep away from women in their courses, and do not approach them until they are clean, but when they have purified themselves, you may approach them in any manner, time, or place, ordained for you, by God."*

Had Reema fought her husband, only to be raped and beaten during a time she was forbidden to him?

I could tell that Nura was thinking of what she was going to say and how she was going to say it. I watched Nura's face as it became white with anger. "Saleem, in a drunken state, became angry at his wife's condition and refusal." My sister took a deep, ragged breath. "Sultana, Reema was badly beaten, and then Saleem raped his wife in a region of her body not allowed to her husband. The physician at the private clinic informed Father that Saleem's attack was so violent and brutal that emergency surgery was performed. For the remainder of her life, Reema will be forced to wear a colostomy bag."

My mouth opened in a soundless howl. Reema? Disabled and encumbered for life? I found myself seething with hostility. Now I understood why Sara had fled the room, for she herself had been subjected to that same type of sexual abuse when wed against her will to her first husband, a man who was sick in his head.

I stood and stamped my foot so hard that a vase tottered and threatened to fall from a tall stand. "If Saleem were in this room, I would attack him with my hands," I shouted. In an uncontrolled rage, I asked, "And Saleem? Has he been jailed?"

Tahani made a clicking sound with her tongue. "Jailed? He is Reema's husband. He is free to do as he likes."

Nura's face was becoming even paler in her grief and bitterness over the fate of our innocent sister.

I protested, "But his conduct was forbidden! Surely, we can make a case for a religious investigation!"

Nura looked at me with great love mingled with sadness. "Sultana, you speak as a child. Who, in our land, will take the side of a woman against her husband? Our own father and brother have directed that this is a personal matter between Reema and Saleem and that no one of our family is to interfere."

Tahani confided, "Father prohibited us from telling you, but we decided that we must, for when you see Reema next, her condition will be obvious."

I insisted, "Reema must divorce him! That, at least!"

Nura reminded me of the reality of Reema's situation. "And lose her children? Both girls have reached puberty, and the boys are now eight and nine. Saleem has the right to take them from their mother. And that he would do. He has already threatened her with their loss. Sultana, Reema would die without her children."

When Nura saw that I was still fiercely angry, she asked, "Tell me, Sultana, could you live if your children were taken from you?"

In my land, in the event of a divorce, the mother has the right to retain her children if they are still suckling. In most cases, a mother maintains custody of daughters until a girl child arrives at puberty. In the case of male children, the boy should be allowed to remain with his mother up until age seven. When he reaches his seventh birthday, he is supposed to have the option to choose between his mother or father. Generally it is accepted that the father would have his sons at age seven. A son *must* go with his father at the age of puberty, regardless of the child's wishes.

Often, in the case of male children, fathers will not allow the mother to retain custody, no matter the age of the child. I have personally known women who have lost custody of their children at young ages, never again seeing those to whom they gave birth. Unfortunately, if a father seizes the initiative and takes his children, there is no authority that will force him to return them to their mother.

I knew that if Saleem refused Reema visitation with her children, my sister would be forever banned from their presence. There was no court of law that would reverse the husband's final decision about the destiny of his children.

I moaned, thinking of the possibilities we would know if we had male support. If only the men of her family, our father and Ali, would stand behind Reema, her position in negotiating for her children would strengthen. Since our father and brother thought that a man should be allowed to do as he wished with the females in his family, they would be of no assistance to Reema.

It was a serious moment.

"Perhaps Saleem will come to his right mind," Nura hopefully suggested.

"Never try to straighten a dog's tail. In vain you

do," Tahani muttered to no one in particular.

After further discussion, my sisters and I decided that we were needed in Riyadh. We would leave our husbands in Monte Carlo with our children, and travel back to Saudi Arabia the following day.

Later that evening, Kareem tried to lift my downcast spirit by reminding me that my sister had not died from her injuries, and where there was life, change might come. He said that a better day would soon be known, that in his opinion, Saleem was suffering from nothing more than a male crisis that would pass.

Kareem became concerned when I promised him that Saleem would suffer for his attack on the gentle Reema.

Trying to ease my murderous rage, he joked, "Sultana, I do not wish to see you made ready for the executioner's sword! You must spare Saleem's life."

My husband continued to speak, but I listened to his words without hearing, thinking how lamentable it was that so much ignorance should prevail in a land that is home to a great religion.

Chapter Twelve:
Home

"A girl possesses nothing but a veil and a tomb."
—Saudi Arabian proverb

Our brother, Ali, met us at the King Khalid International Airport that is located twenty-two miles from Riyadh's city center. Ali seemed preoccupied and curtly informed us that we would be taken directly to the private clinic to visit our sister Reema, for she was suffering a particularly bad day and had been asking for Nura since the early morning.

The traffic was heavy, and the drive took more than an hour. Each of us was lost in our individual thoughts of Reema. At the beginning of the journey, the conversation was strained and sparse, with nothing important spoken.

Ali, tiring of the silence, confided that he, himself, was involved in a family crisis. With a touch of annoyance in his voice, my faithless brother said that Reema's unfortunate injury could not have occurred at a worse time, and that he had been greatly inconvenienced by the necessity of becoming involved in Saleem's private family affair. In all earnestness, Ali wondered aloud what Reema had done to bring forth Saleem's hostility.

Ali was blaming Reema for Saleem's unprovoked attack!

Sara and Tahani looked quickly at Ali, and I detected in their evasive glances faint reprimands at his unfeeling comment.

I could not restrain my tongue and said, "Ali, with each day, your ignorance grows while your intelligence shrinks!"

I felt a keen urge to slap my brother, but not wanting to appear less than admirable in front of Nura and Tahani, I consoled myself with silent criticism. Ali was only a year older than I, but he looked no less than ten years my senior, with lines in his face and pouches under his eyes. In his youth, Ali had been handsome and vain about his looks. In middle age he had grown a bit stout, and his chin had doubled. Ali's affluent, overindulgent lifestyle was clearly evident in his face and form. I was cheered to see his physical appeal decaying.

My eldest sister's face clouded, and in a voice filled with tenderness and concern, she asked Ali what crisis there was in his life.

Out of ten sisters, only Nura truly loves Ali. The emotions of the remaining nine sisters for their only brother range from pity, contempt, and envy to open dislike. We do understand that Nura is protected from acute disapproval of her only brother by the division of many years, for Nura is the oldest child of our mother, and Ali is one year from the youngest. Nura was married with children when Ali was born, and was mercifully spared his spoiled, overbearing conduct. In addition, Nura inherited the kindly character of our mother and belonged to that minority who instinctively make apologies for those around them, while accepting the most feeble explanations for inexcusable deeds. Thus, Nura's reaction to Ali's insensitive statement differed from those of his other three sisters.

Ali frowned slightly. He looked out of the automobile window and then said distantly, "I have divorced Nada."

Nura gasped. "Again?"

Ali looked at Nura and nodded.

"Ali! How could you? You promised Nada that never again would you divorce her!"

Nada was Ali's most beautiful and favored wife. He had married her seven years before, and together they had had three lovely daughters.

Under Muslim law, a man's freedom to divorce his wife is justified in the Koran. This system of the threat of divorce constantly looming over her security is most unsettling to women in my land. It is intolerable that many men stretch this flexible ruling to the utmost, demanding divorce for the most trivial causes, causing the continuous social degradation of their women.

Women do not have the same options, since a divorce in a woman's favor is given only after a thorough investigation into her life. More often than not, women will not be allowed to divorce, even when there is just cause. This female lack of freedom so enjoyed by males creates one-sided, often cruel methods of male control and power over their women. The words of divorce slip most easily off the tongue of any man who wishes to punish his wife. Simply by saying, "I divorce thee," or "I dismiss thee," he sends the woman into exile from her married home, often without her children.

Ali, a man rarely in control of his tongue or his temper, often used divorce as a weapon against his wives.

I knew that my brother had divorced each of his wives at least once, and Nada had been divorced twice.

More times than not, once Ali's anger receded, he would repent the divorce and retain the wife he had divorced the day or night before. Ali had this benefit, for men are not only given the option of divorcing their wives with the greatest of ease but are allowed to take back the divorce and resume their marriage as if nothing out of the ordinary had occurred. Under Muslim law, a man is given this option twice. If he divorces his wife for a third time, the procedure becomes more complicated.

In a fit of anger, Ali had divorced Nada for the third time, and according to our law, he could not resume marriage with her until she had married another man and had then been divorced by him. Through his childlike conduct, Ali had finally and truly divorced himself from the only one of his wives for whom he felt true affection.

I tried not to smile as I quoted the Koran, doing my best to remember every word.

"*You may divorce your wives twice; after that you must either retain them with kindness, or put them away with benefits. If then the husband divorce her a third time, it is not lawful for him to take her again, until she shall have married another husband.*"

I stuck my face into the face of my brother and asked, "Ali, who is Nada now going to wed?"

Ali glared at me with bulging eyes, and answered coldly, "La! La! [no, no] Nada has no desire to wed another!"

"Ha! Nada is famous within the female community for her beauty. Once it is known that she is free, many mothers and sisters will send their sons and brothers to ask for her. Wait and see!"

Sara intervened, not wanting our lifelong, unending feud to lead to a fierce argument in a confined area. "Ali. What led to this divorce?"

Ali was clearly embarrassed. He said that the matter of the divorce was private, but he did ask Sara and Nura if they would visit with Nada, to convince her that the words were spoken in haste, and as such, Ali should be given another opportunity to prove that he had no real desire to divorce her. If Nada chose to ignore the situation and did not notify the authorities, then Ali might be able to avoid an order to allow Nada to leave his home, thereby becoming eligible for another man to pursue.

Nura and Sara agreed to speak with Nada.

The car began to slow down, and Ali peered through the dark blue curtains and then pointed at the black assortment of veils, *abaayas*, and *shaylas* that were spread over the seat. "Hurry. Prepare yourselves. We are there," he commanded.

It was a struggle for the four of us to cover ourselves in the black garb of decency within the small space of the automobile. Ali had met our private airplane on the tarmac, so we had not bothered with our required outer coverings until the last moment.

We had arrived at the private clinic that Ali said was owned jointly by a Lebanese and a Saudi Arabian. The clinic was one often frequented by royal family members when confidentiality was desired. I was acquainted with three princesses who routinely entered the clinic for treatment of drug and alcohol abuse.

Our family was escorted inside the building through a little-used door; we were met there by one of Reema's physicians. The man informed us that he was an internist, a specialist from Beirut, and had recently been hired by the owners of the clinic to care for members of the royal family. It was easy to see why he had been selected to treat influential Saudis, for he was a tall, attractive man, deferential, yet with an air of competence that provided us with a sense of confidence in our sister's safety.

The physician walked between Nura and Ali, and though I made an attempt to lean forward and involve myself in their quiet conversation, I failed to hear the words that he spoke. We passed a group of Asian nurses who were clustered around an elongated nurse's station. I could tell by their accents that they were Filipina.

The windows in Reema's room were still closed, but the blinds were slightly open, allowing a small amount of the sun's glow to penetrate and wash the room in a soft light. The room was completely white, and above Reema's head hung a large pearl-white chandelier that looked strangely out of place in this clinical setting.

Reema was resting, but when she heard us she opened her eyes. I could see that my sister suffered a moment of confusion before reality rushed back to her. Her face was extremely pale, and her eyes were those of a frightened child. My sister was receiving fluids from bottles hanging from metal stands, and I could not count the tubes that had been placed in her arms and nose.

Nura rushed to her side, placing her arms around the form that was Reema. Sara and Tahani held hands, fighting back tears, and I could scarcely see as I flung myself into a white armchair. I bit my lips until I tasted blood, and I pressed my hands into the arms of the chair with such force that I broke three fingernails.

Ali, uncomfortable with our display of grief, whispered to Sara that he would return within the hour to escort us to our homes. Before leaving, he reminded Sara that it was imperative she see Nada that very evening.

I was seething with rage at the sight of my wounded sister and thought to myself that I would like to send the hottest fire raging throughout the whole country. Let the evil of my land die with the flesh of those Saudi men who dared to use the holy Koran as a basis for molesting those of my sex!

I attempted to calm my thoughts, for there was no purpose in creating chaos and adding to Reema's pain. I remembered the Prophet's promises of punishment to those who so sin, but my religion could not soothe me, even in the knowledge that Saleem would suffer everlasting agonies in hell for what he had done to my sister. I had no patience to wait for divine intervention. Nothing would cool my boiling blood but the sight of Saleem's mutilated remains.

Once comforted by Nura, Reema spoke with each of her sisters in turn, pleading with us to treat Saleem with the same courtesy as before, reminding us that one of the duties of good Muslims is to forgive those who do wrong. Seeing the anger in my face, Reema quoted a verse from the Koran. "Sultana, do not forget the words of the Prophet: *Forgive, even when angry.*"

I could not hold back my words. Remembering the text of the Koran that followed, I replied, "*Let evil be rewarded with evil.*"

Sara pinched me on my buttocks, reminding me not to cause further anguish to our sister. I left Reema's side and stared out the window, seeing nothing of what I was looking at.

Reema began to speak once again. I could not believe what I was hearing and was chilled by Reema's words, which were delivered with the impassioned eloquence of a woman whose reason for living was at stake.

I returned to my sister's bedside and stared at her face.

As the intensity of Reema's feelings increased, her brow became furrowed, and her lips grew tight with determination. My sister said that Saleem had repented and had promised there would be no other violence. She was not going to be divorced, nor would she seek a divorce.

Suddenly I realized what was in Reema's heart. My

sister's only fear was deprivation of her children, and those four children were the inspiration for Reema's ability to forgive Saleem for his heinous attack. She would accept any indignity so long as her relationship with her precious children was not severed.

Reema asked us to assure her that no one in our family would seek retribution on her behalf.

It was the most difficult promise ever to pass my lips, and my tongue would scarce obey my mind. But my word was given, and I knew I had no choice but to abide by my sister's sincere wish.

Once recovered, Reema would return to the home of this man who had kept his infinite capacity for cruelty well hidden for many married years. I knew that once unleashed, Saleem's ugly temperament would not soften. There was nothing we could do.

Our frustration only increased when an Egyptian nurse employed by the clinic confided in Nura that Saleem had visited his wife earlier that day. In the presence of that nurse, Saleem had lifted his wife's hospital gown, viewing the opening that had been made in her side for her bodily waste to be expelled, and had expressed shocked disgust at the sight.

The nurse said that Saleem had then made a most callous remark, telling his wife that while he would not divorce her, he would never again come to her bed, for he could not bear the sight or smell of one so repugnant.

I marveled at my ability to control my rage. My sisters and I had entered the clinic as a united force, swelled with determination to snatch our sister from the grasp of her evil husband. Defeated by Reema's legitimate apprehension of the possible loss of her children, we retreated from the clinic as nothing more than a group of black-shrouded and nameless wives, without the ability to force justice upon a single man.

The sting of the defeat was unbearable.

Who could deny that the main bulwark of the Saudi social order remained male dictatorship?

Since our husbands and children were still in Monte Carlo, my sisters and I decided we would stay together in Nura's house. Ali took us there from the clinic. Nura and Sara pledged to our brother that they would have one of Nura's drivers take them to visit Nada that evening and said it would be best for him to stay in the home of another wife that night.

Once we had telephoned our husbands in Monte Carlo, giving them our news of Reema, Tahani pleaded exhaustion and retired early to bed. I insisted on accompanying Sara and Nura to Nada's palace. I was forced to make a second promise, guaranteeing that I would make no suggestion that Nada quit Ali while she had the opportunity.

My sisters know me well. Admittedly, I had already made a plan in my mind to try to convince Nada that she must quickly move to marry another. My brother had treated women with contempt all his life, and in my opinion it was time for him to learn not to use divorce as a weapon. Perhaps if he lost the only wife for whom he felt affection, he would temper his bullying tactics.

Now I had a second difficult promise to keep.

It was nearly nine o'clock in the evening when we arrived. Ali's compound seemed more peaceful than we had ever seen it. We saw none of his wives, concubines, or children as our car made its way along the wide circular drive that wound around the four palaces belonging to our brother. Nada's palace was the third building within the compound walls.

Nada's Egyptian housekeeper informed us that her mistress was having a bath but was expecting us and had instructed the housekeeper to take us to her living quarters.

Nothing about my brother is modest. The influence of Saudi oil wealth was evident in his home at every turn. Conspicuous consumption met my eyes as I entered the white-marbled front hallway that was the width of an airport terminal. The towering staircase gleamed, and I remembered Ali's proud announcement that the columns bracing the structure were coated with real silver. Fifteen-foot-high doors with solid silver doorknobs led into Nada's private living quarters.

I tried not to gloat, recalling that my brother had taken a serious financial loss during the worldwide run on the silver market in the 1980s. In his greed, Ali must have purchased more of the precious metal than we had realized, only to see his fortunes tumble. Now, Ali's financial loss was the gain of a silver-enhanced palace!

I had never visited Nada's bedroom, though I had once received an invitation to view the bedstead. I had been told by a shocked and saddened Sara that the bed was carved in solid ivory, and now I saw that her description was true. Ali had once bragged about the number of elephants that had died to support his bulky frame, but now I could not recall the figure he had quoted.

Looking around my brother's opulent home, I had a vision of justified al Sa'ud exile from the kingdom of Saudi Arabia, for such inherent corruption of wealth deserved no other fate. Would we one day share royal displacement with the likes of King Farouk of Egypt, the Shah of Shahs of Iran, or King Idris of Libya? There was one certainty in my mind, that if the working class of Saudi Arabia ever viewed the private living quarters of Prince Ali al Sa'ud, revolution would be inescapable.

This terrifying idea numbed my body.

At that moment, Nada swept into the room wearing a fashionable hairdo, a haughty expression, and a bulging bosom crammed into a blinding gold lamé dress. It required little imagination to understand how our brother had been infatuated by his most beautiful wife. Nada had achieved fame in our family through her daring fashions and her will to do battle with a man who had met little resistance from women throughout his life. In spite of her ability to torture Ali, I had always thought the expression in her eyes looked subtly malicious and had never veered from my opinion that Nada's itch for gain had been her only purpose in marrying my brother. I did remember Sara saying that it was Nada's insecurity in her marriage that made her appear what she was not, for she had no idea when Ali might dispense with her, as he had other women. Such a position creates the need to ensure one's future economic security. But I still had my lingering doubts about her true nature. I did admit to myself that Nada had paid dearly for the softer luxuries, for married life with Ali surely must be grim.

Nada said, "Ali sent you, did he not?"

I watched her face, thinking that she was pouting and mourning, as if our visit were all a mistake. I alternated between like and dislike, and as Nura and Sara gathered 'round our sister-in-law, I excused myself, saying that I was going to the bar to fetch myself a drink.

The house was completely quiet and there was no one about. After preparing myself a gin and soda, I felt no desire to rejoin my sisters, and I wandered through my brother's palace, finding myself in his private study, which was located on the lowest level of his home.

A childlike curiosity came over me, and I began sifting through my brother's personal belongings, making a discovery that first puzzled me and then brought great amusement.

I opened a small packet on the top of his writing desk, and read with vague curiosity about a set of undergarments my brother had obviously purchased during a recent trip to Hong Kong.

A flimsy sheet of instructions accompanied the underpants, and I read the sheet with interest.

Wonder Garment: Congratulations on the purchase of your new Wonder Garment! The garment that you have purchased should be worn daily. This garment is guaranteed to improve the wearer's sexual performance.

The secret of these miracle underpants lies in the "strategic" pouch, which maintains the sexual organs at the correct temperature and under optimum conditions.

The Wonder Garment is recommended for all men, but most especially for those who maintain an active sexual life and for those who sit down at their work.

I began to giggle, and an evil spirit came over me. I stuffed the slim plastic bag containing the undergarment and instruction sheet under my long dress. I had no thought of what I was going to do with the item but felt an urge to share the secret with Kareem. Feeling as I had in the days of my childhood rivalry with Ali, I gleefully envisioned how my brother would frantically search through his home for the magical pants.

I met my sisters on the staircase and could see from their eyes that they'd had no success with Ali's wife.

Nada was leaving Ali.

Unlike poor Reema, Nada was not worried that her children would be taken, for Ali had little love for his female offspring and had made no secret to his wife that their three daughters were of no value to him and would be allowed to live with their mother.

I left without saying good-bye. In the car, I cradled my gin and tonic. My thievery of Ali's personal possession had brought forth childish emotions, and I felt quite daring as a princess in the House of sl Sa'ud riding down the streets of Riyadh, enjoying an alcoholic drink.

I asked Sara why Nada was leaving the tempting life of an al Sa'ud, for she had a dubious family background, and it would be difficult for her to duplicate the wealth enjoyed as a wife of Ali. It had been Nada's great beauty, not her family connections, that had won her a husband of immense riches.

Nura said that from what she could gather it seemed that Nada and Ali's divorce had come about over an evening of love.

Nada had tearfully confessed to my sisters that she had been divorced on all three occasions over the issue of sex, saying that Ali insisted she accommodate him at odd hours in the night, often waking her from a heavy sleep. The week before, Nada had refused her husband sex, and Ali had insisted, saying that when a man calls his wife to intercourse, she must not resist him even though she might be on a camel! When Nada still refused, Ali had divorced her.

Sara then told me that Nada had made a surprising second declaration, saying that while she had some affection for Ali's other wives, she had grown increasingly weary of the bastards that sprang from his infidelities, for our brother was the father of seventeen legitimate children and twenty-three illegitimate off-spring. The compound that Nada called home was overrun with her husband's concubines and their children.

At the mention of all that sexual activity, which had produced endless offspring, I could not avoid thoughts of Ali's Wonder Garment and laughed until tears streamed down my face, refusing to divulge the source of my uncontrolled merriment to my two sisters, who feared that the day's events now threatened their youngest sister's sanity.

242

Epilogue

O God, make the end of my life the best of my life,
And the best of my deeds, their conclusion,
And the best of my days, the day on which I shall meet Thee.
O God, make death the best of those things we choose not,
But which we await;
And the grave the best dwelling in which we shall dwell,
And, than death, make best which follows death.
—A Pilgrim's Prayer

It had been a week since we left our families in
Monaco. In two days our husbands and children would
return to Saudi Arabia. On this night each of the ten female children of my mother had gathered in the home of
Nura. We were blessed that Reema was among us, for that
morning she had been dismissed from the clinic and had
come to stay in the home of her oldest sister until her
health was further improved.

The occasion was bittersweet, for we had come together on the twentieth anniversary of our dear mother's
death. This was an annual ritual that we had never failed
to commemorate, for our mother was sorely missed, even
after twenty years. On past occasions we had celebrated
our mother's memory by calling to mind our favorite

childhood stories of her—telling of the wonderful influence she had had on our lives. Tonight, because of our sadness over Reema's recent tragedy, our mood was subdued, and our woeful spirits led us to themes more sorrowful than in the past.

"Twenty years?" Sara mused. "It cannot be so long since I looked upon my mother's face."

Each of us agreed that the years had moved more rapidly than we liked to think.

I had a sudden realization that of ten daughters, eight were now older than our mother had been at her death. Sara and I were the two exceptions. When I gave voice to this thought, there were many moans and frowns.

Nura demanded, "Sultana! Say no more! Please!"

Nura now had grandchildren, and our eldest sister's age had become a forbidden topic in the past few years.

Reema asked us to hush, saying that she had a small story about our mother she had never shared, for she had thought I might take offense.

My eyes flashed with interest and surprise, and I agreed that nothing Reema might say would create controversy.

"You must promise, Sultana! And keep your word, no matter your emotions!"

I laughed and agreed, my curiosity aroused.

When I was only eight years of age, Reema was called into our mother's bedroom, and mother asked Reema to give her a solemn promise. Shy Reema was awed at the thought of a special secret that she alone would share with our mother. In great anticipation, she gave her word that no one would know of their conversation.

Mother told her that she had made a disturbing discovery about Sultana. Mother told Reema, "Sultana is a thief!"

My eyes popped in surprise, while my sisters burst into loud laughter.

Reema held her hand in the air, asking for silence so that she could complete her story.

Mother had caught her youngest child stealing from the personal belongings of others in our home. Mother said that I had been discovered stealing toys, books, candy, cookies, and even items for which I had no use, such as Ali's record collection. Mother told Reema that she had tried every tactic and punishment and nothing had succeeded, that I was a child who could not be shamed into obeying her mother. Now Mother needed Reema's assistance in saving my soul.

Mother made Reema swear that each time she prayed, for the rest of her days on earth, she would never cease to ask God to protect Sultana, guide Sultana, and forgive Sultana.

With teary eyes glistening, Reema looked at me and said, "Sultana. I have wearied of worrying about your sinful conduct. That promise has been a great burden, for I am a Muslim who not only prays the five obligatory daily prayers, but who prays on many other occasions. A promise made to my dear mother can never be broken, so I know that I must pray for you until I pass from this earth. But now I pray that you are no longer a thief and my prayers have been answered!"

The room burst with the sound of eight other voices, for each of my sisters was whooping with laughter, screaming over the sounds of the others. Once calm returned, we made the discovery that my mother had requested and received the identical promise from each and every sister! Each had been convinced that she was the only sibling privy to the secret that her baby sister was a little thief! For twenty years, none had broken her promise by telling. When the truth of the situation came over us, our wild and hysterical laughter could be heard throughout Nura's palace.

I felt a keen sense of relief. Surely I was protected by many of God's angels, for each of my sisters was devout and said many daily prayers.

In a joking manner, Tahani asked me point-blank. "Sultana, we would like to know if God has answered our prayers. Have you taken anything not belonging to you since the time of your youth?"

I could see that my sisters expected me to reply in a negative manner, for they could not imagine that I was still a petty thief. I could not keep my face from a trembling smile, and I began to fidget, remembering Ali's Wonder Garment, which was packed away with my belongings in the room that I was occupying.

Surprised at my hesitant reaction, Nura said, "Sultana?"

"Wait a moment," I said, and ran to get the garment I had stolen from Ali's home.

No one could believe her eyes or ears when I returned to the room wearing Ali's underpants, and when I read the instruction sheet and placed two bananas into the special "strategic" pouch, Nura tried to be firm in her disapproval, but hysterical laughter overwhelmed my sisters, and three had to leave the room, while another claimed that she had wet her pants.

We could not control our glee, even after three of Nura's servants came running into the palace, fearful of the tremendous noise they had heard from distant gardens.

After calm returned, the telephone rang, and our thoughts turned to more serious matters. The caller was Nashwa asking for her mother, Sara. It seemed that Nashwa was telephoning from Monaco to complain to her mother about her cousin Amani. My daughter had been following her cousin in Monaco and had appointed herself a one-woman "vice and social corruption committee."

Nashwa's indignation was running high, for Amani had gone so far as to take her cousin's makeup, nail polish, and sunglasses, saying that for Nashwa to wear such things made her a violator of Islamic mores!

Nashwa told her mother that if someone did not control Amani, she was going to have three French friends follow her that evening and strip off her clothes, leaving her clad only in her underwear in an area filled with tourists. That should get the prude's mind set on topics other than Nashwa's morality.

The evening's conversation shifted away from Ali's under pants, and none of my sisters could shake the irony of Sultana's daughter caught in a religious fervor while Sara's child was happily lounging in discos.

I left the room for a moment to call Kareem, advising him of the tension between our child and her cousin. My husband said that he had already decided to keep Amani by his side until she was safely returned to Riyadh, for our daughter had that very day confronted the manager of a hotel in Monte Carlo, demanding that he provide separate elevators in his establishment for men and women, and advising him that unrelated members of the same sex had no business confined together in such close quarters.

I rolled my eyes in disbelief, agreeing when Kareem declared that Amani should be put into counseling when they returned to the kingdom. Maha's successful recovery from her earlier mental unbalance had turned Kareem into a staunch believer of psychiatric counseling.

I lived a short moment of relief, thinking of how Maha had rejoined our family as a responsible girl. My oldest child's thoughts now centered on her education and plans for a normal life.

When I reentered the room, my sisters were involved in a heated discussion of the threat of militant fundamentalism, which was now challenging our family's leadership of Saudi Arabia, and my thoughts returned to Amani and her extreme interest in her faith. Each of my sisters stated that her husband had expressed great fear of the growing gap between the monarchy and the pristine ideological movement now gathering power. The Islamic fundamentalist leaders are known to be young, educated, and urbanized. This group preaches an uncompromising return to the Koran and is on a collision course with our regime, which is linked to the modernization and Westernization of the kingdom.

I said little even though I had done much investigation of the movement, for my own child was a part of an extremist group that had indicated opposition to the monarchy. I felt too close to the subject at hand and made myself busy preparing pillows to place behind Reema's head.

I asked myself, what disturbances would I live to see in the land I called home? Would my own child be a part of the opposition that brought down the legitimate government of Saudi Arabia?

When talk of the Muslim extremists ran dry, Reema said she had another bit of news that she wished to share.

I hoped that another one of my sins was not going to be made public knowledge, and I tried to keep a blank face.

Reema spoke without emotion, saying that Saleem had made plans to take another wife.

While our mother had been greatly humiliated by our father's taking four wives, Reema was the first of my sisters to undergo such an ordeal.

My chest tightened and my eyes flooded with tears, but Reema asked that none of us cry, for she would happily live her life as an ignored wife. Nothing could shake her resolve to live a life of peace, so long as she was not separated from her children. She declared in a strong voice that she was happy, but Reema's eyes spoke a different truth.

I knew my sister had loved Saleem with a true and honest love. Reema's reward for being a faithful wife and loving mother had not come to her on earth.

For her sake, Reema's sisters made a pretense of belief and congratulated our sister on her small victory.

Nura announced that Nada had once more become Ali's wife. Our brother had signed a document giving Nada wealth in her own right, along with a trip to Paris to purchase diamonds and rubies fit for the queen of England.

When Tahani asked how he had overcome the religious edict that forbade him to remarry Nada, I was not surprised to hear that Ali had hired a Saudi cousin to wed Nada without consummating the union. After the marriage, a divorce had taken place. Then Ali and Nada had wed again.

Remembering the teachings of Islam concerning such deeds, I told my sisters that what Ali had done was not allowed. The Prophet himself said that God curses men who are parties to such an arrangement, for it is nothing more than a trick against God and is considered a grave matter.

"Who is going to intervene?" Sara asked.

Nura admitted the truth—no one. "But God knows," she added, and each of us felt great sympathy for Ali, for he had piled yet another sin upon his soul.

The evening was coming to an end when the telephone rang once again. One of Nura's servants came and said that Tahani was wanted on the telephone.

Those of us who had left our loved ones in Monaco thought perhaps there was another crisis and told Tahani to spare us the details of our children's follies.

When we heard her cry out, we rushed to her side. Once she replaced the telephone on the hook, it took us many moments to calm our sister, and our fears were high that a member of our family had met with misfortune.

A grief-stricken Tahani finally spoke. "Sameera has died."

No one could speak, no one could move.

Could it be true?

I counted on my fingers, trying to calculate the number of years that dear girl had spent locked in the woman's room, a padded cell in the home of her savage uncle.

"How long?" Sara asked, seeing me struggle with my memories."

"Almost fifteen years," I told her.

"I have committed a grave sin," Tahani confessed. "For many years I have asked God to take her uncle from this earth!"

We had heard that Sameera's uncle was wrinkled and frail, and that knowledge had given us hope that after his death, Sameera would return to us.

I sarcastically commented, "We should have known that such a one could not be depended upon to die soon enough."

Over the years, many had tried to win Sameera's release, saying that her sin did not merit eternal earthly punishment, but her uncle felt that he alone knew the wishes of God, and his harsh verdict had not been lifted.

Sameera had been brilliant, beautiful, and sweet in temperament. What nature had given her, cruel fortune took away. As a result of her uncle's unbelievable cruelty,

Sameera died, completely alone, locked away in the darkest of rooms, kept from any human contact for fifteen long years.

Tahani began to sob, her cries chopping through her words. It took her many moments to reveal that Sameera had been buried on this day. Her auntie confided that despite her emaciation, Sameera was still beautiful when wrapped in the white linen shroud in which she would appear before God.

How could we bear the pain of her cruel death?

Choking back sobs, I tried to remember a verse from Kahlil Gibran on the question of death. I first whispered it, and as my memory of it returned, I slowly raised my voice, until all could hear me. *"Only when you drink from the river of silence, shall you indeed sing. And, when you have reached the mountaintop, then you shall begin to climb. And, when the earth shall claim your limbs, then shall you truly dance."*

My sisters and I joined hands, remembering that we were as a chain—strong as the strongest link, weak as the weakest link.

As never before, we belonged to a sisterhood more powerful than that of our own blood. Never again would we sit back and wonder at the cruelty of men and the obscene arbitrariness of innocent female death brought about by men's evil.

I said, "Let the world know that the women of Saudi Arabia are gaining strength in the knowledge that they are right."

My sisters looked at me one by one, and for the first time I knew that each of them understood why I do the things that I do.

At that moment I promised myself that somehow the moral order of our world would be changed, and right would triumph someday.

The great human rights movement for women in Saudi Arabia has just begun and it will not be defeated by men of indoctrinated ignorance.

The men of my land will grow to mourn my existence, for I will never cease to challenge the evil precedents they have allowed to prevail against the women of Saudi Arabia.

The End

Appendix A
The Future of Women

The world as we know it was utterly changed on September 11, 2001. Few people were left untouched by the carnage brought against so many by so few. That eventful day even provoked military action. The haunting images of the war against terrorism were often tragic while others were uplifting, and none more so than the endearing smiles on the faces of the previously *burqa* clad women and girls of Afghanistan. Although our purposeful military mission was to seek justice and to stop suicide bombers from future odious acts, I have always believed that the emancipation of women is a freedom worth fighting for. A great imbalance is created in the world when women are treated as liabilities, as they are in many countries.

As the Afghani women celebrated, I rejoiced with them. As I listened to First Lady Laura Bush's now famous radio broadcast about these women, I waited in anticipation, hoping that some golden words of hope would be cast to women in other countries. Consider the fact that women in Saudi Arabia are forbidden to drive or to participate in public life, or that newborn females have their spines snapped in India, or the outrage that men are acquitted for killing women who are raped in Pakistan, or that young girls are routinely forced into prostitution in Thailand.

Much to my sorrow, even after more than ten years, little has changed for women of Afghanistan, a country that remains extremely dangerous for young girls and for women. Afghan Girls and women are so desperate that self-immolation is a common method of suicide. Recently I read of two eight-year-old girls who were given in marriage to men who were aged 36 and 43. Those young girls were expected to have sex with their husbands. How can this be? Why didn't my country fulfill the promises made for women in that land? Why does Afghanistan's own President act as though the plight of women has little to do with him? Women make up half of the citizens of his country.

While women in Saudi Arabia are enjoying some gains in freedom, still women cannot drive in that land, and still women must ask permission from their male guardians to travel, and still women are expected to veil, and still young girls are often wed against their will.

When will this end?

I recently spoke with Princess Sultana and was not surprised when I learned that she, too, has moments of great despair that the gains made are so slow in coming.

While women can strive to bring change, and we do enjoy some successes, until we recruit governments to join our mission of freedom for women, it will be difficult to bring true change to our earth. I believe that every democratic government on this earth should do the responsible thing and proclaim that freedom is just as important for women, as it is for men. Then economic fines should be leveled against countries who allow their females to be so mistreated.

Our governments should act and act now, for we all know that whatever imperils women, imperils the world.

Jean Sasson

Appendix B
Facts about Saudi Arabia

GENERAL INFORMATION
HEAD OF STATE: H.M. King Abdullah ibn Abdul Aziz Al
    Sa'ud
OFFICIAL TITLE: The Custodian of the Two Holy
    Mosques

MAIN CITIES
Riyadh—capital
Jeddah—port city
Makkah—holiest city of Islam, toward which Muslims
    pray
Madinah—burial place of Prophet Mohammed
Taif—summer capital and summer resort area
Dammam—port city and commercial center
Dhahran—oil industry center
Al Khobar—commercial center
Yanbu—natural gas shipping terminal
Hail—trading center
Jubail—industrial city
Ras Tanura—refinery center
Hofuf—principal city of the Al Hasa Oasis

RELIGION

Saudi Arabia is home to Islam, one of the three monotheistic religions. Muslims believe in one God-and that Mohammed is his Prophet. As the heartland of Islam, Saudi Arabia occupies a special place in the Muslim world. Each year, millions of Muslim pilgrims journey to Makkah, in Saudi Arabia, to pay homage to God. For this reason, Saudi Arabia is one of the most traditional Muslim countries and its citizens adhere to a strict interpretation of the Koran.

A Muslim has five obligations, called the Five Pillars of Islam. These obligations are: 1) Profession of faith: "There is no god but God; Mohammed is the messenger of God." 2) A Muslim should pray five times a day, facing the city of Makkah. 3) A Muslim must pay a fixed proportion of his income, called *zakat,* to the poor. 4) During the ninth month of the Islamic calendar, a Muslim must fast. During this time, called Ramadan, Muslims must abstain from food and drink from dawn to sunset. 5) A Muslim must perform the Haj, or pilgrimage, at least once during his lifetime (if he has the economic means).

It is a crime to practice other religions in Saudi Arabia.

PUBLIC HOLIDAYS:
Eid Al Fitr—five days
Eid Al Adha—eight days

SHORT HISTORY
Saudi Arabia is a nation of tribes that can trace their roots back to the earliest civilizations of the Arabian Peninsula. The ancestors of modern-day Saudis lived on ancient and important trade routes and much of their income was realized by raiding parties. Divided into regions and ruled by

independent tribal chiefs, the various warring tribes were unified under one religion, Islam, led by the Prophet Mohammed, in the seventh century. Before the Prophet died at age sixty-three, most of Arabia was Muslim.

The ancestors of the present rulers of Saudi Arabia reigned overmuch of Arabia during the nineteenth century. After losing most of Saudi territory to the Turks, they were driven from Riyadh and sought refuge in Kuwait. King Abdul Aziz Al Sa'ud, father of the present-day king, returned to Riyadh and fought to regain the country. He succeeded and founded modern Saudi Arabia in 1932. Oil was discovered in 1938 and Saudi Arabia began a rapid climb as one of the world's wealthiest and most influential nations.

GEOGRAPHY
Saudi Arabia, with an area of 864,866 square miles, is one-third the size of the United States and is the same size as Western Europe. Saudi Arabia lies at the crossroads of three continents: Africa, Asia, and Europe. The country extends from the Red Sea on the west to the Persian Gulf in the east. It borders Jordan, Iraq, and Kuwait on the north, and Yemen and Oman to the south. The United Arab Emirates, Qatar, and Bahrain lie to the east.

A harsh desert land with no rivers and few permanent streams, Saudi Arabia is home to the Rub Al Khali (Empty Quarter), which is the largest sand desert in the world. The mountain ranges of Asir Province rise to over nine thousand feet in the southwest.

CALENDAR
Saudi Arabia uses the Islamic calendar that is based on a lunar year rather than the Gregorian calendar that is

based on a solar year. A lunar month is the time between two successive new moons. A lunar year contains twelve months, but is eleven days shorter than the solar year. For this reason, the holy days gradually shift from one season to another.

Lunar year dates are derived from A.D. 622, the year of the Prophet's emigration, or Hejirah, from Makkah to Madinah. The Islamic holy day is Friday. The work week in Saudi Arabia begins on Saturday and ends Thursday.

ECONOMY
More than one quarter of the world's known oil reserves lie beneath the sands of Saudi Arabia.In 1933, Standard Oil Company of California won the rights to prospect for oil in Saudi Arabia. In 1938 oil was discovered at Dammam Oil Well #7, which is still producing oil today. The Arabian American Oil Company (ARAMCO) was founded in 1944 and held the right to continue to search for oil in the kingdom. In 1980 the Saudi Government assumed ownership of ARAMCO.

The kingdom's oil wealth has ensured that the citizens of that country live an opulent life-style enjoyed by few. With free education and interest-free loans most Saudis prosper. All Saudi citizens, as well as Muslim pilgrims, receive free health care. Government programs provide support for Saudi Arabians in the case of disability, death, or retirement. The entire country is an impressive socialist state. Economically, Saudi Arabia has developed into a modern, technologically advanced nation.

CURRENCY
The Saudi riyal is the basic monetary unit in Saudi Arabia. The riyal consists of 100 halalahs and is issued in notes

and coins of various denominations. The riyal is 3.7450 to the American dollar.

LAW & GOVERNMENT

Saudi Arabia is an Islamic state and the law is based on the *Shari'a,* the Islamic code of law taken from the pages of the Koran, and the *Sunna,* which are the traditions addressed by Prophet Mohammed. The Koran is the constitution of the country and provides guidance for legal judgments.

Executive and legislative authority is exercised by the king and the Council of Ministers. Their decisions are based on *Shari'a* law. All ministries and government agencies are responsible to the king.

DEMOGRAPHICS (2011)

Population
26,131,703 (July 2011 est.) includes 5,576,076 non-
   nationals

Age Structure:
0-14 years: 29.4% (male 3,939,377/female 3,754,020)
15-64 years: 67.6% (male 9,980,253/female 7,685,328)
65 years and over: 3% (male 404,269/female 368,456)
   (2011 est.)

Median age:25.3 years
      male: 26.4 years
      female: 23.9 years (2011 est.)

Population growth rate: 1.536% (2011 est.)

Birth rate: 19.34 births/1,000 population (2011 est.)

Death rate: 3.33 deaths/1,000 population (July 2011 est.)

Net migration rate: -0.64 migrant(s)/1,000 population
(2011 est.)

Urban population: 82% of total population (2010)

Rate of urbanization: 2.2% annual rate of change
(2010-15 est.)

Sex ratio
at birth: 1.05 male(s)/female
under 15 years: 1.04 male(s)/female
15-64 years: 1.27 male(s)/female
65 years and over: 1.03 male(s)/female
total population: 1.17 male(s)/female (2011 est.)

Infant mortality rate
total: 16.16 deaths/1,000 live births
male: 18.54 deaths/1,000 live births
female: 13.65 deaths/1,000 live births (2011 est.)

Life expectancy at birth: 74.11 years
male: 72.15 years
female: 76.16 years (2011 est.)

Total fertility rate: 2.31 children born/woman (2011 est.)

Nationality
noun: Saudi(s)
adjective: Saudi or Saudi Arabian

Ethnic groups
Arab 90%, Afro-Asian 10%

Religions

Muslim 100% with majority Sunni and minority Shiite
Languages
Arabic (official although English is widely spoken in business circles.)

Literacy (age 15 and over who can read and write)
    total population: 78.8%
    male: 84.7%
    female: 70.8% (2003 est.)

School life expectancy (primary to tertiary education)
    total: 14 years
    male: 14 years
    female: 13 years (2009)

Education expenditures
    5.6% of GDP (2008)

Maternal mortality rate
    24 deaths/100,000 live births (2008)

Health expenditures
    5% of GDP (2009)

Physicians density
    0.939 physicians/1,000 population (2008)

Hospital bed density
2.2 beds/1,000 population (2008)

Appendix C
Glossary

ABAAYA: a black, full-length outer garment worn by Saudi women.

ABU: father.

AL RAS: school for girls in Saudi Arabia.

AL SA'UD: ruling family of Saudi Arabia.

ARABIC: language relating to Arabs or Arabia.

ASSIUT: village in southern Egypt.

BACKGAMMON: board game popular in Middle East.

BAHRAIN: island nation in the Arabian Gulf.

BEDOUIN: a nomadic desert people, the original Arabs.

BIN (or Ibn): following a man's given name and preceding a man's father's or grandfather's name. Means "son of."

CAIRO: capital of Egypt.

CHRISTIANITY: religion derived from the teachings of Jesus Christ.

DHU AL HIJAH: the twelfth month of the hejira calendar.

DHU AL QIDA: the eleventh month of the hejira calendar.

DUBAI: a city located in the federation of the United

Arab Emirates bordering Saudi Arabia.

EGYPT: country in Africa and on Sinai Peninsula.

EMIRATES: United Arab Emirates, which is a federation of small emirate states located on the Arabian Peninsula.

FRENCH RIVIERA: fashionable Mediterranean resort area in southeastern France famed for its scenery, warm climate, and excellent beaches.

GAMAA AL ISLAMIYA: Islamic extremist group formed in Egypt in the early 1980s.

GREEN BOOK: Qaddafi's Green Book: Philosophy of Colonel Qaddafi of Libya.

HADITHS: sayings and traditions of Prophet Mohammed that help to formulate Islamic law.

HAJ: annual pilgrimage to Makkah made by those of the Islamic faith.

HAJJI: pilgrim who makes the pilgrimage to Makkah (a title that denotes honor).

HEJIRA: Islamic calendar that started on the date that Prophet Mohammed fled Makkah and escaped to Madinah (622).

IHRAM: special time during Haj that all Muslims refrain from normal life and dwell on nothing but religious matters.

IMAM: person who leads communal prayers and/or delivers the sermon on Fridays.

INFANTICIDE: practice of killing an infant. In pre-Islamic times a common practice in Arabia of ridding the family of unwanted female children.

ISLAM: religious faith of Muslims of which Mohammed was the Prophet. Islam is the last of the three great monotheistic religions to appear.

JEDDAH: Saudi Arabian city located on the Red Sea.

JUDAISM: religion developed among the ancient Hebrews.

KAABA: Islam's holiest shrine, a sacred sanctuary for all Muslims. The Kaaba is a small building in the Holy Mosque of Makkah,nearly cubic in shape, built to enclose the Black Stone, which is the most venerated Muslim object.

KOHL: a black powder used by Saudi Arabian women that goes on the eyelid of the eye to enhance the beauty of a woman.

KORAN: the Holy Book of all Muslims that contains the words of God as they were given to Prophet Mohammed.

KUWAIT: small sheikhdom that borders Saudi Arabia that has more than 10 percent of the world's oil reserves.

LA: Arabian word meaning "no."

MADINAH: second holiest city of Islam. The burial place of Prophet Mohammed.

MAHRAM: males to whom a woman cannot be married, such as her father, brother, or uncle, who are allowed to be a woman's escort when traveling. Must be a close relative.

MAKKAH: holiest city of Islam. Each year, millions of Muslims travel to Makkah to perform the annual pilgrimage.

MONOTHEISM: belief that there is only one God.

MORALS POLICE: religious authorities in Saudi Arabia who have the power to arrest those they believe commit moral wrongs or crimes against Islam or go against the teachings of Islam.

MUEZZIN: the crier who calls the faithful to pray five times a day.

MUSLIM: adherent of the religion founded by Prophet Mohammed in the year 610.

MUT'A: temporary marriage allowed to those of the Islamic faith.

MUTAWWA: the religious police, also known as the morals police. Men who seek out, arrest, and punish those who do not abide by Saudi religious law.

NAJD: the traditional name for central Arabia. The inhabitants of this area are known for their conservative behavior. The ruling family of Saudi Arabia are Najdis.

PLO: Palestine Liberation Organization.

POLYGAMY: Marriage to more than one spouse at the same time. Men of the Muslim faith are legally allowed four wives at one time.

PURDAH: practice of confining women to their homes. This total seclusion of females can occur in some Muslim countries.

PURIFICATION: the ritual of cleansing prior to offering prayers to God practiced by Muslims.

RED SEA: the sea between Arabia and Africa.

RIYADH: the capital city of Saudi Arabia, which is located in the desert.

RIYAL: Saudi Arabian currency. The exchange varies but was recently about 3.75 to the dollar.

RUB AL KHALI: an enormous desert wilderness that occupies the southeast portion of Arabia. It is often referred to as the "Empty Quarter."

SAN'A: the capital city of Yemen.

SAUDI ARABIA: country in Asia that occupies most of Arabia. Saudi Arabia has at least one quarter of the world's known oil reserves.

SECULAR: not religious.

SHAWARMA: popular sandwich sold in Saudi Arabia and other Arab countries made of lamb, beef, or chicken wrapped in pita bread, mixed with sauces and tomatoes and peppers.

SHAYLA: black gauzy scarf worn by women of the Muslim faith in Saudi Arabia.

SHIITE: the branch of Islam that split from the Sunni majority over the issue of Prophet Mohammed's successor. One of two main sects.

SUNNA: traditions of the Islamic faith as addressed by Prophet Mohammed.

SUNNI: the majority orthodox branch of Islam. Saudi Arabia is 95 percent populated by those of the Sunni sect. The word means "traditionalists." One of two main sects.

TAIF: mountain resort city in Saudi Arabia that is located close to Makkah.

TEHRAN: the capital city of Iran.

THOBE: a long shirt-like dress that is worn by Saudi men. It is usually made of white cotton, but can be made of heavier, darker colored fabric for the winter months.

UMM AL QURRAH: "Mother of Cities" or "The Blessed City" that is Makkah.

UMRAH: a short pilgrimage (to Makkah) undertaken by those of the Muslim faith that can be made anytime of the year.

VEIL: black fabric that is used to cover a Saudi Arabian Muslim woman's face. The material can be sheer or thick.

WOMAN'S ROOM: room in a man's house used to confine Saudi Arabian women who go against the wishes of their husbands, fathers, or brothers. The punishment can be for a short period or a life sentence.

YEMEN: country located in the southwest corner of the Arabian Peninsula, neighboring Saudi Arabia.

ZAKAH: obligatory alms giving required of all Muslims that is the third pillar of Islam.

Appendix D
Chronology of Key Events
in Saudi Arabia

570 A.D. Prophet Mohammed is born in Makkah, Saudi Arabia.

610 Prophet Mohammed sees a vision from God proclaiming him to be the messenger of God. Islam is born.

622 Prophet Mohammed flees an angry mob in Makkah and escapes to Madinah. This flight is forever after known as, "the Hegira", the great crisis of Mohammed's mission on earth. The Muslim calendar begins on that date and is called Hegira in honor of that journey.

632 Prophet Mohammed dies in Madinah.

650 The sayings of Prophet Mohammed are collected and written. Known as the Koran, this book, which recorded the word of God as told by Mohammed, became the holy book of Muslims.

1446 The first documented Al Sa'ud, ancestor of Sultana, leaves the nomadic life of the desert and settles in Dar'iyah (old Riyadh).

1744 Mohammed Al Sa'ud establishes a partnership with Mohammed Al Wahhab, a teacher who believes in the strictest interpretation of the Koran. Combined forces of a warrior and a teacher unleash a rigid system of punishment upon the people.

1802–1806 Sons of Mohammed Al Sa'ud and Mohammed Al Wahhab, inspired by the teachings of the Koran, attack and capture Makkah and Madinah. They were ruthless, massacring the entire male population of Taif, a settlement above Makkah. With this victory, most of Arabia united under one authority.

1843–1865 The Al Sa'uds extend authority southward to Oman.

1871 The Ottomans take control of the province of Hasa.

1876 Sultana's grandfather, Abdul Aziz ibn Sa'ud, founder of the kingdom, is born.

1887 The city of Riyadh is captured by the Rashed's.

1891 The Al Sa'ud clan flees Riyadh into the Empty Quarter.

1893–1894 The Al Sa'ud clan marches across the desert to Kuwait.

1901 (Sept.) Abdul Aziz, now twenty-five years old, along with his warriors departs Kuwait for Riyadh.

1902 (Jan.) Abdul Aziz and his men capture Riyadh. The new Al Sa'ud dynasty begins.

1912 The Ikhwan (Brotherhood) is founded based on Wahhabism; it grows quickly and provides key support for Abdul Aziz ibn Sa'ud.

1913 Hasa is taken from the Ottomans by Abdul Aziz

1915 Abdul Aziz Al Sa'ud enters into an agreement with the British government to receive five thousand pounds per month to fight the Turks.

1926 Abdul Aziz is proclaimed King of the Hejaz in the Grand Mosque of Makkah.

1932 Unification of the dual kingdoms of Hejaz and Najd. Named the Kingdom of Saudi Arabia, it becomes the twelfth largest country in the world.

1933 King Abdul Aziz's eldest son, Sa'ud, is named Crown Prince.

1933 (May) America wins concessions (over the British) to search for oil in Saudi Arabia.

1934 Saudi Arabia goes to war against Yemen; peace is established one month later.

1934 (May 15) In revenge for the Yemen war, King Abdul Aziz is attacked at a holy mosque in Makkah by three knife-wielding Yemenis. His eldest son, Sa'ud, flings himself in front of his father and is wounded instead.

1938 (March 20) Oil is discovered in Dammam, Saudi Arabia.

1939 War in Europe halts oil production.

1944 Oil production in the kingdom rises to eight million barrels a year.

1945 (Feb. 14) President Roosevelt meets with King Abdul Aziz aboard the USS *Quincy.*

1945 (Feb. 17) Winston Churchill, the prime minister of Great Britain, meets with King Abdul Aziz aboard the USS *Quincy.*

1946 Oil production soars to sixty million barrels a year.

1948 (May 14) The state of Israel is established.

1948 (May 14) The first Arab-Israeli war begins.

1948 Radio Makkah, the first radio station in the kingdom, is opened despite fierce opposition from the Ulema (religious men).

1952 King Abdul Aziz bans alcohol imports for nonbelievers.

1953 (Nov. 9) King Abdul Aziz, Sultana's grandfather, dies at age seventy-seven.

1953 (Nov. 9) The late king's eldest son, fifty-one-year-old Sa'ud, becomes King. His half-brother Faisal becomes Crown Prince.

1960 Saudi Arabia is a founding member of the Organization of Petroleum Exporting Countries, known as OPEC.

1958 (March) With the kingdom in financial turmoil, Crown Prince Faisal takes administrative control of the government.

1960 (Dec.) King Sa'ud dismisses his brother from administrative duties and assumes control of the government.

1962 Slavery is abolished in the Kingdom of Saudi Arabia. Most slaves continue to live with the families that owned them.

1963 The first girls' school opens; religious factions riot.

1964 (Nov. 3) King Sa'ud abdicates and departs the kingdom for Beirut. Faisal is declared King, and his half-brother Khalid, Crown Prince.

1965 Despite protests, the first television station is opened in Riyadh.

1965 (Sept.) Prince Khalid ibn Musaid, nephew of King Faisal, is killed as he leads an armed protest against the opening of the television station.

1967 (June) The Six-Day War begins between Israel and its Arab neighbors. Saudi Arabia sends forces.

1969 (Feb.) Deposed ex-king Sa'ud ibn Abdul Aziz dies in Athens, Greece, after spending more than fifteen million dollars each year of his exile.

1973 (Oct. 6) The October 1973 war begins between Israel and its Arab neighbors. Saudi Arabia sends troops.

1973 (Oct. 20) Furious at America's military assistance to Israel, King Faisal announces a holy war and an oil embargo against America.

1975 (March 25) King Faisal is assassinated by his nephew Prince Faisal ibn Musaid, brother of the prince who was shot and killed during a riot in 1965.

1975 (March 25) Crown Prince Khalid is declared King. His half-brother Fahd is named new Crown Prince.

1977 King Khalid issues a government decree that forbids women to travel outside their homes unless accompanied by a male family member. A second order follows that forbids women to travel abroad to study. Both decrees resulted from the international incident of Princess Misha'il, who was publicly executed after meeting and falling in love with another Saudi student at the American University in Lebanon. Her lover was beheaded.

1979 Saudi Arabia severs diplomatic relations with Egypt after it makes peace with Israel.

1979 (Nov.) The Grand Mosque in Makkah is attacked. Protestors complain of women working outside the home in the kingdom. In the months to follow, freedoms for women are curtailed, in response to government fear of increased fundamentalist unrest.

1980 Saudi Arabia takes full control of ARAMCO from the United States.

1982 (June) King Khalid dies of a heart attack. Fahd, his half-brother, is declared King; his half-brother Abdullah is named new Crown Prince.

1987 Saudi Arabia resumes diplomatic relations with Egypt (severed since 1979).

1990 (Aug. 5) Kuwait is invaded by Iraq.

1990 Saudi Arabia condemns the Iraqi invasion of Kuwait. The Saudi government asks the United States to intervene. Although the Saudi government allows foreign troops and Kuwaiti citizens to remain in the country, they expel citizens of Yemen and Jordan due to their governments' support of Iraq.

1991 *Mutawah* react with fear and hostility to the presence of foreign female soldiers. Pressure increases to force the Saudi government to tighten restrictions on the female population of all nationalities as religious factions return to strict interpretation of the Koran.

1991 Saudi Arabia is involved in the war against Iraq.

1994 Islamic dissident Osama bin Laden is stripped of his Saudi nationality.

1995 King Fahd suffers a stroke. The day-to-day running of the country is entrusted to Crown Prince Abdullah bin Abdul Aziz al Sa'ud.

1996 A bomb explodes at the US military complex near Dhahran killing 19 and wounding over 300.

1999 Twenty Saudi women attend the session of the Consultative Council for the first time in Saudi history.

2000 The London-based human rights group Amnesty International describes Saudi Arabia's treatment of women as "untenable" by any legal or moral standard.

2001 (September 11) America is attacked by Al-Qaida. 15 of the 19 hijackers involved are Saudi nationals. Tension develops between Americans and Saudi Arabians when the Saudi government fails to cooperate fully with American investigators.

2001 Western media focuses on Saudi Arabia and their archaic system of repression against women. The Saudi government reacts angrily and goes on to finance a widespread propaganda program praising the Al-Sa'ud and Saudi Arabia in the Western media.

2001 When the media uncovers the fact that the Saudi government has been spending millions of dollars annually to foster the Wahhabi message of hate and violence, a sect repugnant to most of the world's Muslims, a number of Western governments and media outlets call for the Saudi royal family to end its exclusive alliance with the fanatical Wahhabi sect. Once again, the Saudi government reacts with denial and anger.

2001 (Dec.) The Saudi government takes the unprecedented step of issuing identity cards to women.

2002 Saudi investors redraw funds from the United States in angry protest at a lawsuit filed by relatives of the 9/11 victims that claim the Saudi government conspired with Al-Qaida.

2002 The government of Saudi Arabia refuses to endorse

President Bush's plan to invade Iraq and depose Iraqi President Saddam Hussein.

2003 The United States announces that it will pull out almost all its troops from the Kingdom, ending America's military presence back to 1991.

2003 Domestic criticism of the royal family spreads across the Kingdom. In September, more than 300 Saudi intellectuals (women as well as men) sign a petition calling for political reforms.

2003 (Oct.) Saudi Arabia hosts its first ever human rights conference. The government announces it will hold the first elections ever within a year.

2003 (Nov.) King Fahd grants greater power to the Consultative Council, enabling the Council to initiate legislation without first seeking permission from the King.

2004 (Jan.) Saudi female business professionals shed their veils and storm the stage at the international gathering of 1,000 men at the Jeddah Economic Forum, demanding reforms for women. Saudi Arabia's highest religious authority issued a thunderous condemnation, denouncing the women, saying that the mixing of men and women without the women wearing the Islamic hijab ordered by God was forbidden. Members of the Al-Sa'ud said that the liberals were moving too fast. Crown Prince Abdullah warned that he "will not permit anyone to interfere with reform, be it by appeals to ultra-conservatism and stagnation or to ill-considered adventure."

2004 Prince Sultan bin Turki bin Abdul-Aziz Al-Sa'ud, calling for democratic reform in the Kingdom says he was lured to a meeting with a member of the Saudi ruling family (in Geneva). During the meeting he was attacked by five masked men, drugged and taken by force back to the Kingdom where he is under house arrest.

2004 (Dec.) An attack on the US consulate in Jeddah leaves five staff members dead as well as four attackers.

2004 Two car bombs explode in Riyadh. Saudi security forces kill seven suspects.

2005 (Feb. – Apr.) there are nationwide municipal elections. This is a first in the kingdom, although only men can vote.

2005 (Aug.) King Fahd bin Abdul Aziz Al Sa'ud, Saudi Arabia's king since 1982 dies at the age of 84. He is succeeded by his half-brother, Abdullah bin Abdul Aziz Al Saudi.

2005 (Nov.) The World Trade Organization allows Saudi Arabia to join.

2006 (Jan.) There is yet another tragedy during the Haj when 363 Hajj pilgrims are killed in a crush during the stone-throwing ritual in Mecca. Another 70 pilgrims are killed when a hotel in the city of Mecca collapses.

2006 (Oct.) The Saudi Arabian government formalizes the royal succession in an attempt to prevent infighting among Saudi princes.

2007 (Feb.) Four French nationals are killed in a terror attack near the tourist popular ruins of Madain Salen.

2007 (Apr.) Saudi police announce the arrests of 172 terror suspects who were training as pilots for suicide missions.

2007 (July) Saudi religious police come under attack after being the deaths of people under their custody.

2007 (Sept.) Great Britain and Saudi Arabia sign a deal for 72 Eurofighter combat jets.

2007 (Oct.) There is a Royal decree ordering an overhaul of the judicial system, although little changes.

2008 (Dec.) Saudi Arabia and neighboring Qatar finally agree on the final delineation of shared border.

2009 (Feb.) Interpol issues a security alert for 83 Saudi men suspecting of plotting terror attacks.

2009 King Abdullah fires the head of the religious police, the most senior judge, and the head of the central bank in a rare government reshuffle. At the same time he appoints Saudi Arabia's first female government minister.

2009 Amnesty International accuses Saudi Arabia of abuses against prisoners held for years without charge or trial.

2009 The Human Rights Watch group criticizes Saudi Arabia of failing to keep their pledge to free women from the institution of male guardianship, a practice which prevents women from receiving medical treatment with the permission of a male family member.

2010 The United States confirms plans to sell $60 billion military arms to Saudi Arabia. This is the most lucrative arms deal in the history of the United States.

2010 King Abdullah travels to the United States for back surgery.

2011 (Jan.) The president of Tunisia seeks and finds sanctuary in Saudi Arabia after being forced to flee his own country.

2011 (Feb.) King Abdullah increases welfare spending as a way of soothing Saudi unrest in the wake of revolutions spreading across the Arab world.

2011 (March) King Abdullah bans public protests in the kingdom, warning that such protests will not be tolerated.

2011 (May 2) Osama bin Laden, who was on the FBI's list of ten most wanted fugitives for his involvement in the 1998 US Embassy bombings and for the terror attack of September 9, 2001, was shot and killed in Abbottabad, Pakistan by U.S. Navy Seals and CIA operatives ordered by President Barack Obama. Bin Laden was buried at sea, to the horror and protest of Muslims worldwide. Three wives and numerous children and grandchildren were arrested by the Pakistani government.

2011 (June) Saudi women once again mount a protest drive in defiance of ban on female drivers.

2011 (Sept.) King Abdullah announces that women will be given the right to vote and to run in municipal elections in the year 2015.

2011 A Saudi woman is sentenced to be lashed after being found guilty of driving her son to school. To the fury of the religious clerics, King Abdullah overturns the sentence.

2011 Prince Naif bin Abdul Aziz al Saud is named as heir to the throne after Crown Prince Sultan bin Abdul Aziz al Saud dies of cancer.

2011 (Dec.) A Saudi woman is executed for practicing sorcery. The Chief of Religious Police reports that the woman tricked people into believing that she could cure illnesses.

2011 (Dec.) The Saudi royal family has a lavish royal locomotive built for the royal family to be transported back and forth to Mecca during religious festivals.

2012 (March) Hillary Clinton travels to Saudi Arabia for talks about the Syrian situation.

2012 (Apr.) Pakistan announces that the three widows and nine children arrested at the time of Osama bin Laden's death will be deported from Pakistan to their home countries. Two of the wives are Saudi Arabian.

2012 A girls' school in the Eastern province defies the religious clerics by installing basketball hoops and allowing girls to play.

2012 (Apr. 26) Saudi Arabia announces that 14 members of Osama bin Laden's family have arrived in Saudi Arabia.

2012 (Apr.) Saudi Arabia and Egypt are involved in a diplomatic battle after Saudi Arabia arrests Egyptian Ahmed el-Gezawi.

2012 (May) A group of courageous Saudi women climb Mount Everest in support of breast cancer treatment.

Index

The Princess Trilogy

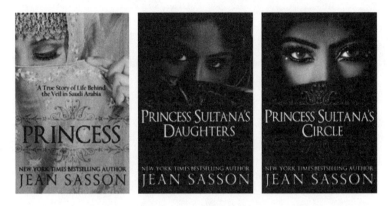

"Absolutely riveting and profoundly sad..."
—People magazine

"Must-reading for anyone interested in human rights."
—USA Today

"A chilling story...a vivid account of an air-conditioned nightmare..." *—Entertainment Weekly*

"Shocking...candid...sad, sobering, and compassionate..."
—San Francisco Chronicle

In Jean Sasson's international best sellers, the books about Princess Sultana Al Sa'ud vividly depict the harsh reality of life lived behind the black veil. Through Sasson, Princess Sultana tells the world about the lives of women who live in a society where they have few rights, little control over their own lives or bodies, and have no choice but to endure the atrocities perpetrated against them. Years have passed, and despite the Arab Spring and the call for new freedom for men and women, too little has changed for the women of Saudi Arabia.

NEW YORK TIMES BESTSELLING AUTHOR OF
Princess: A True Story of Life Behind the Veil in Saudi Arabia

JEAN SASSON

DAUGHTER OF IRAQ

MAYADA

One Woman's Survival Under Saddam Hussein

From the *New York Times*
bestselling author of
*Princess: A True Story
of Life Behind the Veil
in Saudi Arabia*

"Fascinating."
—*The Washington Post*

Growing Up
bin Laden

OSAMA'S WIFE AND SON TAKE US
INSIDE THEIR SECRET WORLD

Najwa bin Laden | Omar bin Laden | Jean Sasson

"The most vivid look the American public has had at Bin
Laden's family life...The most complete account available."
—*New York Times*

"Fascinating." –*The Washington Post*

JEAN SASSON

AMERICAN
CHICK IN
SAUDI ARABIA

When Jean Sasson, a young Southern woman living in
Jacksonville Beach, Florida, answers a call to work in the
royal hospital in Saudi Arabia, what should have been a
two-year stay turns into a life-changing adventure span-
ning   over   a   decade.

JEAN SASSON

FOR THE LOVE
OF A SON

One Afghan woman's quest
for her stolen child